Aristocratic Encounters

Aristocratic Encounters: European Travelers and North American Indians relates how an aristocratic discourse on American Indians took shape in French and German writing in the late eighteenth and early nineteenth centuries. Titled and educated French and German visitors to North America, with the background of the French Revolution in mind, developed a new belief in their affinity with the warrior elites of Indian societies, whom they viewed as fellow aristocrats. The book alternates between chapters on major figures such as Chateaubriand and Tocqueville and chapters on numerous lesser, but often instructive, travelers. For European historians, the book offers fresh evidence for the creation of a post-Revolutionary "aristocratic" culture through overseas travel. To the interdisciplinary audience of readers interested in colonial encounters, it opens up a Romantic vision of aristocrats from two worlds struggling to defend their code of valor and honor in an age of democratic politics. This book differs from other books about the European vision of the United States in its concentration on American Indians as the dramatic focus of European–American encounters. *Aristocratic Encounters* is a contribution to a burgeoning transatlantic, and even transnational, form of historical writing; it moves across national boundaries to ask how Europeans understood cultures vastly different from their own.

Harry Liebersohn is the author of *Fate and Utopia in German Sociology, 1870–1923*. His article "Discovering Indigenous Nobility: Tocqueville, Chamisso and Romantic Travel Writing" in *The American Historical Review* won the William Koren Jr. Prize of the Society for French Historical Studies. He is currently an Associate Professor of History at the University of Illinois, Urbana-Champaign.

Aristocratic Encounters

European Travelers and
North American Indians

Harry Liebersohn

CAMBRIDGE
UNIVERSITY PRESS

PUBLISHED BY THE PRESS SYNDICATE OF THE UNIVERSITY OF CAMBRIDGE
The Pitt Building, Trumpington Street, Cambridge, United Kingdom

CAMBRIDGE UNIVERSITY PRESS
The Edinburgh Building, Cambridge CB2 2RU, UK
40 West 20th Street, New York, NY 10011-4211, USA
10 Stamford Road, Oakleigh, VIC 3166, Australia
Ruiz de Alarcón 13, 28014 Madrid, Spain
Dock House, The Waterfront, Cape Town 8001, South Africa

http://www.cambridge.org

© Harry Liebersohn 1998

First published 1998
First paperback edition 2001

Printed in the United States of America

Typeset in 10/12 Stempel Garamond, in Quark XPress™ [BB]

*A catalog record for this book is available from
the British Library*

Library of Congress Cataloging-in-Publication Data
Liebersohn, Harry.
Aristocratic encounters : European travelers and North American
Indians / Harry Liebersohn.
p.   cm.
Includes bibliographical references and index.
ISBN 0-521-64090-3 (hardbound)
1. Indians of North America – Public opinion.   2. Travelers – North
America.   3. Romanticism – Europe.   4. Aristocracy (Social class) –
Europe.   5. Public opinion – Europe.   I. Title.
E98.P99L54   1998
970'.004'97 – dc21   98-29057
CIP

ISBN 0 521 64090 3 hardback
ISBN 0 521 00360 1 paperback

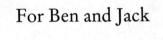

For Ben and Jack

Contents

List of Illustrations	*page*	viii
Acknowledgments		ix
Introduction		1
Part I From Neoclassicism to Romanticism: France and American Indians, 1682–1815		11
1 Indians in the French Enlightenment		13
2 Chateaubriand and the Fiction of Native Aristocrats		39
Part II Ending a Tradition: The French Romantic Travelers, 1815–1848		61
3 Critics and Nostalgics		63
4 Tocqueville and the Sociology of Native Aristocrats		92
Part III Founding a Tradition: The German Romantic Travelers		113
5 Immigrants and Educated Observers		115
6 Maximilian of Wied and the Ethnography of Native Aristocrats		135
Epilogue: A World of New Aristocrats		165
A Note on Guides to Research		171
Index		173

Illustrations

1. *Sauvage du Canada,* 1784   *page* 15
2. *Femme sauvage du Canada,* 1784   16
3. *Un Roi Sauvage,* 1768   29
4. *... Je crus que c'était la Vierge des dernières amours,* 1805   44
5. *Horse Shoe of Niagara, from the Canada Side,* 1828–1829   67
6. *Les Natchez,* 1824–1835   77
7. *Lake George and the Village of Caldwell,* 1828–1829   85
8. *Wissigong, Indien Chippeway,* 1842   88
9. *Massika – Wakusásse,* 1839–1841   152
10. *Council of the Sacs and Foxes at Washington City,* 1842   153
11. *The Dying Tecumseh,* 1856   154
12. *Péhriska-Rúhpa,* 1839–1841   155
13. *Mató-Tópe,* 1839–1841   156
14. *Mató-Tópe, geschmückt mit den Zeichen seiner Kriegsthaten,* 1839–1841   158
15. *Péhriska-Rúhpa, Mönnitarri Krieger im Anzuge des Hundetanzes,* 1839–1841   160
16. *Bisontanz der Mandan Indianer,* 1839–1841   161
17. *A North American Indian,* 1878   169

Acknowledgments

This book has at times resembled a voyage in its own right, taking me to unfamiliar places and cultures. I could neither have ventured so widely, nor interpreted what I saw, without the generosity of others. Institutions have supported my work, and colleagues and friends have shared their knowledge with me from beginning to end. I am grateful to them all, including many whose names I have not mentioned.

I am indebted to Roger Chickering, Philippe Despoix, Peter Reill, Donald Ritchie, Guenther Roth, Jerrold Seigel, and Theodore Ziolkowski for their encouragement of my work over the past nine years. James Boon corrected ethnological errors and lightened my spirits; a master theorist, he never let me forget that this was to be a work of history. Natalie Z. Davis has been a special source of inspiration, prodding me to deeper sympathy with my historical subjects and demonstrating how biography can bring together seemingly alien worlds. Thomas Head set an example of how to combine dedication to European history with wide chronological and comparative perspectives. Carl Schorske, cherished mentor and friend, encouraged from the start my inclination to wander from Europe to new worlds and provided an ongoing model of professional dedication and integrity. Daniel Segal played a special role when he invited me in the late 1980s to learn more about anthropology by teaching two courses and organizing a conference with him. His rare commitment to mediating between history and anthropology has benefited me then and since; toward the end, our dialogue intensified once again when he read the entire manuscript. Bernard Smith's *European Vision and the South Pacific* came to my attention when my research was just beginning, and it has never ceased to influence the way I have asked questions about travel, especially in its relationship to art and science. I am thankful to Nicholas Thomas and Diane Losche for inviting me to take part in a most stimulating conference held in his honor and to meet Professor Smith at the Australian National

University, Canberra. William Truettner has been an invaluable guide to the art of the American West, deepening my understanding of aesthetic conventions and quickening my sensitivity to the ethical dimensions of studying American art and history.

The book was largely completed during my 1996–1997 stay as a Dilworth Member of the School of Historical Studies in the Institute for Advanced Study, Princeton, New Jersey. The Institute's atmosphere of conviviality and intellectual dedication contributed immeasurably to its final form. I am grateful to Phillip Griffiths, the Director of the Institute, and to the late J. Richardson Dilworth for their roles in making such a year possible. Peter Paret ensured a peaceful and productive work atmosphere and read the entire manuscript, sharing with me his expertise in early-nineteenth-century culture and offering judicious suggestions for the introduction and epilogue. Irving and Marilyn Lavin expanded my understanding of the art historical traditions underlying the illustrations. The faculty of the School of Social Science permitted me to make a presentation at one of their Thursday luncheons. Bonnie Smith read a large part of the manuscript and helped me place the French travelers in the larger context of pre-1848 French intellectual life. My thanks to Brigitte Bedos-Rezak, Sabine MacCormack, Charlotte Schoell-Glass, and Mark Turner for discussing various aspects of the book with me; and to Fernando Cervantes, Carlos Forment, and Donald Kelley for reading individual chapters. Old friends and new in the History Department of Princeton University attended a presentation in their European history colloquium in April 1997 and offered valuable criticisms then and on other occasions. I am especially indebted to Philip Nord for commenting on the chapters on Tocqueville and French travelers. Peter Brown read the entire manuscript and brought his universal historical knowledge and luminous psychological insight to bear on this extension of European history to the Plains of North America; his advice, and Betsy Brown's thoughtful reflections on the entire manuscript as well, were precious gifts in a bountiful year.

At the University of Illinois at Urbana-Champaign, my home institution, David Prochaska and the other members of the Cultural Studies Group provided fellowship and frank criticism of my work. Richard Burkhardt, Jr., shared with me his erudition in the naturalist tradition, indispensable for my comprehension of the scientific travelers. Alma Gottlieb's anthropological insight and Philip Graham's literary imagination enlivened numerous conversations and drew my attention to an overlooked choice of cover illustration. Jean-Philippe Mathy encouraged my interest and shared his own expertise in the history of French travelers. A research semester granted by the History Department, a semester in residence at the Center for Values and Ethics, and grants from the Research Board supported portions of the research for this book. A subvention from the Oliver M. Dickerson Fund of the History Department supported the publication costs. Elise Moentmann and Brent Maner served as conscientious research assistants.

For assistance in the use of their collections I am indebted to numerous librarians and archivists. Its staff, with their special dedication to scholarship, as well as its holdings, make the University of Illinois Library a great center for scholarly research. Mary Stuart was endlessly patient and helpful in answering my questions; John Hoffmann took special care to make available the resources of the Illinois Historical Survey; Nancy Romero and the Rare Books staff efficiently placed their collection at my disposal; and the Interlibrary Loan Office responded speedily to my requests. At The Newberry Library, John Aubrey shared with me his unequaled knowledge of the Ayer Collection. At the Institute for Advanced Study, Elliot Shore, Marcia Tucker, and other staff members worked wonders to fill my requests for books and microforms. I am grateful, too, to helpful library and other staff members at the American Philosophical Society, the Art Institute of Chicago, the Bayerische Staatsbibliothek of Munich, the Chicago Historical Society, the Deutsche Staatsbibliothek of Berlin, the Geheimes Staatsarchiv of Merseburg, the Geheimes Staatsarchiv of Berlin-Dahlem, the German Society of Pennsylvania, the Library of Congress, the Metropolitan Museum of Art, the National Museum of American Art, the New York Public Library, Princeton University, Southern Illinois University at Edwardsville (Research Collections), the United States Capitol (Office of the Architect of the Capitol), the University of Pennsylvania, and Yale University. At Cambridge University Press, Frank Smith has been a wonderfully attentive editor and Camilla Knapp as production editor carried the book on a smooth passage from manuscript to finished form.

Affectionate thanks to my wife Dorothee for her enthusiasm for the whole project and her readiness to criticize countless manuscript drafts alongside our adventure of raising the two dedicatees.

Introduction

One of Tocqueville's discoveries on his trip to the United States was an affinity between European aristocrats and American Indians. Here is his testimony from *Democracy in America:*

He thinks hunting and war the only cares worthy of a man. Therefore the Indian in the miserable depths of his forests cherishes the same ideas and opinions as the medieval noble in his castle, and he only needs to become a conqueror to complete the resemblance. How odd it is that the ancient prejudices of Europe should reappear, not among the European population along the coast, but in the forests of the New World.[1]

The statement distills a generational experience. Many other travelers of the early nineteenth century, too, felt a sense of kinship with American Indians. A few of them – the most ambitious ones, like Tocqueville, also aristocrats – actually hunted and rode with Indians. Others glimpsed them from afar or simply repeated earlier travelers' tales. These gentlemen on tour – scientists, soldiers, and political refugees – were not just visiting the frontier for pleasure; out of their encounters with American Indians they were helping to shape a new aristocratic culture.

Their aristocratic vision opened up at a moment of peculiar affinity between the destiny of warrior elites from two worlds. On the European side, an elite formed after the end of the Napoleonic Wars that brought the successful survivors of the old order's collapse together with wealthy and educated members of the upper middle class. This new aristocracy was adept at taking up symbols of the old noble way of life and streamlining them into an acceptable culture for an increasingly industrial, commercial, and emanci-

---

1. Alexis de Tocqueville, *Democracy in America*, ed. J. P. Mayer, trans. George Lawrence (Garden City, N.Y., 1969), 328. Cf. Alexis de Tocqueville, *Oeuvres complètes*, vol. 1, part 1, *De la Démocratie en Amérique*, ed. J. P. Mayer, introd. Harold J. Laski (Paris, 1961), 343–344. See also Harry Liebersohn, "Discovering Indigenous Nobility: Tocqueville, Chamisso, and Romantic Travel Writing," in *The American Historical Review* 99 (1994): 746–766.

pated society. For members of this elite, travel to the North American frontier was a passage to a world of male warrior virtue.[2]

On the other side of the encounter were the native peoples who dwelt along the East Coast and Southeast, the Great Lakes, and the Mississippi and the Missouri Rivers. Indian societies seemed to their admirers more aristocratic than Europeans themselves in their cultivation of warrior virtues. Among peoples favored by European travelers such as the Crows, the Mandans, the Osages, the Sauk and Fox, and the Blackfeet, boys learned from earliest youth on to cultivate qualities of courage, strength, bravery, and self-control that would bring success in hunting and battle. Myths and ceremonies were difficult for travelers to comprehend; horticulture and the role of women were uninteresting. But precisely their own background permitted elite Europeans to appreciate the brilliant dress of Crow warriors or the bravura of Osage hunters. These native peoples had the warrior's charisma that they had lost and wished to regain.[3]

European visitors could find parallels, too, between their own experiences of terror and exile in the years 1789 to 1815 and American Indians' struggle for survival. Peoples like the Iroquois and Hurons had thrived in the early eighteenth century by playing off the French, British, and Anglo-American invaders against one another. Later, the withdrawal first of the French and then of the British was for them a disaster. The Anglo-American victors pushed Indians westward from their native lands. Titled Europeans had themselves been recent victims of popular land hunger, and they knew how democratic societies could invent new laws to give legitimacy to expropriation. They could readily see through the deceptions of written treaties for Indian lands and knew the hardship of being driven from one's home. To be sure, many

2. The terms "aristocracy" and "nobility" do not admit of easy distinction. "Nobility" in pre-1789 Europe referred to a corporate, legally distinct, privileged elite. "Aristocracy" referred to the upper ranks within the nobility. Yet both "nobility" and "aristocracy" referred simultaneously to idealized personal qualities such as bravery, selflessness, adherence to a code of honor, and refined manners. After 1789–1790 the nobility no longer existed as a separate legal order in France; in Central Europe, privilege diminished over the course of the nineteenth century but persisted until 1918. For the nineteenth century I have generally preferred the term "aristocracy" to describe a social ideal that appealed to the educated and wealthy middle classes as much as to persons descended from families with pre-1789 noble origins. This emphasis on the newness of post-1789 aristocratic culture sets my interpretation apart from that of Arno J. Mayer, *The Persistence of the Old Regime: Europe to the Great War* (New York, 1981), which argues for an economic, political, and cultural continuity of the old regime until 1914. Mayer's book remains a valuable starting point for reconsideration of the aristocracy's role in the nineteenth century.
3. For a recent scholarly perspective see Frederick E. Hoxie, *Parading Through History: The Making of the Crow Nation in America, 1805–1935* (Cambridge and New York, 1995). The classic description of Plains warrior culture remains Robert H. Lowie, *Indians of the Plains* (1954; Garden City, N.Y. 1963).

titled Europeans clambered back to status and comfort despite the loss of legal privileges. Some identified with the expansion of Anglo-American civilization and felt no special regard for its victims. The trials of revolution and dictatorship for over a quarter century nonetheless stimulated others to develop a tragic perspective on the human costs of the settlement of a new continent.

This book relates in three parts how an aristocratic discourse on American Indians took shape: in the transition from old regime to Revolutionary France, in French travel writing from 1815 to 1848, and in German travel writing of the same era. Each part includes one survey chapter and one chapter on a major writer. The major figures memorialize the aristocratic character of Indians in fiction, social science, and ethnography; the minor travel writers document a broad revitalization of aristocratic ideals. It is primarily a book of European cultural and intellectual history, but it examines how extra-European experiences tinctured century-old traditions of behavior and belief.

Part I relates how the Romantic discourse took shape in response to Enlightenment debates on Indians. Our story starts with the philosophes' turn to the native peoples of Canada as natural democrats. After 1789 members of the old privileged elite, determined to tear down the philosophy of Rousseau that they blamed for the Revolution, took a new look at American Indians, sometimes denigrating figures elevated by the philosophes, sometimes discovering that Indians too were victims of revolutionaries. Chateaubriand, the subject of Chapter 2, dramatized the parallel between his personal suffering and the fate of American Indians in his novellas *Atala* and *René*. These works provided subsequent travelers with a style, a vocabulary, a cast of characters, and a set of landscapes for imagining Indians as native aristocracy.

The background to Parts II and III is the unsteady balance between elite control and democratic protest on both sides of the Atlantic. In France the restoration of the Bourbon monarchy after 1815 raised conservatives' hope that the movement of modern history toward democracy could be contained. Their confidence was jolted by the Revolution of 1830, which replaced the Bourbon monarch Charles X with his cousin of the Orléanist line, Louis Philippe. Modern society had lurched; it had a forward motion, felt by both French and German contemporaries, that could end in new catastrophes.[4] Travelers to the United States received a second shock: the era of political rule by Virginia plantation owners and patrician Bostonians was over. Andrew Jackson practiced a populist politics, American society a disregard for status

4. On the unsettling effect of the Revolution of 1830, see Karl Löwith, *Von Hegel zu Nietzsche: Der revolutionäre Bruch im Denken des neunzehnten Jahrhunderts* (Hamburg, 1986), 40–43.

distinctions, that rankled elite visitors. This conjuncture of events is the setting for the climax of our story, the visits of a cluster of elite observers in the early 1830s. They came just in time to observe Jackson's policy of forced removal of native peoples to territories beyond the Mississippi. The exterminating logic of democracy as they knew it already from the Terror once again displaced classes and peoples as part of the cost of progress.

French Romantic travelers in America, the protagonists of Part II, were an unusually politicized group, their nerve ends sensitized by the rapid succession of regimes since 1789. In our overview of French travelers in Chapter 3 they debate the pros and cons of American democracy, with some of them criticizing the chaos of popular rule and others defending a free society. Memories of cooperation in New France, as well as ambivalence toward Anglo-America, fed into French fondness for their former native allies. Tocqueville (who visited North America in 1831–1832) made a special trip to visit Ojibwas in the wilds of Michigan. No one more pointedly made the analogy of Indian and European aristocratic ethos; no one more effectively linked the condition of native peoples to a critique of Anglo-American conquest. He synthesized the insights of a generation of travelers with singularly trenchant sociological analysis.

Just when Tocqueville and his contemporaries were taking the measure of the end of their colonial involvement, Germans began an era of mass migration to the New World. Their debates are the subject of Chapter 5. At home the German ruling classes after 1815, like their French counterparts, faced the uncertainties of reestablishing their authority after decades of revolutionary challenge. While not hit as directly by the French Revolution, they had to contend with more drastic social and economic changes, including a rise in population, the decay of artisanal modes of production, and overseas migration. Germans of all classes (in contrast to the predominantly elite French authors) argued over whether America offered dignity or misery to German immigrants. Indians were a regular topic of discussion within this controversy. While farmers and artisans and their middle-class defenders saw in them only an obstacle to settlement, elite travelers were scandalized by Anglo-American injustices. A few actually ventured into frontier territory, and one of them, Prince Maximilian of Wied, traveled with the artist Karl Bodmer to make a rigorous ethnographic record of Plains and Prairie Indians. Their words and images were as faithful to the original as human circumstances would permit, yet they embodied a distinctly Romantic vision of native aristocracy.

This is a story that crosses many borders, temporal and geographic, and I have attempted both to delineate and to keep open the movement of people and ideas across them. One such border has to do with intellectual style: from the late eighteenth to the early nineteenth century, European descriptions of North American Indians shifted from a Neoclassical to a Romantic discourse. Enlightenment thinkers used classical allusions as a continuation of politics by other means: dressing up Indians in classical descriptions was a way to endow them with republican virtues. At the beginning of the nineteenth century, Romantic writers turned this use of native societies upside down: developing their aesthetic and political ideas in response to the French Revolution, and anxious about their status as members of learned elites in a democratizing Europe, they discovered in American Indians an aristocratic ethos. Man in his original condition was no longer Rousseau's exemplar of equality but a being of rank and honor. In other respects, however, the legacies of the eighteenth century and Romanticism were not rigorously opposed in travel writing; one could uphold an enlightened scientific ethos while elevating natives' social status.

Another border is geographic. The differences between French and German travelers are great enough to recommend discussion of them in separate chapters. Pride in belonging to a great nation set the French apart from their neighbors across the Rhine, while the mass overseas migration of Central Europeans later conditioned the observations of German visitors to the United States. It would be anachronistic, however, to separate the elite cultures of France and Germany during the Romantic era without indicating, too, their many points of transition. French émigrés from the Revolution took refuge in Germany, and German artists and writers made themselves at home in Paris. This was the time, too, when Mme. De Staël wrote *De L'Allemagne* with the help of a lover who was one of the founders of Romanticism in Germany, August von Schlegel; when a French refugee, Adelbert von Chamisso, became one of the arbiters of German literary life; and when Alexander von Humboldt spent years living in Paris as a leader of its scientific establishment (and publishing his account of his voyage to South America in French) before returning to play the same role in Berlin. National loyalties mattered, but so did cosmopolitan conversations that transcended linguistic and state-imposed borders.

British travelers inhabited a world farther apart. The ex-colonial relationship between the United States and England was a love-hate affair without a Continental counterpart. The worldwide success of their commerce and empire-building encouraged an aloof British view of native peoples. Evangelicalism added a religious motive for repudiating the kind of enlightened curiosity that had inspired the members of Captain Cook's voyages in the late eighteenth century and condemning indigenous sexual and religious practices. Above all, the British ruling class never knew the French and German experience of persecution, exile, and loss of status. While English travelers sometimes complained about American mistreatment of Indians, they more typically had the unromantic attitude of successful colonial masters. It was a bitter quarter century of seeing the world upside down that prepared Continental travelers for a sense of identification with the nobility and suffering they observed among Native Americans.[5]

While the accounts of English travelers diverge more than one might expect at first sight, Anglo-Americans offer more notable cases of convergence with French and German discovery of native aristocracy. Although many took pride in their countrymen's westward expansion and expulsion of native inhabitants, one needs to treat European condemnations of American heartlessness with critical caution. Others were moved to moral indignation by the government-sanctioned injustices culminating in Andrew Jackson's policy of forced appropriation of Indian lands. They, too, could indirectly criticize democratic hypocrisy and bolster their own sense of superior status by sympathizing with the peoples whom the artist George Catlin called "nature's noblemen."

The Romantic travelers to North America seem at first to take us to a sought-after destination: a zone of encounter between European and non-European cultures. Critics in recent years have challenged interpreters of European history to be less insular and to recognize the steady traffic of ideas going into and out of the subcontinent, steadily enriching its stores of art and thought.[6] With their interest in Indians, the travelers appear to open up one avenue and permit us to acknowledge the flow of foreign influences. All that we have to do for an exercise in cosmopolitan history, it seems, is to take up the travel accounts and read.

5. For a general orientation to British attitudes toward native peoples in the late eighteenth and early nineteenth centuries, see George W. Stocking, Jr., *Victorian Anthropology* (New York, 1987); and Bernard Smith, *European Vision and the South Pacific*, 2nd ed. (New Haven, Conn., 1985). Although it lies beyond the scope of this book, the early history of New England offers striking evidence for the "aristocratic" character of Indians in European eyes. Karen O. Kupperman has made a sustained argument for the priority of status categories in the thinking of seventeenth-century English settlers, whose leaders could treat elite Americans as their status equals and describe them in the language of nobility. See idem., "Presentment of Civility: English Reading of American Self-Presentation in the Early Years of Colonization," in *The William and Mary Quarterly* 54 (1997): 193–227. James Axtell notes that Puritans found the long hair of Indian men an abhorrent symbol of personal pride and independence that reminded them of their Cavalier enemies. See Axtell, *The European and the Indian: Essays in the Ethnohistory of Colonial North America* (New York and Oxford, 1981), 59–62.
6. See, for example, Mary Louise Pratt, *Imperial Eyes: Travel Writing and Transculturation* (New York, 1992).

Anyone who follows this advice, however, discovers that travelers do not tell straightforward stories. How and what do they "see"? Travelers' perceptions can never be neutral; they are formed by their home culture. What one scoops out as meaningful from the chaos of new impressions depends on unconscious processes of selection that have been formed since infancy. The clearest example of this is linguistic competence: what we hear is affected by the set of sounds we have grown up to hear. While our ears will absorb some of the sounds in a foreign language system, they will also miss significant distinctions. English speakers may be unable to hear the difference between *Ratten* and *raten* ("rats" and "advise") in German, since they have not been trained to make a comparable distinction in their mother tongue. We can only sort out so much, and what we notice may be different from what natives think is important. The same is true for the whole range of human activities, from something as trivial as closing a door (not trivial in Germany if you forget to do it) to respecting religious taboos. As an isolated individual, no traveler can observe another culture without making systematic errors; as a member of one culture in regular contact with another, a traveler relies on predecessors from home and finds confirmation of his own misperceptions by reading them and seeing what they have seen. There is no sure-fire way for travelers to correct their perceptions, just as there is no guarantee that present-day scholars do not impose a modern belief system on past travelers.[7]

The Romantics themselves were the ancestors of our deliberations over these difficulties of cultural communication. Historians do well to turn to an era for guidance to its peculiar preoccupations, and we can look to the

---

7. On the tradition of linguistic relativity, see John A. Lucy, *Language Diversity and Thought: A Reformulation of the Linguistic Relativity Hypothesis* (Cambridge and New York, 1992); and Roger Langham Brown, *Wilhelm von Humboldt's Conception of Linguistic Relativity* (The Hague and Paris, 1967). See also the classic essay by Franz Boas, "On Alternating Sounds" (1889), in *A Franz Boas Reader: The Shaping of American Anthropology, 1883–1911,* ed. George W. Stocking, Jr. (Chicago and London, 1974), 72–77.

The intellectual historians of anthropology, too, have made an effective critique of anthropology's knowledge of "others" that makes us both more wary of the discipline's claims to scientific status of a positivist kind and more sympathetic to the reports of pre–twentieth-century travelers. Travel writing no longer seems just like a prescientific or protoscientific prelude to anthropology, but may instead be examined as a form in its own right of knowledge about foreign cultures. From the large recent literature see the *History of Anthropology* series (Madison, Wisc., and London, 1983–); Marc Manganaro, ed., *Modernist Anthropology: From Fieldwork to Text* (Princeton, N.J., 1990); and James Clifford, *The Predicament of Culture: Twentieth-Century Ethnography, Literature, and Art* (Cambridge, Mass., and London, 1988). Accomplished anthropologists have recently turned to travel writing as an alternative to the monograph. See Alma Gottlieb and Philip Graham, *Parallel Worlds: An Anthropologist and a Writer Encounter Africa* (New York, 1993); and Richard Price and Sally Price, *Equatoria* (New York and London, 1992). For a more detailed discussion of the relationship between travel writing and anthropology see Harry Liebersohn, "Recent Works on Travel Writing," in *The Journal of Modern History* 68 (1996): 617–628.

Romantics for a special form of engagement with language that can guide our understanding of them.[8] It is no accident that theirs was a great age not only of curiosity about foreign cultures and expansion of the European canon of world literature, but also of translation, an art that the German Romantics in particular practiced with special creative skill. We may find in their traveling a parallel to the task of the translator. Travel writing is a labor of translation – literally, of "carrying over" from one place to another. To be sure, translations leave the original more or less behind, stuffing all the materials of a foreign language into differently organized cubicles. The self-centeredness of translations, though, does not entirely subvert communication. Otherwise we would not argue over good and bad translations, ones that get the original wrong and ones that get it right, ones that drain the spice and ones that keep it, ones that impose iamb and rhyme and ones that invigorate our own language with alien forms. And as Walter Benjamin argued, a translation can also be an *expansion* of the original, bringing out new dimensions of meaning in the medium of a new tongue. So it is with travel writing. Some of it is bad translation borrowed from older bad translations. Some shows a working knowledge of the foreign culture but is still too dependent on homegrown prejudice to yield original insight. Some leans on intuition without evidence. The best travel testimony combines insight and evidence, imagination and science. We shall encounter all of these kinds of writing in the accounts of Europeans who visited North America a century and a half ago.[9]

It is difficult to adopt a method of analyzing travel encounters that is supple enough to follow the movement of travelers and their writings across the many borders I have named. One school of writing about cross-cultural encounters, beginning with Edward Said's *Orientalism*, has emphasized the moment of pure projection of Western power onto non-Western societies, in which Western scholars and artists have used other parts of the world as a *terra incognita* on which to write their fantasies of pleasure or cruelty while constructing an antithetical Western identity. Works in this tradition have had

8. This methodological precept is one of the enduring insights of Clifford Geertz, *The Interpretation of Cultures* (New York, 1973). For two brilliant historical examples, see the use of Hegel's theory of personal development as a guide to Marx's biography in Jerrold Seigel, *Marx's Fate* (Princeton, N.J., 1978); and of Oedipal conflict as a model for understanding cultural modernism in Carl E. Schorske, *Fin de Siècle Vienna: Politics and Culture* (New York, 1980).
9. For a starting point in English, see Walter Benjamin, "The Task of the Translator," in *Illuminations*, ed. and introd. Hannah Arendt (New York, 1968), 69–82; and "On Language as Such and on the Language of Man" in *Reflections*, ed. and introd. Peter Demetz (New York and London, 1978), 314–332. Important background for understanding Benjamin's theory of translation and its derivation from the Romantics is his dissertation, "Der Begriff der Kunstkritik in der deutschen Romantik," in *Gesammelte Schriften*, ed. Rolf Tiedemann and Hermann Schweppenhäuser (Frankfurt am Main, 1974), vol. 1, part 1, 7–122.

a critical function of challenging their readers to scrutinize the habits, language, and presumptions of the literary past for participation, voluntary or involuntary, in the work of colonialism.[10] This kind of radical critique occupies a place comparable to the role of Georg Lukács's *History and Class Consciousness* (1923), whose universal suspicion of bourgeois thought revolutionized the Marxian cultural criticism of the 1920s and 1930s. Just as the brilliant clarity of Lukács's analysis gave way to the Frankfurt School's more differentiated and diffident investigations, however, the contention of an inherent colonialism in Western culture has given way to a blurrier map of cultural encounters.[11] The early modern era has been particularly fertile ground for this kind of reexamination. Each side, native and European, approached the other with what Stuart Schwartz has called "implicit understandings," a set of cultural assumptions that shaped its perceptions of foreigners; those assumptions underwent transformation in initial meetings and continued to change over later periods of time. In recent years the scholarship of early encounters has turned into a series of subtle and unpredictable adventures, restoring something of our own sense of wonder at the diverse stories that cultures tell about one another.[12]

Romantic travelers have a story of their own to tell, related to yet removed from the world of their predecessors. The early sense of wonder, of experiencing things new and fresh and marvelous to the point of incomprehensibility, had given way to back-and-forth borrowings.[13] Richard White has recovered the history of a "middle ground" that was neither French nor native but

10. Edward W. Said, *Orientalism* (New York, 1978). Cf. Dennis Porter, *Haunted Journeys: Desire and Transgression in European Travel Writing* (Princeton, N.J., 1991), and Timothy Mitchell, *Colonising Egypt* (Cambridge, 1988), for two stimulating recent interpretations of Western colonization of "others." Ruel W. Tyson, *"Live by Comparisons": A New Home for Reason in the University,"* Sixth Annual Memorial Lecture of the Society for Values in Higher Education, introd. Agnes M. Jackson (Knoxville, Tenn., 1988), is an especially thoughtful meditation on the critique of colonialism as a challenge to inherited cultural habits.

11. For a fuller critique of *History and Class Consciousness*, see Harry Liebersohn, *Fate and Utopia in German Sociology, 1870–1923* (Cambridge, Mass., and London, 1988), 190–196.

12. Stuart B. Schwartz, ed., *Implicit Understanding: Observing, Reporting, and Reflecting on the Encounters Between Europeans and Other Peoples in the Early Modern Era* (Cambridge and New York, 1994), especially the editor's introduction, 1–3, 15. Cf. Karen O. Kupperman, ed., *America in European Consciousness 1493–1750* (Chapel Hill, N.C., and London, 1995), especially the editor's discussion of the subtle changes in identity among groups on both sides of the Atlantic, 4–5, 22–24; and Stephen Greenblatt, ed., *New World Encounters* (Berkeley and Los Angeles, 1993). Natalie Zemon Davis, *Women at the Margins* (Cambridge, Mass., and London, 1995), suggests a new kind of global history that can capture the localness of European lives and their overseas transformation.

13. See the splendid evocation of the early encounters in Stephen Greenblatt, *Marvelous Possessions: The Wonder of the New World* (Chicago, 1991), which, as its title suggests, balances its account of Europeans' sense of wonder with recognition of their imperial ambitions.

a new constellation formed out of earlier cultures in the Lower Great Lakes region. The Romantic travelers who are the main focus of this book arrived after this middle ground had been torn apart and had given way to the deadly opposition of "Indian" and "white," but they could still observe, and frequently comment on, the bits and pieces of it that survived, especially in the form of Indian friendliness toward French visitors and knowledge of their language.[14] By their time, travel experiences had become, in James Boon's term, "echoey": their perceptions of Indian societies were inseparable from wave after wave of historical experience carried back and forth across the Atlantic.[15] Old legends, learned prejudices, memories of colonial partnership, revolutionary traumas, shrewd Indian role playing for their visitors, and travelers' posing for audiences back home came together in their testimony. The travelers themselves did not always like to see it that way; in their less ironic moments, they were convinced that one could meet pristine peoples if only one pushed far enough into the interior of North America. Paradoxically, they sought out a place they called a "wilderness" while selectively translating to merge its features with European memories of a high and ancient way of life. Discreet editing fashioned for themselves and their readers the fiction of natural aristocrats, unchanged since the creation, whom one could glimpse just before the democratic civilization of Anglo-America surged over and forever buried them. Their travel writings offered a vision of aristocracy as the natural condition of man before the turmoil and decay of historical time.

14. See Richard White, *The Middle Ground: Indians, Empires, and Republics in the Great Lakes Region, 1650–1815* (Cambridge and New York, 1991).
15. See James A. Boon, "Cosmopolitan Moments: Echoey Confessions of an Ethnographer-Tourist," in Daniel Segal, ed., *Crossing Cultures: Essays in the Displacement of Western Civilization* (Tucson, Ariz., and London, 1992), 226–253. My understanding of travel in an "echoey" age has also been enriched by idem., *Affinities and Extremes: Crisscrossing the Bittersweet Ethnology of East Indies History, Hindu-Balinese Culture, and Indo-European Allure* (Chicago and London, 1990); *Other Tribes, Other Scribes: Symbolic Anthropology in the Comparative Study of Cultures, Histories, Religions, and Texts* (Cambridge and New York, 1982); and *The Anthropological Romance of Bali 1597–1972: Dynamic Perspectives in Marriage and Caste, Politics and Religion* (Cambridge and New York, 1977).

PART I

From Neoclassicism to Romanticism:
France and American Indians,
1682–1815

1

Indians in the French Enlightenment

A 1780s guide to costumes from around the world included a chapter on the manners and customs of Canadian "savages."[1] The compiler, Jacques Grasset de Saint-Sauveur, made the Iroquois polity a political reproach to his countrymen. "The form of their government," he wrote, "has a simplicity and at the same time a wisdom that our profound legislators have not yet been able to achieve in their sophisticated codes." Each tribe chose a military leader for his valor, a civilian leader for his eloquence. One representative from each family served the two chiefs, who were in turn but the general expression of the assembled nation. The paterfamilias kept unchallenged control over his household. "Is it necessary then to go to the Iroquois," Grasset asked in conclusion, "to find a model of legislation?"[2]

1. Montaigne had already questioned the pejorative connotations of the term *sauvage* in his essay on cannibals, but his countrymen continued their un-self-conscious, usually contemptuous use of it. Germans used an equally contemptuous term, *wild*, to describe indigenous peoples of North America and other parts of the world. Unless the context otherwise makes it clear, I have used either quotation marks or the French or German word in order to signal its historical status. See Michel de Montaigne, *Essais*, ed. Alexandre Micha (Paris, 1969), 1: 254; cf. Montaigne, *Essays*, trans. and ed. J. M. Cohen (London and New York, 1958), 108–109. It is especially relevant to the concerns of this book that Montaigne tried to make the Tupinamba Indians admirable to his contemporaries as the upholders of a chivalric ethos. Cf. David Quint, "A Reconsideration of Montaigne's *Des cannibales*," in Karen O. Kupperman, ed., *America in European Consciousness, 1493–1750* (Chapel Hill, N.C., and London, 1995), 166–191; and the discussion of the chivalric code in the splendid editor's introduction to one of Montaigne's probable sources, Jean de Léry, *History of a Voyage to the Land of Brazil, Otherwise Called America*, ed. and introd. Janet Whately (Berkeley and Los Angeles, 1990), esp. xxiv–xxvii.

2. Jacques Grasset de Saint-Sauveur with Sylvain Maréchal, *Costumes civils actuels de tous les peuples connus, dessinés d'après nature, gravés et coloriés, accompagnés d'une notice historique de leurs coutumes, moeurs, religions, sciences, arts, commerce, monnoies &c.&c.* (1784; Paris, 1788), "Moeurs et coutumes des sauvages du Canada," 6. Grasset himself was born in Canada. See E. Hubert, "Grasset de Saint-Sauveur," in *Dictionnaire de biographie française* (Paris, 1933), 7: cols. 1076–1077.

Perhaps our first impulse today is to smile at Grasset's question. His praise of the Iroquois belonged to a broader stream of eighteenth-century novels, stories, poetry, plays, and art that praised non-Europeans in order to point out the shortcomings of European society and government.[3] Despite his question he did not seem to be traveling at all, just idealizing European qualities and wrapping them up in native costume. In his illustrations the Iroquois man fits heroic or even godlike conventions of European art, and the woman's dress and raised hand suggest the delicacy of a middle-class matron. These "Indians" look at first sight like Frenchmen in drag[4] (Figs. 1 and 2).

Enlightenment fables, like myths from other times and places, may have a surface implausibility that disguises deeper layers of meaning. And so it is with Grasset's remarks. His book does not *just* impose European conventions on alien peoples. Rather, it gives indirect expression to the challenge posed by native forms of authority. French visitors came from an absolute monarchy attempting to impose its authority on society; they encountered peoples like the Iroquois who conducted war and peacemaking on the basis of consensus, permitted divorce, and raised their children without beating them. We need to consider more closely the historical shaping of hierarchy in Europe in order to understand how Grasset's contemporaries, even if they did not have to go to the Iroquois, found it worthwhile to talk about them.

Liberal societies of the nineteenth and twentieth centuries, beneficiaries of the age of revolution, are founded on the idea of legal equality. Vast differences in

---

3. See Gilbert Chinard, *L'Amérique et le rêve exotique dans la littérature française au 17. et au 18. siècle* (Paris, 1913); Geoffroy Atkinson, *The Extraordinary Voyage in French Literature Before 1700* (New York, 1920), especially the discussion of Fénélon's *Aventures de Télémaque* (1699), 144ff.; Atkinson, *The Extraordinary Voyage in French Literature from 1700 to 1720* (Paris, 1922); Benjamin Bissell, *The American Indian in English Literature of the Eighteenth Century* (New Haven, Conn., 1925); Hoxie Neale Fairchild, *The Noble Savage: A Study in Romantic Naturalism* (New York, 1928); Lois Whitney, *Primitivism and the Idea of Progress in English Popular Literature of the Eighteenth Century* (Baltimore, 1934); Henri Baudet, *Paradise on Earth: Some Thoughts on European Images of Non-European Man*, trans. Elizabeth Wentholt (New Haven and London, 1965); Hayden White, "The Noble Savage Theme as Fetish," in Fredi Chiappelli et al., eds., *First Images of America: The Impact of the New World on the Old*, 2 vols. (Berkeley and Los Angeles, 1976), 1: 121–135; Robert Berkhofer, Jr., *The White Man's Indian: Images of the American Indian from Columbus to the Present* (New York, 1978), 77–79; Tzvetan Todorov, *On Human Diversity: Nationalism, Racism, and Exoticism in French Thought*, trans. Catherine Porter (Cambridge, Mass., 1993), 270–277.

4. The model for the male figure is the Apollo Belvedere, a Roman sculpture probably going back to a Greek original, which was found at the beginning of the sixteenth century and celebrated thereafter as an exemplar of male beauty. See Luca Leoncini, "Apollo Belvedere," in *The Dictionary of Art* (London, 1996), 2: 226–227. There is a picture of the sculpture in *Encyclopedia of World Art* (London, 1971), 3: pl. 383. I thank Irving Lavin, Marilyn Lavin, and the participants in the art history seminar at the Institute for Advanced Study for pointing out the resemblance.

1. *Sauvage du Canada.* From Jacques Grasset de Saint-Sauveur with Sylvain Maréchal, "Moeurs et coutumes des sauvages du Canada," in *Costumes civils actuels de tous les peuples connus, dessinés d'après nature, gravés et coloriés, accompagnés d'une notice historique de leurs coutumes, moeurs, religions, sciences, arts, commerce, monnoies &c.&c.* (1784; Paris, 1788). Courtesy of Art and Architecture Collection, Miriam and Ira D. Wallach Division of Art, Prints and Photographs, The New York Public Library, Astor, Lenox, and Tilden Foundations.

2. *Femme sauvage du Canada.* From Grasset, "Moeurs et coutumes des sauvages du Canada," in *Costumes civils.* . . . Courtesy of Art and Architecture Collection, Miriam and Ira D. Wallach Division of Art, Prints and Photographs, The New York Public Library, Astor, Lenox, and Tilden Foundations.

wealth may separate rich and poor, but all are supposed to enjoy one set of laws and rights. Pre–Revolutionary European societies worked on the opposite principle of legal inequality. Each individual belonged to a corporate body (or several overlapping bodies), and membership determined one's place in society: as part of a household, follower of a religious confession, noble, bourgeois, peasant, practitioner of a trade, inhabitant of a region, or citizen of a town. To each of these groups attached privileges, particular advantages jealously guarded from outsiders. It was not just the elite that had status and privileges; lesser groups too enjoyed freedoms specific to their rank. The peasants who took part in a village council, the artisans entitled to practice their craft, the bourgeois licensed to trade, the judges who owned their court seats – groups like these vied for advantage in a world where some walked with the pride of command, others with the humility of obedience.[5]

The divisions between nobility and nonnobility ran deep but were permeable. Whoever was lucky enough to have a title enjoyed substantial material privileges, like freedom from taxation, as well as honorific privileges like hunting rights that dramatized social superiority. While the legal distinction was substantial and visible, the nobility was never a caste closed off from the rest of society. Despite an ideology propagated by extreme defenders of exclusiveness that the true nobility was a separate race descended from Germanic conquerors, only a minority of all noble families by the eighteenth century were descended from the medieval warrior estate. In social practice, the upper reaches of nonnoble society – in particular wealthy financiers and distinguished members of learned professions – could gain noble status for themselves and their descendants. Revising the Marxian image of a radical conflict of economic interest between the two groups, historians have in recent decades emphasized their interpenetration, and indeed the consolidation of noble and nonnoble elites, in the decades leading up to 1789.[6]

5. For a discussion of privilege in eighteenth-century France, see Gail Bossenga, *The Politics of Privilege: Old Regime and Revolution in Lille* (Cambridge and New York, 1991), 4–8. See also the valuable comparative interpretation of C. B. A. Behrens, *Society, Government, and the Enlightenment: The Experiences of Eighteenth-Century France and Prussia* (New York, 1985); and the discussion of Germany in Werner Conze, "Stand, Klasse," part 7, in Otto Brunner, Werner Conze, and Reinhart Koselleck, eds., *Geschichtliche Grundbegriffe* (Stuttgart, 1990), 6: 200–217. For a European-wide survey, see Jerome Blum, *The End of the Old Order in Rural Europe* (Princeton, N.J., 1978). Cf. Max Weber, *Economy and Society: An Outline of Interpretive Sociology*, ed. Guenther Roth and Claus Wittich, trans. Ephraim Fischoff et al. (Berkeley and Los Angeles, 1978), 932–933, 1087, 1105. Weber anticipated the current preoccupation with cultural history by emphasizing that honor was the specific characteristic of *Stände* (estates or status groups) and that honor was linked to "a specific *style of life*" (932).
6. For the social history of nobility in the old regime, see Guy Chaussinand-Nogaret, *The French Nobility in the Eighteenth Century: From Feudalism to Enlightenment*, trans. William Doyle (Cambridge and New York, 1985); and William Doyle, *Origins of the French Revolution* (Oxford, 1988), 116–127.

Nobility was more than just a form of social advantage, however. It signified a *culture* as much as a social rank. It was not just a way of ordering society, efficient or inefficient, but also a way of life manifest in the man with the
right to duel, the wife who led a salon, the child reared to public prominence.
It looked back to ancient traditions of military service, which eighteenth-
century nobles clung to as their proper calling; it included the social grace and
conversational skills perfected at court; it demanded honorable and dignified
behavior of the judges and administrators whose offices conferred noble
rank; it announced itself in the dress and comportment of social leadership.
Moreover, nobility was never just a synonym for ancient lineage; those born
into noble families had to prove their noble qualities through personal acts of
merit. The most recent round of scholarship suggests a deep ambivalence of
nonnoble public opinion toward society's designated superiors. In the twi-
light years of the old regime, radical pamphleteers eroded its legitimacy by
accusing it of corruption and sexual profligacy, while members of the middle
class developed their own distinctive ideology of domesticity and utility. Yet
the qualities of an idealized nobility entranced the imagination of nonnobles
too. Ambitious nonnobles who felt themselves to be within reach of it made
strenuous efforts to lift themselves into its ranks.[7]

Court and counselors in Paris took it for granted that they would transplant
their privileged order when they colonized across the sea. By the late seventeenth century, France had successfully established a colonial society in
present-day Canada with a rich fur trade, settlers firmly established on New
World soil, a wealthy and aristocratic merchant elite, and a cultivated and
energetic church – a distinctively French society, though with opportunities
greater than those in the metropolis for social mobility. This was a colonial
modification of the kind of seigneurial system that existed in France.[8] From

---

7. On the nobility's understanding of the relationship between birth and merit, see Jay M. Smith,
   *The Culture of Merit: Nobility, Royal Service, and the Making of Absolute Monarchy in
   France, 1600–1789* (Ann Arbor, Mich., 1996); and Ellery Schalk, *From Valor to Pedigree: Ideas
   of Nobility in France in the Sixteenth and Seventeenth Centuries* (Princeton, N.J., 1986).
   Smith's work is an ingenious corrective to that of Chaussinand-Nogaret, which treats conceptions of merit as a foreign import into the nobility.
      On the old regime's legitimation crisis, see Sarah Maza, *Private Lives and Public Affairs:
   The Causes Célèbres of Pre-Revolutionary France* (Berkeley and Los Angeles, 1993). On the
   ideology of the middle class, see David Garrioch, *The Formation of the Parisian Bourgeoisie
   1690–1830* (Cambridge, Mass., and London, 1996), especially the discussion of middle-class
   ideology, 281. See also the delineation of the explosion of hatred against the nobility in the
   opening stages of the Revolution in Timothy Tackett, *Becoming a Revolutionary: The
   Deputies of the French National Assembly and the Emergence of a Revolutionary Culture
   (1789–1790)* (Princeton, N.J., 1996).
8. See Guy Frégault, *La Civilisation de la Nouvelle-France, 1713–1744* (Montreal, 1969),
   132–153, and W. J. Eccles, *Canada Under Louis XIV, 1663–1701* (Toronto and New York,

the beginning, it was difficult to make the colonial reality fit the seigneurial ideal. French explorers and settlers moved westward and began filtering down the Mississippi Valley in the late seventeenth century. The French government only sporadically supported the new outposts. It was afraid that the *coureurs de bois*, the "runners through the woods" who actually hunted, trapped, and traded with Native Americans, would corrode the whole social order if they were allowed to run free the length of the Mississippi. But by the beginning of the eighteenth century these men had forced the government to recognize them as a free and independent force, and the ministers in Paris followed their trails into the interior of the continent.[9] They were also unavoidable allies if the French wished to have any chance of competing with British settlement and trade. One of the costs of empire was this tension between imposed hierarchy and freedom on the ground.

The economy and diplomacy of New France depended on French partnership with native peoples. Without Indians there could be none of the furs that were the chief source of surplus wealth. Indians were invaluable allies against the English and fearsome foes of soldiers and settlers. Yet Indians were not just strangers; they were also neighbors and relatives. During the first half of the eighteenth century, the Lower Great Lakes region was the center of a new culture emerging from French and Indian encounters: French military governors encouraged it with gifts and dispensation of justice, Indian leaders accepted it to bolster their own power, and the region's villages housed *métis* families and a blend of European and native cultural practices.[10]

Indian ways of doing things were different enough to resist any simple application of European categories to them. If we turn to our opening example of Grasset's Iroquois, for example, we find societies in which there were households, but not of a kind to appeal to a would-be French paterfamilias. The Iroquois traditionally inhabited so-called longhouses, structures that might be forty-two meters long and hold five pairs of nuclear families facing one another across a central isle of hearths. Husbands lived in their wives' household, within which the dominant authority figures were the respected senior women of a lineage.[11] As for Iroquois political organization, in contrast to European decision-making structures it rested on persuasion. At both the village level and in the great council that united members of the different

1964), 48–52. For general background see also Denys Delàge, *Bitter Feast: Amerindians and Europeans in Northeastern North America, 1600–64*, trans. Jane Brierley (Vancouver, 1993).

9. See Eccles, *Canada Under Louis XIV*, 246–248.

10. The formation of a Franco-Indian world is described in Richard White, *The Middle Ground: Indians, Empires, and Republics in the Great Lakes Region, 1650–1815* (Cambridge and New York, 1991).

11. Dean R. Snow, *The Iroquois* (Cambridge, Mass., and Oxford, 1994), 43–44, 129.

peoples comprising the Iroquois, a leader worked through his eloquence, his reputation for good judgment, and his generosity, not coercion.[12] Elements of both aristocratic and democratic rule entered into government. Iroquois peoples honored personal achievement and were impatient with claims to authority that were not backed up by it. Those who did live up to cultural models of heroism in hunting, warfare, and spiritual quest were venerated. The sachems who fulfilled this ideal displayed the kind of self-confidence that Europeans associated with their titled elites. Whether Europeans discovered Iroquois to be aristocratic or democratic depended on the observer's perspective. And this perspective, in turn, usually emerged from a traveler's reasons for going to North America.

One widely read group of eighteenth-century writings was the reports of missionaries. In particular the Jesuits, with their commitment to understanding non-Christian cultures and their willingness to wander far beyond the limits of European settlement, were in an unusually favorable position to report on native peoples. The missionaries who worked beyond the security of Quebec and Montreal endured lives of unremitting hardship. After thirty years in Canadian missions, François de Crepieul summed up his life in 1697 as "a long and slow martyrdom" of exposure to the cold and sleeping on the frozen ground, of contending with dogs, vermin, and smoke-filled Indian cabins, of drinking dirty water and eating half-cooked meat. "Holy but arduous" he called the missions – as if the test were almost too severe for even the most dedicated servant to bear.[13] Five years later, Étienne de Carheil wrote a long letter complaining about the two evils of trade in alcohol and sex between French and Indians. "Both," he commented,

are carried on in an equally public manner, without our being able to remedy the evil, because we are not supported by the Commandants. They – far from attempting, when we undertake to remonstrate with them, to check these trades – themselves carry them on with greater freedom than do their Subordinates; and so sanction them by their example that, on witnessing it, a general permission and an assurance of impunity are assumed, that cause them to become Common to all the french who come here to trade.[14]

---

12. See Daniel K. Richter, *The Ordeal of the Longhouse: The Peoples of the Iroquois League in the Era of European Colonization* (Chapel Hill, N.C., and London, 1992), 39–49.
13. Father François de Crepieul, "The Life of a Montagnaix Missionary, Presented to his Successors in the Montagnaix Mission for Their Instruction and Greater Consolation," April 21, 1697, in *The Jesuit Relations and Allied Documents: Travel and Explorations of the Jesuit Missionaries in New France, 1610–1791 . . .*, vol. 65: *Lower Canada, Mississippi Valley (1696–1702)*, ed. Reuben G. Thwaites (Cleveland, 1900), 43, 49.
14. Carheil to Louis Hector de Callières, governor, August 30, 1702, ibid., 193–195.

Trappers and traders imported alcohol as one of the most sought-after commodities. Women, as Carheil himself admitted, performed crucial household tasks for their French partners, pounding corn and cooking, cutting their wood, washing their clothes, and making shoes and other garments, and their physical proximity led to sexual relations.[15]

Jesuit views on Indians were anything but uniform. They ranged from satisfaction with the modest and friendly character of some peoples to frustration over others' sexual morality, witchcraft, and willfulness. Their Christianity provided them with a firm standard of judgment; they sized up Indians according to how closely they held to their own religious principles and their need for successful conversion work.

This point of view is highly evident in the writing of the most able Jesuit ethnographer, Jean-François Lafitau. He went to New France after receiving a thorough humanist education and spent nearly six years, from 1712 to 1717, as a missionary among the Iroquois. Lafitau believed that all mankind originally had had one religion, and he drew parallels between Greco-Roman and Iroquois religious practices. The classical analogies did not preclude close observation of Iroquois mores (including prescient insight into Iroquois kinship relations, later a chief theme of modern anthropology developed by Lewis Henry Morgan from the Iroquois example). They also permitted him to drive home to European readers his conviction that Indians were not merely repositories of superstition, but were receptive to Christian doctrine and moral precept.[16] At first sight, he wrote, Europeans might not get a favorable impression of Indians. They lacked letters, science, laws, temples, the external apparatus of religion, and the comforts of European material culture; travelers had gone on to paint them as stupid, crude, ignorant, and lacking in religious or humane sensibility. But this was a false portrait. He thought they

---

15. Ibid., 231.
16. See the editors' introduction to Joseph-François Lafitau, *Customs of the American Indians Compared With The Customs Of Primitive Times*, ed. and trans. William N. Fenton and Elizabeth L. Moore, 2 vols. (Toronto, 1974), 1, esp. xxix–xxxi and xlvi–xlviii, which praises Lafitau as a founder of modern anthropology. Anthony Pagden, *European Encounters with the New World* (New Haven, 1993), comes to the skeptical conclusion that "Lafitau's comparative method subsumes two or more unrelated cultures beneath a single, culturally specific, gaze" (149). Michel de Certeau suggests that Lafitau was indeed a founder of an anthropological "science" – one that abstracts from its subjects and from history. See De Certeau, "Writing vs. Time: History and Anthropology in the Works of Lafitau," in *Yale French Studies* 59 (1980): 37–64, esp. 47–49, 59–60. An especially differentiated appraisal of Lafitau is to be found in Sabine MacCormack, "Limits of Understanding: Perceptions of Greco-Roman and Amerindian Paganism in Early Modern Europe," in Karen O. Kupperman, ed., *America in European Consciousness 1493–1750* (Chapel Hill, N.C., and London, 1995), 108–114, which simultaneously recognizes Lafitau's flattening of native religions into a classical mold and his genuine curiosity about Native American religious and social practices.

had good minds, were more judicious in managing their lives than ordinary Europeans, were sober and patient in reaching their goals, had their own form of civility toward one another, and, though not demonstrative, were affable and showed a hospitality toward strangers and charity toward the unfortunate that put Europeans to shame.[17]

The missionary propaganda of Lafitau and others fed into Enlightenment discussions. Reform-minded social critics readily secularized the clerical message and declared that Indians needed only the benefits of colonization or education (or both) to be the cultural equals of the French.[18] Philosophes took the same admiration a step further and declared Indians to be a model of natural reason. In either case there was a straightforward transition from religious to secular admiration of indigenous models of natural virtue.

A contrasting group of writings came from the men who went abroad to administer and defend the new colony. From the early seventeenth century, the great explorer Samuel de Champlain and his successors were keen observers of their surroundings, with their eyes on very different problems from the ones that preoccupied missionaries – the resources for trade, the difficulties facing new settlements, the military uses and dangers of native peoples.[19] Governors and soldiers were not sentimentalists, but they appreciated early on the importance of cooperation with their native neighbors and the need to gain some understanding of their culture.

The military memoir most cherished by the Enlightenment was the travel account of Baron Lahontan. He taught his contemporaries to look to Indian societies for the freedom that absolute government had squeezed out of France. Mishaps at home and abroad taught this querulous adventurer that a state infested with bureaucrats and lawyers was not the best of all possible worlds. Creditors took away his patrimony after he went as a soldier to

---

17. Joseph François Lafitau, *La Vie et les moeurs des sauvages amériquains, comparées aux moeurs des premiers tems* . . . (Amsterdam and Paris, 1724–1732), 97–98.
18. On the Jesuits and their influence on Enlightenment thinkers, see Catherine M. Northeast, *The Parisian Jesuits and the Enlightenment, 1700–1762* (Oxford, 1991), 171–175. Cf. Chinard, *L'Amérique et le rêve exotique,* 187, 314–338. On the relationship between enlightened notions of a colonizing mission and the thinking of French policymakers, see Michèle Duchet, *Anthropologie et histoire au siècle des lumières. Buffon, Voltaire, Rousseau, Helvétius, Diderot* (Paris, 1971).

Enlightenment writers could also secularize another corpus of religious writings: the comments of sixteenth-century Huguenots on the European conquest of the New World. See Frank Lestringant, "The Philosopher's Breviary: Jean de Léry in the Enlightenment," in Stephen Greenblatt, ed., *New World Encounters* (Berkeley and Los Angeles, 1993), 127–138.
19. See Samuel de Champlain, *Voyages of Samuel de Champlain,* trans. Charles P. Otis, 3 vols. (1880; New York, 1966). The authenticity of Champlain's writings is contested. They may have been authored or edited in some degree by Jesuits. See R. Le Blant, "Champlain, Samuel de," in *Dictionnaire de biographie française* (Paris, 1959), 8: cols. 343–345.

Canada in 1683, and he found it impossible to get back to France in time to straighten out his affairs. While overseas he also found it difficult to follow what he claimed were the cruel and stupid orders of his superiors and ended up accused of insubordination. His experiences transformed him into a kind of homespun philosophe who turned his quarrels with authority into the stuff of a generalized critique of French society and state.[20]

What a contrast there was between Montreal and the forest! Cooped up in town, Lahontan suffered the tyranny of priests who watched over the women, expected everyone to take the sacrament once a month, and tore up his copy of Petronius.[21] Out hunting with his Indian friends, Lahontan savored a nobleman's paradise, filled with game and enlivened by male camaraderie. When he finally sat down to write, he wanted his audience to know that there was a world not yet monitored. His preface prays for the reader's prosperity "in preserving him from having any business to adjust with most of the Ministers of State, and Priests; for let them be never so faulty, they'll still be said to be in the right, till such time as Anarchy be introduc'd amongst us, as well as the *Americans,* among whom the sorryest fellow thinks himself a better Man, than a Chancellour of *France.*"[22] Lahontan reports that when de la Barre, the governor-general of New France, tried to demand reparations for damages to French traders from an Iroquois leader, the latter replied: "We are born Freemen. . . . We have a power to go where we please, to conduct who we will to the places we resort to, and to buy and sell where we think fit."[23] The Indian puts his European contemporaries to shame, reminding them of how a free man behaves in the face of authority.

The contrasts between Jesuit and soldier are a reminder of the diversity of eighteenth-century traditions of writing about Indians. Lafitau emphasized their quasi-Christian, Lahontan their quasi-noble qualities. These two writers, in turn, were part of a larger number of reports that made their way back to the home country, some published, others memoranda that circulated in court and governing circles. "Noble savage" is a shorthand term that too tightly compresses the perspectives of witnesses with diverging occupations

---

20. There is a brilliant interpretation of the conflict between civic and primitive man in Lahontan, organized around their conflicting uses of language, in Pagden, *European Encounters,* chap. 4. On Lahontan, see the editor's introduction to Lahontan, *Oeuvres complètes,* 2 vols. (Quebec, 1990), 1: 11–16; and the sympathetic article by David M. Hayne, "Lom d'Arce de Lahontan, Louis-Armand de," *Dictionary of Canadian Biography,* vol. 2 *(1701 to 1740)* (Toronto, 1969), 439–445. Cf. the critical evaluation in Gilbert Chinard, *L'Amérique et le rêve exotique,* 167–187, which dislikes Lahontan for embodying the libertine and anarchist tendencies of the philosophes and preparing the way for the Revolutionary ideology of Rousseau's *Discourse on Inequality.*
21. Lahontan, *New Voyages to North America . . .,* vol. 1 (London, 1703), 46.
22. Ibid., preface.   23. Ibid., 41.

and experiences. Enlightenment writers needed to make selections from these overlapping, at times conflicting reports in order to put together an interpretation of New France's native peoples.

The struggle to wriggle loose from a ranked society in New France was a colonial counterpart to the tensions that were taking shape in the metropolis. The inefficiencies and injustices of a birth-ranked social hierarchy stimulated Enlightenment thinkers to consider fundamentally different principles of social organization. How far one pushed the critique of hierarchy varied from thinker to thinker. It might imply political participation by a large body of enlightened citizens or an elite group of peers. Discussion might take the form of reflection on classical antiquity or speculation on the remote origins of society. For their own time "the republic of letters" was a favorite phrase used to describe the free association of the learned from Philadelphia to St. Petersburg, one that suggested an alternative to hierarchical and dogmatic organization of knowledge. The notion of a republic shimmered in turn with ambiguities, for it could refer to an aristocracy or a democracy of competing talents. There were many reasons for dissatisfaction with the existing order: religious persecution, oppressive regulation, the perceived inefficiency of government in an age of scientific and commercial rationalization, and disillusionment with a court and an aristocracy believed to be corrupt. Philosophes sometimes experimented with radical alternatives but often were reformers who wished to put social hierarchy in better working order and were disturbed by democratic noises. Whether radical or tempered in their expectations, however, they looked to other times and places in order to conceive of a society that would give greater room to social efficiency and personal merit.[24] One of the most obvious sources for them to turn to was the reports from overseas.

Controversy over one work's portrayal of indigenous societies resounded through the Enlightenment, Revolutionary, and Romantic eras: Jean-Jacques

---

24. The creation of a new political culture on the eve of the Revolution has recently attracted considerable comment from French historians. See, for example, François Furet, *Interpreting the French Revolution,* trans. Elborg Forster (Cambridge and New York, 1981); Keith M. Baker, *Inventing the French Revolution: Essays on French Political Culture in the Eighteenth Century* (Cambridge, 1990); and Roger Chartier, *The Cultural Origins of the French Revolution,* trans. Lydia G. Cochrane (Durham, N.C., and London, 1991).

On the emergence of republican and democratic opinion in the world of letters, see Dena Goodman, *The Republic of Letters: A Cultural History of the French Enlightenment* (Ithaca, 1994); Ann Goldgar, *Impolite Learning: Conduct and Community in the Republic of Letters, 1680–1750* (New Haven, Conn., 1995); and Robert Darnton, "The High Enlightenment and the Low-Life of Literature," in *The Literary Underground of the Old Regime* (Cambridge, Mass., 1982), 1–40.

Rousseau's *Discourse on Inequality*. From its publication in 1755 to our own time, Rousseau is said to have idealized a state of nature filled with virtuous people called "noble savages." Yet Rousseau's argument was not so simple. The "state of nature" in Rousseau had a double status as thought experiment and historical reality. Using a familiar strategy of modern Western philosophy, he tried to imagine a pure or original state of nature by stripping away later accretions until he arrived at an elementary form. This was, as Rousseau understood it, a humanity so devoid of cultivation that one could only imperfectly conceive of it, since, among other things, it would lack language. "Savages" belonged not to this original state of nature, but to a later historical stage of development. In this second stage, the family emerged as a simple form of social organization. There were personal possessions, but they had not yet degenerated into the inequalities of wealth that set some human beings above others. This was not a perfect world, according to Rousseau, but it was the state best suited to human beings. It was also, he believed, the state in which humanity had existed for most of its history. The invention of agriculture and metallurgy disrupted this equilibrium and set humanity on a dynamic path of development completed by the formation of the state. In Rousseau's ironic vision of progress, advances in technology and state power only made human beings ever more divided and enslaved. Nonetheless, far from calling for a return to a primitive state of equality, his discourse acknowledged the irreversibility of history. It concluded with fatalism in the face of history's perverse evolution.[25]

Rousseau did not make more than incidental mention in this work of North American Indians. For his contemporaries, though, they readily came to mind as test case of his argument that at an earlier stage of development human beings had lived together without birth-ordered ranks. Native Americans were supposedly anarchic, or at least lacked the higher form of social

---

25. Jean-Jacques Rousseau, *Oeuvres complètes*, ed. Bernard Gagnebin and Marcel Raymond, vol. 3: *Du Contrat social – Écrits politiques* (Paris, 1964); see the valuable introduction by Jean Starobinski, which discusses the status of Rousseau's original state of nature as a regulative idea and his reductive philosophical method, lv–lxvii. See also the editor's introduction to the translation, *A Discourse on Inequality*, trans. and ed. Maurice Cranston (1755; London, 1984); and the biographical interpretation of the Second Discourse in Maurice Cranston, *Jean-Jacques: The Early Life and Work of Jean-Jacques Rousseau, 1712–1754* (New York and London, 1983), especially his observation on 308–309 that Rousseau's prime target was not the old aristocracy, with whom he felt rather at home, but the newly rich of his century and their alliance with the monarchy. See also the classic critique of the interpretation of Rousseau as glorifier of the state of nature by Arthur O. Lovejoy, "The Supposed Primitivism of Rousseau's *Discourse on Inequality*," in *Essays in the History of Ideas* (Baltimore, 1948), 14–37. Carol Blum, *Rousseau and the Republic of Virtue: The Language of Politics in the French Revolution* (Ithaca, N.Y., and London, 1986), emphasizes the destructive tone of the *Discourse on Inequality* and Rousseau's idealization of Geneva, 50–56.

organization that Europeans called the "state." They were wandering hunter-gatherers without settled forms of agriculture. And their lives had an appealing freedom from chains of subordination and command. Rousseau's defense of indigenous societies had an effect on intellectuals comparable to the effect of Marx's defense of the industrial working class: it gave them an unprecedented dignity by endowing them with philosophical significance in the high intellectual language of the time. Subsequent writers could not seriously criticize "savages" without taking on their philosophical defender.

North American Indians figure more directly in the Abbé Raynal's celebrated *Philosophical and Political History of the Establishments and Commerce of Europeans in the Two Indies.* Diderot and other philosophes collaborated with Raynal on this ten-volume work, which was a compendium of the late, radical phase of the Enlightenment and its reckoning with European colonialism.[26] With their natural reason intact, according to Raynal, Indians governed themselves without compulsion; reason guided their councils of government and permitted them to cooperate without submission to authority. At their somber assemblies one was never interrupted; public affairs were managed with a disinterest unknown in Europe; they never quarreled over ownership of land, but only against external enemies; they took good care of orphans, widows, and the infirm; they shared the little they had and won esteem by giving it away.[27] The encounter with indigenous societies revealed that European social institutions were not rooted in nature and that many people lived without any need for organized religion.

Raynal's assertions are a good illustration of the mixture of truthful reporting and tendentiousness that entered into Enlightenment writing on Indians. Some of the qualities that he mentioned – for example, the high regard for generosity and care of the weak – were indeed features of Indian societies. He worked them up into absolute virtues, however, and surrounded them with an Enlightenment ideology of natural reason that divested them of their local meaning: for example, a virtue like generosity was not necessarily disinterested, but instead satisfied a sachem's dependents and advanced his political ambitions. The impact of the Canadian experience was ambiguous: it did help Raynal shake off his European assumptions about society, *and* he distorted what he learned in order to score debating points.

All sorts of late Enlightenment writings took up the praise of Indians. A

---

26. Guillaume-Thomas Raynal, *Histoire philosophique et politique des établissemens et du commerce des Européens dans les deux Indes,* 10 vols. (Geneva, 1780). On the composition of Raynal's work, see Michèle Duchet, *Diderot et L'histoire des Deux Indes, ou l'Écriture Fragmentaire* (Paris, 1978). According to Duchet, Diderot was involved in the *Histoire* from around 1770 to 1780.

27. Raynal, *Histoire,* 8: 28–32.

universal history ticked off the standard philanthropic wisdom about Canadian Indians: they had no criminal laws, but few people committed crimes; they thought that man was born free and no one dared take away their freedom; with the exception of their cruel behavior in war, they were always happy and wise. A dictionary of dance praised the Iroquois for their courage, love of freedom, and self-discipline as manifest in their war dances. A satirist used the persona of an Indian spy in England to denounce English hardness and cunning one year after France's defeat in the Seven Years' War.[28] Iroquois and Hurons were at times subjects of genuine curiosity, at times figures for enlightened fables, their stories retold to satisfy a French audience's need for entertainment and instruction.

Travelers carried Enlightenment commonplaces back to North America. Declaring that he was but a simple soldier and sailor who strove only to write a straightforward account of what he had observed, Pierre de Pagès, naval captain and correspondent of the Académie des Sciences of Paris, claimed to have set out from New Orleans in 1767 on a voyage that took him across Asia and the Middle East before his arrival in Marseille in 1771.[29] He confessed to his readers his hope of finding a better sort of human being among savages – "the simpler and cruder people are, the less they are bad" was his belief.[30] He found just the serene and civil beings he was looking for among the natives of Louisiana. "Savage" was a misnomer for these people, he wrote, and continued, "We have only named them thus because of their manner of living hardier than we: I admired above all the phlegm and serenity that they always maintained, without the lively interest or disquietude that we feel toward good or bad consequences."[31] Jean-Bernard Bossu, an army captain who served in Louisiana from 1750 to 1757 and again from 1758 to 1762, proclaimed a philosophy of enlightened philanthropy: "Man is the same everywhere; he is equally prone to good and evil; education corrects his vices, but cannot give him virtues; the same author has created civil and savage man (*l'homme policé et l'homme Sauvage*), and has endowed them with like qual-

28. André Guillaume Contant d'Orville, *Histoire des différens peuples du monde contenant les cérémonies religieuses et civiles, l'origine des religions, leurs sectes & superstitions, & les moeurs & usages de chaque nation . . .,* (Paris, 1771), 5: 435, 445; Charles Compan, *Dictionnaire de danse, contenant l'histoire, les règles & les principes de cet art, avec des réflexions critiques, & des anecdotes curieuses concernant la danse ancienne & moderne . . .* (Paris, 1787), 150–151; [Anonymous], *L'Espion des Sauvages en Angleterre* (London, 1764), esp. 69.

29. For Pagès's itinerary see "Pagès, Pierre-Marie-François, Vicomte de," in *Biographie universelle, ancienne et moderne* (Michaud), nouvelle édition (Paris, 1843–1865), 31: 612. For his self-description, see Pierre Marie François de Pagès, *Voyages autour du monde et vers les deux pôles, par terre et par mer, pendant les années 1767, 1768, 1769, 1770, 1771, 1773, 1774 et 1776* (Paris, 1782), 1: 7.

30. Ibid., 11.   31. Ibid., 28.

ities. . . . "[32] The frontispiece of his book showed Indians in the first days of French colonization, when their happy innocence had not yet been corrupted and their chief had only contempt for the lucre spilling from the box beneath his feet[33] (Fig. 3). On his own romps through Louisiana, Bossu still found plenty of *bons sauvages*. The Arkansas Indians, who according to Bossu resembled all other Indians, were "big and well made, brave, good swimmers, very skilled at hunting and fishing, and highly devoted to the French. . . ."[34] Since the arrival of the French, they had given up their obscene dances.[35] As for their religion, they believed in a Great Spirit, whom they worshiped in the form of a serpent or a crocodile.[36] As one reviewer noted: "Everything here is true, and yet the truth sometimes appears here to have the air of fiction."[37] The truths of a Lafitau and the truisms of the philosophes descended here into parody.

Not all French travelers were constructing fables for the amusement of salon guests. There were also travelers to North America who developed serious programs of scientific study. The American Philosophical Society in Philadelphia served as the institutional partner for exchange between such French scientists and their American counterparts. With Benjamin Franklin as its first president and Thomas Jefferson as one of its leading members, the Society was in the hands of men passionately interested in cooperation between French and American scientists. It chose the French naturalist André Michaux to serve as leader of a scientific expedition that was to cross North America "from the Mississippi along the Missouri, and Westwardly to the Pacific ocean." So wrote Thomas Jefferson in his preamble to a subscription list written in his own hand, which included pledges from George Washington, John Adams, Alexander Hamilton, and James Madison, as well as Jefferson himself.[38] In the end the expedition did not materialize, but the Society continued to turn to foreigners for their scientific expertise. Franklin's successor, Peter Duponceau, was a naturalized American of French birth who

32. Bossu, *Nouveaux voyages aux Indes occidentales; Contenant une relation des differens peuples qui habitent les environs du grand fleuve Saint-Louis, appellé vulgairement le Mississipi; leur religion; leur gouvernement; leurs moeurs; leurs guerres & leur commerce* (Paris, 1768), 1: 19.
33. Ibid., xv–xvi.   34. Ibid., 109.   35. Ibid., 110–111.   36. Ibid., 121.
37. "Tout y est vrai, et cependant la vérité y a paroit quelque fois avec l'air de la fiction." Transcription of an article in *L'Avant Coureur*, March 21, 1768. Folios 2–276, handwritten transcripts of Ms. 12262, Archives de la Bastille, Bibliothèque de l'Arsenal, Paris. Affaire de la Louisiane, 1765–1770, 267ᵛ, copy in the Library of Congress.
38. Thomas Jefferson, Autograph subscription list for Michaux Expedition, 1793, American Philosophical Society. The Society also possesses a manuscript of four pages of instructions to Michaux for exploring the American West.

3. *Un Roi Sauvage . . .* From Jean-Baptiste Bossu, *Nouveaux voyages aux Indes occidentales; contenant une relation des differens peuples qui habitent les environs du grand fleuve Saint-Louis, appelé vulgairement le Mississipi; leur religion; leur gouvernement; leurs moeurs; leurs guerres & leur commerce* (Paris, 1768), frontispiece. Courtesy of University of Illinois Libraries, Urbana-Champaign.

had a deep interest in the languages of American Indians.[39] Reaching back
into the eighteenth century and continuing in the early decades of the nineteenth, the Society's philological tradition was an important starting point for
further linguistic and ethnological studies.[40]

Less sympathetic views of American Indians circulated too among the
learned. While French culture included an unusual strand of curiosity about
native peoples, the word *sauvage* connoted contempt. Disdain was not
unusual among the colonial administrators and officers who tolerated them
as allies. As for the philosophes, many repudiated the fuzzy humanitarianism
of a Raynal. Theorists of history assigned American Indians a lowly place as
hunters and gatherers on a scale ascending to the commercial societies of
modern Europe.[41] If some commentators commended Native Americans in
order to criticize European society, others responded by putting them far
down on the human hierarchy.

Voltaire made ingenious use of noble savage imagery to counter the despair
that underlies Rousseau's critique of inequality. The Huron hero of his tale,
L'Ingénu, disrupts polite expectations in eighteenth-century France with his
direct expressions of feeling, his insistence on justice, and his indifference to

---

39. Duponceau played an important role in helping the missionary John Heckewelder write his
    famous account of his years among the Delaware Indians. See Heckewelder to Peter Dupon-
    ceau, Letters, 1816–1822, American Philosophical Society. See in particular Heckewelder's
    discussion of Duponceau's editing of the manuscript in Heckewelder to Duponceau, Octo-
    ber 7, 1818, October 10, 1818, and October 13, 1818.
40. See André Michaux, "Journal of Travels into Kentucky; July 15, 1793–April 11, 1796," in
    Reuben G. Thwaites, *Early Western Travels 1748–1846* ... (Cleveland, 1904), 3: 27–104.
        On the origins of the American Philosophical Society, see Brooke Hindle, *The Pursuit of
    Science in Revolutionary America, 1735–1789* (Chapel Hill, N.C., 1956). See also James E.
    McClellan III, *Science Reorganized: Scientific Societies in the Eighteenth Century* (New
    York, 1985), 141–144, which emphasizes the modest place of the American Philosophical
    Society in the late-eighteenth-century world of scientific societies.
        A second center for contact between European and American scientists was Peale's
    Museum. On Peale, his museum, and his contacts with Europeans, see Charles Willson Peale,
    The Selected Papers of Charles Willson Peale and His Family, vol. 2, parts 1 and 2: *The Artist
    as Museum Keeper, 1791–1810,* ed. Lillian B. Miller with Sidney Hart and David C. Ward
    (New Haven and London, 1988). See also Lillian B. Miller and David C. Ward, *New Per-
    spectives on Charles Willson Peale: A 250th Anniversary Celebration* (Pittsburgh, 1991); and
    Charles Coleman Sellers, *Charles Willson Peale*, 2 vols. (Philadelphia, 1947). On the next
    generation see Lillian B. Miller et al., *The Peale Family: Creation of a Legacy, 1770–1870*
    (New York, 1996).
        No late-eighteenth-century French scientist attempted a serious ethnographic study of
    an American Indian people. Palisot de Beauvois made an extended stay among the Creek and
    Choctaw Indians, yet his observations scarcely went beyond the clichés that one could gather
    from the existing missionary and memoir literature of the period. See the modern reprint
    edited and with a valuable introduction by Gilbert Chinard: Palisot de Beauvois, *Odérahi,
    Histoire Américaine. Une soeur aîné d'Atala* (1795, 1801; Paris, 1950). Palisot's essay on the
    Creeks and Cherokees is reprinted on 221–230.
41. Ronald L. Meek, *Social Science and the Ignoble Savage* (Cambridge and New York, 1976).

titles. The royal government replies to his request for an audience with the king by throwing him into the Bastille. When his beloved tries to help him, she can do so only by submitting to the advances of a bureaucrat. While her cynical friend prostitutes herself to further her husband's career and advises her to do the same, she dies of shame after her self-sacrifice. What begins as a mocking fable turns by the end into a rather uneasy tale of corruption.[42] Yet Voltaire does not write to condemn French society. During his stay in the Bastille the hero receives a snap course in world civilization from a Jansenist fellow prisoner. Reading changes the unformed savage into an ideal blend of nature and culture, a frank character bred to civilized restraint. Voltaire's tale reveals that while natural man has goodness and strength, he is in need of an education.

Other writers were more vehement. A so-called degenerationist school of European writers gave the notion of hierarchy a biological turn, assigning the American environment and its inhabitants a degraded place in the world order.[43] A celebrated catalogue of the arguments for the inferiority of American and Native Americans was Cornelius De Pauw's *Philosophical Research On the Americas*.[44] De Pauw was following the lead of Buffon, who had applied a hierarchical imagination to the study of nature and had catalogued the inferiority of the American climate and the flora and fauna it produced. Buffon did not, however, draw racialist conclusions about the peoples of the Americas.[45] De Pauw was less cautious. He imagined a place of such utter

---

42. Voltaire, *L'Ingénu: Histoire véritable,* ed. William R. Jones (1767; Geneva and Paris, 1957). I have also consulted the introduction to Voltaire, *L'Ingénu* and *Histoire de Jenni,* ed. J. H. Brumfitt and M. I. Gerard Davis (Oxford, 1970). John S. Clouston, *Voltaire's Binary Masterpiece L'Ingénu Reconsidered* (Berne, Frankfurt am Main, and New York, 1986), brings out the tensions between spoof and seriousness in the tale, 30, 39.

43. See Antonello Gerbi, *The Dispute of the New World: The History of a Polemic, 1750–1900,* rev. ed., trans. Jeremy Moyle (Pittsburgh, 1973). For an overview of the degenerationist controversy, see also Gilbert Chinard, "Eighteenth-Century Theories on America as a Human Habitat," *Proceedings* of the American Philosophical Society, 91 (1947): 27–57.

44. Cornelius De Pauw, *Recherches philosophiques sur les Américains, ou mémoires intéressants pour servir à l'histoire de l'espèce humaine. Nouvelle édition, augmentée d'une dissertation critique par Dom Pernety; & de la défense de l'auteur des recherches contre cette dissertation,* 3 vols. (Berlin 1771).

45. Buffon assigned the human species the role of nobility within the hierarchy of nature: "Son port majestueux, sa démarche ferme et hardie, annoncent sa noblesse et son rang" George Louis Leclerc de Buffon, *Oeuvres complètes* (Paris, 1853), 3: 193. Buffon did not think highly of "savages." He criticized them for their oppression of women while praising *peuples policés* for furthering equality between the sexes and permitting women to teach men politeness and appreciation of beauty. Nonetheless, Buffon avoided making racial distinctions between peoples. While recognizing differences caused by climate, nourishment, and mores, he insisted on the original and enduring unity of the human species (320). In particular, American Indians had migrated from older human habitats (315). An addition specifically opposed De Pauw's degenerationist views (457–458).

depravity that his book read like a piece of secularized Calvinist theology. American Indians were stunted, vitiated, and enervated. Venereal disease was natural among them, and their daughters communicated "a kind of virus that eventually perverts the quality of blood."[46] Their men were poor, sickly creatures with feeble sexual desire and no hair on their chests. Their women had too much milk and nourished their children until the age of seven, while menstruating rarely. This, plus the presence of milk in the male breast, were further signs of "a vice manifest in the blood."[47] Pederasty was "very fashionable" (*fort en vogue*) in America, human sacrifice to the gods was universal, and cannibalism was widespread.[48] De Pauw's climatological views shaded over into a conviction of the racial inferiority of the Americans. In a section entitled "Concerning the Brutal Character of the Americans" (*Du géni abruti des Américains*), he wrote: "Stupefaction (*une insensibilité stupide*) forms the basic character of all the Americans. . . . Higher than the animals because they have the use of their hands and of language, they are really inferior to the least of the Europeans."[49] De Pauw wrote as a critic of European colonialism – an isolationist who urged Europeans to shun the toxic fruit of distant shores. According to De Pauw, contact between the two worlds, Old and New, had resulted in mutual disaster, massacre of the natives and venereal disease for the conquerors. Europe had abused its superior strength and been punished for its invasion of the other side of the Atlantic. If disaster on this scale happened again, it would lead to extinction of the human species. De Pauw warned the princes of Europe to leave the recently explored lands of the South Pacific (the "Australian" lands) in peace and cultivate their own gardens.[50]

After the outbreak of the French Revolution, the circumstances for writing about America changed.[51] No longer was America the testing ground for the-

On Buffon, De Pauw, and American Indians see Duchet, *Anthropologie et histoire*, 246–248, 265–266; and Durand Echeverria, *Mirage in the West: A History of the French Image of American Society to 1815* (Princeton, N.J., 1957), 7–9.
46. De Pauw, *Recherches*, 1: 49.   47. Ibid., 55.   48. Ibid., , 214.   49. Ibid., 2: 154.
50. Ibid., 1: iv–vii.
51. The older view of America as a republican utopia persisted in some writers. See François Marquis de Barbé-Marbois, "Discours sur les États-Unis D'Amérique," in *Complot D'Arnold et de Sir Henry Clinton contre les États-Unis D'Amérique et contre le général Washington, Septembre 1780* (Paris, 1816), i–xliv. On Barbé-Marbois see René Rémond, *Les États-Unis devant l'opinion française, 1815–1852* (Paris, 1962), 1: 318. Lafayette and his admirers upheld the same ideal in the 1820s. See Lafayette, *Mémoires, correspondance et manuscrits* (Paris, 1838), 6: 165–211. Cf. Charles Barbaroux and J. A. Lardier, *Voyage du général Lafayette aux États-Unis d'Amérique en 1824 . . .*, 3 vols. (Brussels, 1824). Barbaroux later named his son Charles-Jean-Washington. See E. Franceschini, "Barbaroux (Charles-Ogé)," *Dictionnaire de biographie française*, 5: cols. 226–227.
French naturalists continued to come and work, with little regard for the social and polit-

ories unrealizable at home: suddenly the ancient society of orders had collapsed in Europe and given way to ever more radical forms of democratic
social organization. America took on new significance as the Revolution
expelled wave after wave of political opponents – families in flight from the
spontaneous urban and rural violence that began in the summer of 1789, supporters of the king, liberals in flight from Jacobin terror, settlers endangered
by the revolution in Saint Domingue, and later, critics of Napoleon.[52] Cut off
from home and often impoverished, they now scrutinized the United States
for clues to the movement of modern history that had upset their lives.

In this new political context, the meaning of American Indians changed too.
Critics began tearing down received images of the Indian as emblem of natural
equality. Louis-Narcisse Baudry des Lozières illustrates the kind of counterrevolutionary career that resulted in a hatred of Rousseauist admiration for
indigenous peoples. Baudry (his real name – he made the noble addition himself during the Restoration) went to Saint Domingue in 1777, served as a military and political leader of the colony, defended it against the revolutionaries
until he was wounded in late 1792, and after briefly returning to France left for
the United States in November 1793.[53] A man of scientific aspirations, in 1784
he was one of the founders of the Cercle des Philadelphes, which constituted
itself in Saint Domingue as a learned academy for natural science ("la
physique"), natural history, and literature.[54] His address of the following
week to the Cercle was a passionate defense of scientific knowledge that

ical changes taking place in the United States. See François André Michaux, *Travels to the West of the Alleghany Mountains . . . Undertaken in the Year 1802, Under the Auspices of his Excellency M. Chaptal, Minister of the Interior*, 2nd ed. (London, 1805), reprinted in Reuben G. Thwaites, *Early Western Travels 1748–1846* (Cleveland, 1904), 3: 107–306. François-André was the son of André Michaux, discussed earlier.

Charles Alexandre Lesueur, who had traveled with the Baudin expedition to the Pacific of 1800–1804, stayed in the United States from 1816 to 1837. He was widely admired in his own time for his scientific activities: he produced valuable sketches and paintings, gathered an enormous amount of information about North American flora and fauna, and collected specimens for museums. On Lesueur see Adrien Loir, *Charles-Alexandre Lesueur, artiste et savant française en Amérique de 1816 à 1839* (Le Havre, 1920); R. W. G. Vail, *The American Sketchbooks of Charles Alexandre Lesueur 1816–1837* (Worcester, Mass., 1938); and Waldo G. Leland, "The Lesueur Collection of American Sketches in the Museum of Natural History at Havre, Seine-Inférieure," *Mississippi Valley Historical Review*, 10 (1923): 53–78.

52. See H. Forneron, *Histoire générale des émigrés pendant la révolution française*, 3 vols. (Paris, 1884); and Rémond, *Les États-Unis*, 1: 31ff.
53. See "Baudry des Lozières" in *Nouvelle biographie générale* (Hoefer) (Paris, 1852–1866), 6: cols. 796–798; and "Baudry des Lozières, Louis-Narcisse," in *Dictionnaire de biographie française*, 5: cols. 905–906.
54. See Cercle des Philadelphes, Cap-François, 1784–87, nos. 1 and 2, American Philosophical Society.

On the Cercle des Philadelphes see James E. McClellan III, *Colonialism and Science: Saint Domingue in the Old Regime* (Baltimore and London, 1992), 181–297.

might have been applauded by any philosophe. It is hard to recognize the same writer in his works on Louisiana of 1802 and 1803. There he raged against the philosophes' notion of the Native American as natural egalitarian:

These men of nature, whom they [the philosophes] don't know, and whom they raise so high, looked to me, despite the resemblance I find between them and our sages of [the Revolutionary] year Two, looked to me, who knows them, like the dullest beings, with whom only our impious philosophes could live, all our atheist intellectuals (*savants*), who would like, imitating Rousseau, that we go on all fours nibbling lettuce.[55]

While the ideas were abstract, the passions of men like this were directed against equality as a real and present danger.

One of the most influential observers of American Indians after 1789 was Constant-François Chassebeuf de Volney. Already a prominent figure in French letters and politics on the eve of the Revolution, in touch with the radical philosophes Holbach and Helvétius, he turned into a dedicated revolutionary but also a conciliator and defender of freedom of the press. In 1793 he was imprisoned for ten months. After his release, he was elected to the chair in history at the École Normale in 1795 and visited the United States in 1795–1798. Volney planned a work on the United States that would build up from environmental conditions to the study of American society. While that work never materialized, he did publish a volume on American climate and soil that included a lengthy appendix on American Indians.[56] He had originally hoped to spend time among them, he wrote, but when he discovered that they had no hierarchy or government, "that in a word their social condition was one of anarchy and of a wild and brutal nature," he gave up the project.[57] They seem to have activated traumatic memories of the Jacobin France

---

55. Louis Narcisse Baudry des Lozières, *Second voyage à la Louisiane faisant suite au premier de l'auteur de 1794 à 1798*, 2 vols. (Paris, 1803), 1: 211–212. Cf. Baudry des Lozières, *Voyage à la Louisiane, et sur le continent de l'Amérique septentrionale, fait dans les années 1794 à 1798 . . .* (Paris, 1802).

56. See the article "Volney" in *Nouvelle biographie générale*, 46: 347–351, and "Volney, Constantin-François Chassebeuf de," in Edna Hindie Lemay et al., *Dictionnaire des constituants, 1789–1791* (Paris, 1991), 2: 942–943.

    For evidence of Volney's importance for subsequent travelers and commentators see J. Milbert, *Itinéraire pittoresque du fleuve Hudson et des parties latérales de l'Amérique du Nord, d'apprès les dessins originaux pris sur les lieux* (Paris, 1828), 1: xix, xxi; Prince Maximilian of Wied, *Reise in das innere Nord-America in den Jahren 1832 bis 1834* (Coblenz, 1839), 2: 103, 133–34; G. E. Schulze, "Vorrede des Uebersetzers," in Johann Heckewelder, *Nachricht von der Geschichte, den Sitten und Gebräuchen der Indianischen Völkerschaften, welche ehemals Pennsylvanien und die benachbarten Staaten bewohnten*, trans. Fr. Hesse (Göttingen, 1821), xxvi; Alexis de Tocqueville, *De la Démocratie en Amérique*, vol. 1, part 1, in *Oeuvres complètes* (Paris, 1961), 338, 343.

57. C. F. Volney, *Oeuvres*, vol. 4: *Tableau du climat et du sol des États-Unis d'Amérique . . .*, 2nd ed. (Paris, 1825), 375.

he had left behind, as if the Revolutionary anarchy had its counterpart in the supposed anarchy of American Indians. They looked weird, and their drinking bouts disgusted him.[58] Hearing from an informant that Indians were capable of envy, he could not resist scoring a point against thinkers like Rousseau who maintained that social evolution bred competitiveness: "What!, I responded with an air of astonishment, is it the case that *these men of nature* know jealousy, hatred, base motives of vengefulness? At home we have brilliant minds who assure us that these passions can only arise in our civilized societies."[59] Removed from France by thousands of miles, he could not distance himself from the errors that had led to the revolutionary catastrophe and appeared to have nothing more important to do than to sound off against his former conversation partners in Paris salons. Volney was doing more than just lashing out at the philosophes, however. His account helped to clear away eighteenth-century truisms that had lost their relationship to any reality, European or American.

The Duke de la Rochefoucauld-Liancourt was also singed by the violence of the early Revolutionary years but was better able to maintain a dispassionate view of American affairs. From a famous family with close connections to the court, he supported political reform in the early stages of the Revolution but felt himself endangered by the summer of 1792 and left, first for England, then in the fall of 1794 for the United States, where he stayed until 1797.[60] One emotional trial after another preceded his arrival. The intrigues of the other émigrés made England an uncomfortable place of refuge; at the beginning of September he learned of relatives massacred at home; the news of Louis XVI's death hit him as the loss of a beloved monarch.[61] He arrived in the United States saddened and homesick.[62] Nevertheless he showed an unusual determination to make something out of his exile. Imbued with the philanthropic ethos of the late eighteenth century, he worked to gather observations useful for humanity, turning his particular impressions into the evidence for general reflections. He met with high and low, founding fathers and backwoods farmers, and commented on government, agriculture, education, slavery, and the condition of roads and towns.[63] His experience foreshadowed the liberating effect of America on Tocqueville, who similarly used his trip to break out of his social confinement. He also anticipated Tocqueville's

58. Volney, *Tableau du climat*, 372–374.   59. Ibid., 403.
60. See Fernand Dreyfus, *Un Philanthrope d'autrefois: La Rochefoucauld-Liancourt, 1742–1827* (Paris, 1903); and David J. Brandenburg and Millicent H. Brandenburg, "The Duc De La Rochefoucault-Liancourt's Visit to the Federal City in 1797: A New Translation," in *Records of the Columbia Historical Society of Washington, D.C.* (1973–1974), 35–60.
61. Dreyfus, 201–208.   62. Ibid., 222.   63. Ibid., 211, 213–218.

careful questioning of informants in the interest of accurate empirical reporting.[64]

Liancourt was a critical observer who achieved a fine balance between sympathetic understanding of a new society and its underlying principles, and frankness about its shortcomings. Anglo-American behavior toward Indians provoked his indignation:

All that I have been able to learn of these Indians interests me in their favour. The Americans are waging war against them, in order to drive them out of a country, which belongs to them; and the Americans, who inhabit the frontiers, are greater robbers, and more cruel than the Indians, against whom it is alleged as a crime, that they exercise the right of retaliation.[65]

Liancourt's perspective was that of a liberal aristocrat detached from the logic of commercial success. The special sympathy of Indians for the French added to his liking for them, while the hypocrisy of American justice left him astonished and angry.[66] When an American soldier murdered two natives, the man's captain settled the incident by paying a hundred dollars per head to the party that came in search of justice. In the reverse case, noted Liancourt – if an Indian had killed a white man – he would have been hanged. Such uneven treatment was a disgrace to a society that claimed to honor justice and equality.[67] The greed of the settlers, he added, had led them to degrade the Indians "to the lowest rank in the scale of human beings," ruining them with whiskey and money in order to advance their own interests. "As long as they were suffered to remain in their savage state, they were warlike and independent, wild, perhaps, yet humane"; it was their contact with whites that had brutalized them. Reflecting on the odious means that *les nations policées* used to advance their interests, he concluded that one had little reason to appreciate their supposed superiority.[68] This was a remarkable revaluation of native and settler societies, uncompromising in its critique of civilized amorality and sympathetic to native claims on humanity. When it came to a conflict between the warrior and commercial ethos, Liancourt sided with the vanquished Indians against the vulgar conqueror.

Equally remarkable were the mature reflections of Michel Guillaume St. Jean de Crèvecoeur. This famous observer of American life first came to the

64. See François de La Rochefoucauld-Liancourt, *Voyage dans les États-Unis d'Amérique, fait en 1795, 1796 et 1797* (Paris, 1799), 1: viii–xi.
65. François de La Rochefoucauld-Liancourt, *Travels Through the United States of North America, the Country of the Iroquois, and Upper Canada, in the Years 1795, 1796, and 1797; With an Authentic Account of Lower Canada*, trans. H. Neuman (London, 1799), 1: 45. Cf. Liancourt, *Voyage*, 1: 78.
66. Liancourt, *Travels*, 1: 178; cf. Liancourt, *Voyage*, 1: 305.
67. Liancourt, *Travels*, 1: 149.   68. Ibid. Cf. Liancourt, *Voyage*, 1: 254–255.

New World with Montcalm's army, leaving his Norman home to serve in Canada from 1755 to 1759. Staying on and developing an intimate knowledge of frontier life, he married and settled down as a gentleman farmer in Orange County, New York, in 1769. Crèvecoeur's *Letters from an American Farmer* were an instant literary success after their publication in 1782 and enjoyed a second success when Crèvecoeur published a revised French edition two years later. He was intensely aware of the need to capture the novelty of the American experience. His famous letter, "What is an American?," describes how the Europeans who made the passage to America become new men as they go from a state of dependence to one of individual freedom.[69] Even in this work Crèvecoeur writes with knowledgeable anger about the backwoodsmen's fraud, drinking, and use of force in their dealings with Indians, which in turn lead to Indian acts of antisettler violence.[70] These remarks are but an aside, however, to the *Letters'* purpose of portraying an idyllic republic. Dissent becomes the dominant note of a lesser-known work of 1801, Crèvecoeur's *Journey into Northern Pennsylvania and the State of New York*. Gone is the concise and direct style of the *Letters;* instead, a rambling, disjointed narrative conveys the experience of travel through a troubled land. The narrator's persona shifts too: instead of the plain-spoken farmer of the *Letters,* Crèvecoeur assumes the role of an Indian – "an adopted member of Oneida" (one of the Iroquois tribes). In the form of a dialogue among the different characters, Crèvecoeur records his contemporaries' dispute over the destiny of Native Americans. At one point his narrator recalls the violence and stupidity of savage life and repudiates the illusions of sentimental writers: "They assumed a type of primitive man, whom they didn't know at all – in order to satirize their contemporaries."[71] When the illusions are discarded, however, a more admirable being emerges, one superior to Europeans: "What a gap there is between the noble pride, independence, steadfastness, courage of these war-like hunters, and the baseness and vice of most of the inhabitants of the frontiers!"[72] It was a striking sign of the changing mood of the times that of all people Crèvecoeur, the famous celebrator of the American farmer, now contrasted Indian aristocrats to plebeian pioneers.

Liancourt and the later Crèvecoeur wrote as nobles in a post-noble age. Unlike Volney, they were no longer fixated on old battles with the philosophes. Rather, they had landed in the new world of democratic politics

69. J. Hector St. John [Michel-Guillaume St. Jean de Crèvecoeur], *Letters from an American Farmer* (London, 1782), 53.
70. Ibid., 68–69.
71. Michel-Guillaume St. Jean de Crèvecoeur, *Journey into Northern Pennsylvania and the State of New York,* trans. Clarissa Spencer Bostelmann (Ann Arbor, 1964), 52.
72. Ibid., 316.

and saw familiar objects in a new light. Even though they accepted the political revolution of their times, they sought to preserve the aristocratic values nurtured by the old privileged order and endangered by democracy, whether in the capitals of Europe or on the American frontier. American Indians now took on new interest as fellow victims of historical tragedy and fellow upholders of an aristocratic ethos.

2

◁ ═══════════════════════════════ ▷

Chateaubriand and the Fiction
of Native Aristocrats

Year IX of the Revolution (Christian calendar year 1801): François-René, Chevalier de Chateaubriand, publishes the tale *Atala*. The author has barely returned to France after years of poverty, obscurity, and exile. But with this work he reverses his fortunes; he creates a new Romantic style, enduring fame for himself – and a vision of aristocracy to enchant a post-Revolutionary world. Chateaubriand's story fulfills the promise of authors like Liancourt and Crèvecoeur: it creates a new world of estrangement from Europe, ardor for honor, and kinship with Indians.[1]

Like Liancourt and Crèvecoeur, Chateaubriand came from the old nobility. Born in 1768 into a Brettanese family with a seafaring tradition, he became a second lieutenant in the royal army in 1786. Three years later he was made a Knight of Malta, an office that included a sizable income. During the early months of the Revolution, Chateaubriand was a listless onlooker, disaffected from the old regime but unwilling to join its attackers. As the Revolutionary mood spread from the populace to the troops in Rouen, where his regiment was stationed in 1790, the commander and senior officer decided to emigrate, and Chateaubriand was left to decide for himself how to shape his future.[2]

---

1. On the historical significance of *Atala* for the Romantic era, see Hugh Honour, *The New Golden Land: European Images of America from the Discoveries to the Present Time* (New York, 1975), 220.
2. The preceding biographical description is taken from Richard Switzer, *Chateaubriand* (New York, 1971), 13, 16–21. Gilbert Chinard, *L'Exotisme américain dans l'oeuvre de Chateaubriand* (Paris, 1918), is still indispensable reading for anyone interested in Chateaubriand's relationship to America, though it needs to be supplemented with Switzer's revised conclusions about the length and route of Chateaubriand's American journey.

Where should a young aristocrat go at a moment like this – with the state falling apart and his own status making him a doubtful friend of the Revolution? The man he turned to for guidance was Chrétien-Guillaume Lamoignon de Malesherbes. Generous, tolerant, concerned with improving the legal status of Protestants and Jews, protector of Rousseau, and advisor to the king, he was the epitome of the liberal aristocratic reformer. Chateaubriand's relationship to him exemplifies the kind of kinship network that structured a privileged elite. Malesherbes's elder daughter, Antoinette-Thérèse-Marguerite, married Louis Le Peletier de Rosanbo in 1769: a good marriage, for he belonged to another of the great clans of the *noblesse de robe*. Their daughter Aline-Thérèse married Jean-Baptiste Auguste de Chateaubriand, older brother of François-René. Through his brother and sister-in-law, the would-be man of letters François-René made the acquaintance of this important cultural broker of the old regime.[3]

Malesherbes's advice was to go to America. Chateaubriand made the voyage in mid-1791, arriving on July 10 and returning to Le Havre in early January 1792. After arriving in Baltimore he departed the next morning for Philadelphia; from there he went to New York, sailed up the Hudson to Albany, and engaged a Dutch guide to lead him to Niagara. Probably he then returned along the East Coast to Philadelphia.[4] (His own later retellings of the journey were so vague and inaccurate that they kept generations of scholars busy reconstructing his actual itinerary.) The chapters of his memoirs dedicated to his American voyage make much of the shock of the new. Like other French travelers to North America during the 1790s, he soon lost the utopian illusions of Enlightenment propaganda. The commercial society of the East Coast dispelled French fantasies of a Roman republic arising on American shores.[5] As for Indians, his encounters with them did away with Rousseauist notions of indigenous peoples in a state of pastoral tranquility. Instead he became a witness to the arrogance of settlers pushing an Indian woman away from the meadow where her cow used to graze. A scene like this one worked powerfully on the young aristocrat's imagination as he struggled to comprehend the injustices of modern history.

Learning of the king's failed attempt to flee into exile, he felt honor bound

---

3. On Malesherbes, see the insightful remarks in Gerald N. Izenberg, *Impossible Individuality: Romanticism, Revolution, and the Origins of Modern Selfhood, 1787–1802* (Princeton, N. J., 1992), 268–269; George Armstrong Kelly, *Victims, Authority, and Terror: The Parallel Deaths of d'Orléans, Custine, Bailly, and Malesherbes* (Chapel Hill, N.C., 1982), 213–277; and Pierre Grosclaude, *Malesherbes, témoin et interprète de son temps* (Paris, 1961), especially the genealogical table, 20–24, the description of Malesherbes's family in chap. 1, and the remarks on Malesherbes and Chateaubriand, 698–701.

4. Switzer, *Chateaubriand*, 21–23.

5. Chateaubriand, *Mémoires d'outre tombe* (1849; Paris, 1951), 1: 220.

to return and defend the monarchy. What awaited him was sickness and long years away from home. In mid-1792 he joined the Koblenz army of exiles, then at Trier; in the course of battle he was wounded in the leg, got dysentery, and contracted smallpox or chickenpox. After the army dissolved, he made his way to Brussels and to England, where he arrived in 1793 and stayed for the next seven years. A weary time, but an inwardly productive one too, in which he found his Romantic style and themes.

In 1800 Chateaubriand returned to Paris and took up with the liberal aristocratic circle around Benjamin Constant and Mme. de Staël. The publication of *Atala* the following year brought instant literary celebrity. Following up on this initial success, *The Genius of Christianity,* published in 1802, announced a return by the cultural elite from skepticism to religious faith. *Atala* was included in this work as a sample of Christian art. So was a companion piece, *René,* which was equally stirring to generations of French Romantics. A year later Chateaubriand was named secretary to the French ambassador in Rome. The period of immaturity and suffering was over. Chateaubriand, the Romantic man of letters, diplomat, and larger-than-life personality, took his commanding place in French public affairs.[6]

What kinds of works were the tales that made Chateaubriand a French and, before long, a European name, one of those personalities that (like his fellow aristocrat Byron) symbolize a whole epoch? He wrote a full-length prose epic, *Les Natchez,* during his years in England. The manuscript was lost there, however, and what he published on the French and Indians at the time was the two novellas. On a later trip to England Chateaubriand recovered *Les Natchez,* and he included it in 1826–1827 as part of his complete works. It remained unpolished and inchoate, a document of the imaginative labors leading up to the shorter masterpieces. One can observe his struggle in the epic to develop a new idiom out of older literary conventions. The human characters are the same cast as in the novellas. A young Frenchman, René, arrives at a village of the Natchez, an Indian people of the lower Mississippi. There he is adopted by their aged leader, Chactas. God's original plan was to prepare a renewal of humanity in this part of the world, restoring paradise lost. As in Milton, however, Satan meddles. After René is betrothed to a Natchez maid, Céluta, the Prince of Darkness implants jealousy in the heart of Ondouré, a young Natchez warrior. He picks a fight with René and loses, but he incites others until the young Frenchman in their midst divides the

6. For the dates and other information about Chateaubriand's life, see the chronology in François-René de Chateaubriand, *Atala/René/Les Aventures du dernier abencérage,* ed. Fernand Letessier (Paris, 1962), lxxxi–xci.

Natchez. René is a hated figure, and his presence only gives the evildoers among the Natchez a chance to urge on warfare against the European invaders. The outcome is a second fall: a massacre of the French, extermination of the Indians, and paradise forever spoiled.[7]

Atala and *René* were fragments that Chateaubriand rescued from the ambition of an epic of the New World. While the larger work remained an experiment, never adequately shaping older literary forms to encompass the experiences of a new age, the novellas realized a fresh Romantic vision. They challenged Neoclassicism in fiction as surely as *The Genius of Christianity* assailed the intellectualism of the late Enlightenment. The setting was a different North America: not the eighteenth century's republic of reason, but a wilderness of unsuspected shadow and light in which mythic forces of good and evil struggled for control of the modern world. The tales offered novel Romantic subjects, too. Atala is an Indian maid. Plenty of those already existed as exemplars of natural virtue, but she is something different: a woman of passion, torn between her devotion to her lover and her promise of chastity to her mother, between her uncompromising soul and the teachings of Christianity. Instead of eighteenth-century oppositions of savagery and civilization, she exemplifies a quest for synthesis. The same is true of *René*, the story of how the hero flees an ignoble France and an illicit love for his sister to seek a new home among the Natchez. These are tales of sacrifice, exile, and defeat. They draw strength from their author's personal suffering and discover a counterpart among Native Americans; they express the mood of a generation, yet link its experiences to universal themes of love and loyalty.

Atala opens with a magnificent description of the valley of the Mississippi ("Meschacebé" in his pseudo-archaizing rendering). There René listens to Chactas, now old and blind, as he tells his life story. As a boy, Chactas follows his father into warfare against the Muscogulges, a Florida nation. After his father is killed in battle, a kindly Spaniard, Lopez, takes him in, but Chactas can't stand the constraints of civilized life and leaves for the forest. Here he is promptly captured by the Muscogulges. Their chief tells him that he will be burned by them, and they take him on a long march. The young captive and Atala, the chief's daughter, fall in love. While the sentry set over him is asleep, she frees him – at first, he mistakes her for a virginal apparition come to visit him in the hour of his death – and they make their way over the Alleghanies

---

7. Chateaubriand, "Les Natchez," in *Oeuvres complètes*, nouvelle édition, ed. Sainte-Beuve, vol. 3 (Paris, 1859) (hereinafter cited as "Les Natchez"). On the background and significance of this work, see the critical edition, François-René de Chateaubriand, *Les Natchez*, ed. and introd. Gilbert Chinard et al. (Baltimore, 1932).

to the Tennessee River (Fig. 4). As they wander through the forest, she is torn between her Christian faith (her mother was a convert) and her longing for union with Chactas. She, too, is now an exile from her homeland, indeed doubly so, for as she now confesses, her real father is Lopez. A missionary, Father Aubry, discovers them as they make their way through the forest and takes them in. Just when they seem on the verge of marriage, Atala swallows a poison; her mother swore her to eternal virginity, and she decides to sacrifice herself rather than betray her vow. On their return from a visit to a nearby mission, Chactas and Father Aubry find her weakened, and she reveals the reason for her deed. Father Aubry tells her that he could have written to Montreal for an exemption, but it is too late. After her death, the missionary urges Chactas to return to his mother on the Mississippi and to seek there the education that will allow him to fulfill his vow to Atala to become a Christian.

The narrator introduces himself in the epilogue. He is the grandson of René and encounters the last of the Natchez near Niagara Falls – erring, wretched exiles. From them he learns that Chactas and René both died in a massacre by the French. The homeless narrator recognizes his counterpart in the homeless Indians. He concludes with an invocation to their shared suffering: "Hapless Indians whom I have seen wandering in the wildernesses of the New World with the ashes of your ancestors, you who showed me hospitality in the midst of your misery, today I could not return your kindness, for, like you, I wander at the mercy of men. . . ."[8] Never had a Frenchman had occasion to write lines like these before the Revolution. To be sure, every European in North America was an immigrant, and many left behind personal difficulties by traveling to North America. But the exile from France after 1789 had lost not only his personal possessions, but also a world. The crisis of the nobility provided a starting point for generalized insight into historical defeat, and the cataclysmic defeat of North American Indians served as a symbol of destruction of nobility in the European imagination.

The crisis of nobility haunts *René*, too, which takes the topic back to its old-world origins. A well-born European, Réne has been driven by a secret sorrow to leave his home. Only after several years among the Natchez does he agree to share the story of his misfortune with Chactas and Father Souël, a missionary to the local French fort. His mother dies in childbirth, his father favors his older brother, and he grows up isolated, his one human bond his sister. He travels; he contemplates the ruins of Greece and Rome. Returning home, he languishes in an extended state of disenchantment. René is estranged from the frivolity of the early eighteenth century and the necessity

8. François-René de Chateaubriand, *Atala/René*, trans. Irving Putter (Berkeley and Los Angeles, 1960), 82 (hereinafter cited as *Atala/René*, trans. Putter).

4. . . . *Je crus que c'était la Vierge des dernières amours.* From Chateaubriand, *Atala – René* (Paris, 1805). Courtesy of McCormick Library of Special Collections, Northwestern University Library.

of earning a living; his is the kind of noble soul for which the age has no use. Amélie, his sister, leaves home too but eventually agrees to come back, only to grow weaker and weaker, until finally she flees to a convent. René pursues her and is to witness her ceremony of taking vows. She looks sexier than ever to René, who recounts that on seeing her in full dress, "I suddenly felt my passion flame up within me"! And there, in the midst of the ceremony, she announces her *passion criminelle* for her brother. After giving her a final embrace, René flees across the ocean.[9]

With their sibling kinship and near-twinship ("We were closely bound together by our tender affinities in mood and taste; my sister was only slightly older than I"), Amélie and René belong to a long line of highborn couples in Indo-European and world literature whose affinity suggests their separation from and superiority to the rest of humanity.[10] There is, however, a modern twist to the story: sociocultural conditions have separated these siblings from their class. René and Amélie are in flight from a Enlightenment culture that has no room for their kind of high seriousness. With their shared aversion for their age, they turn inward.

With their passion forbidden, they search for other forms of heroism. Amélie replaces earthly with spiritual love. As for René, he elects affinity with the wilds of the New World. Chactas becomes his adoptive father, and to conform to Indian mores he takes a wife (though he doesn't live with her). This constructed community takes the place of his failed relationship to his native society and to his sister. Almost cut off from the community of men, he spends most of his days alone in the woods, "a savage among the savages." And yet Chactas, accompanied by saintly Father Souël, rescues him from his solitude. The kinship of souls transcends national boundaries; René is closer to the Indian sage than to his own people. Nobility has its last refuge on the shores of the Mississippi.

Chateaubriand's novellas are a striking departure from his contemporaries' treatment of similar themes. The return to nature was a well-established subject of eighteenth-century literature, as were works offering sympathetic portrayals of Indians and other native peoples. The most obvious model for Chateaubriand was *Paul et Virginie* by Jacques Henri Bernardin de Saint-Pierre, first published in 1788 and steadily reprinted for decades to come. In Bernardin's tale two women travel from their French homes to Mauritius, one

9. Ibid., 107–109.
10. Ibid., 87. On the Indo-European tradition see James A. Boon, *Affinities and Extremes: Crisscrossing the Bittersweet Ethnology of East Indies History, Hindu-Balinese Culture, and Indo-European Allure* (Chicago and London, 1990), 105–112.

abandoned by her lover, the other by her family after marrying beneath her social rank. They raise their children, Paul and Virginie, in a state of nature, innocents washed free of the sins of society. They seem to be an Adam and Eve destined for marriage in their Pacific paradise. But they cannot escape the long reach of the mother country: a selfish aunt calls Virginie back to France in order to turn her into a proper lady, and she dies in a shipwreck on her return to the island.[11]

Bernardin has little in common with Chateaubriand beyond an interest in exotic places. His story is a sentimental protest against privilege. It seeks a nature that will be free of the pretensions and destructive ambitions of society. Nature, preaches Bernardin in lines that could have come straight from his friend Rousseau's tract *Émile,* can serve as educator: "Far from turning savage by living alone," he writes of the isolated mothers and children, "they had become more human."[12] One can hardly imagine a nature more at odds with Chateaubriand than this tender, taming paradise. Passion, extremes, excess, a *recovery* of the "savage" within man – this is the quest of the Natchez novellas. *Paul et Virginie* captures the longing of a hypercivilized audience for a country vacation; *Atala* and *René* initiate a nineteenth-century mood of rebellion.

At first sight, a closer comparison to Chateaubriand is *Odérahi.* The anonymous author thought so too; six years after its first appearance, he had it published in 1801 with the subtitle "Odérahi is Atala's older sister." Themes that recur in Chateaubriand are announced here: an Indian maid's faithfulness to her lover, romance between French and Indians, and the charms of going native. Yet these thematic similarities cannot disguise the deeper differences.[13] When the hero is captured by Indians, he returns to a Rousseauist state of nature:

Boredom withered my mind during the first eight moons of my captivity, for my soul was not yet accustomed to a savage way of life, but little by little I found it a thousand times preferable to that of Europeans. I was no longer astonished that so many of the latter left their homes to rest on the mats of the Indians who, free as birds, knew no ties except those that unite men for general utility and [knew no] ardent passion except the love of country that directs all their actions. My needs diminished to the degree that I accommodated myself to nature.[14]

11. Jacques Henri Bernardin de Saint-Pierre, *Paul et Virginie* (1788; Paris, 1964).
12. Ibid., 108.
13. *Odérahi, Histoire Américaine; contenant une peinture fidelle des moeurs des habitans de l'intérieur de l'Amérique septentrionale. Odérahi est la soeur aîné d'Atala* (1795; Paris, 1801). The work has been attributed to the naturalist Palisot de Beauvois. Cf. idem., *Odérahi, Histoire Américaine. Une soeur aîné d'Atala,* ed. Gilbert Chinard (1795, 1801; Paris, 1950).
14. Palisot de Beauvois, *Odérahi* (1801), 58–59.

There is no hint here of Romantic extremes. Life among Indians simply subtracts the burdens of civilization, with *l'utilité commune,* a core Enlightenment conception, creating a free society of individuals. The story line, too, points up the contrast to Chateaubriand. The hero begins the process of going native but cannot go through with it; the tragedy of the story turns precisely on the ineradicable difference between savage and *homme policé.*

By contrast, characters like Atala and René are tragic precisely because they cannot remain at home and try instead to enter a foreign culture. Atala only half understands the Christianity she has adopted, and the conflict between her loyalty to a vow and her love of Chactas cannot find a worldly resolution. René is more "savage" than civilized and finds a refuge among the Natchez, but he brings the evils of his countrymen in his wake; like the beachcombers and adventurers and anthropologists and other dropouts from civilization who will follow, he destroys the very thing he seeks merely by being there.[15]

Chateaubriand's achievement was not merely original; it was a revolutionary rethinking of the relationship between Indians and Europeans. To comprehend the transformation, we need to step back in time and compare his tales to previous generations of French writings on the Natchez, who were a historical people before they became a literary artifact. The relationship between Natchez and French culminated in a conflict of the 1720s that led to the extermination of the Natchez and the failure of the Louisiana colony. The war persisted in French memory as a colonial trauma, comparable to the Vietnam War for the United States, one of those episodes that erode the moral authority of empire. By turning back in time, we can better distinguish the elements of fact, fantasy, stereotype, and innovation that gave Chateaubriand's retelling of the Natchez story its hold over the Romantic imagination.

Three types of writing about the Natchez preceded the work of Chateaubriand. There was the correspondence between leaders in the colony and administrators in Paris. While most of these communications passed into the archives, the substance of the debates entered public opinion as different factions tried to make a winning case for their views. Missionary writings included numerous reports on the Louisiana colony that were also a powerful shaper of French sentiment. And finally, a few memoirs tried to explain the conflict that set a course of decline for the Louisiana colony. We shall con-

---

15. Setting them in the revolutionary context of the early nineteenth century, Jean Gillet contrasts Chateaubriand's heroic idealization with Volney's degrading portrayal of Indians. See idem., "Chateaubriand, Volney et le Sauvage américain," in *Romantisme: Revue du dix-neuvième siècle* 36 (1982): 15–26.

trast these genres to Chateaubriand's interpretation of the political aims, religious meaning, and historical significance of French and Indian encounters.

The Natchez war belongs to the larger story of France's attempt to create a colony in the lower Mississippi Valley. The first leader to open up the region to French occupation, Réné-Robert Cavelier de La Salle, was a restless visionary who pushed across Canada and down the Mississippi. Although he fell short on his first two attempts, La Salle and his friends at court worked hard to create the mirage of a southern paradise with temperate climate, abundant game, fertile soil, wild grapes, and mineral wealth, all inviting French settlement.[16] Finally, on his third expedition, La Salle and his party sighted the Gulf of Mexico on April 6, 1682.[17]

The colonial reality turned out to be very different from the advance publicity. A Canadian-born governor, Le Moyne de Bienville, held together the colony for several decades after 1702 by building up Indian alliances, favoring his friends, and terrorizing merchants and administrators from France.[18] After watching Louisiana flounder for a decade and a half, the royal authorities handed over all rights of commerce within it to a newly founded enterprise, the Company of the West, headed by the famous financial speculator John Law. The problems of the preceding years did not go away. Quarreling continued between company men and Bienville, with the governor accusing the merchants and landholders of disloyalty and the merchants and land-

---

16. "Un ami de Cavelier de La Salle présentant la relation officielle de l'entreprise de 1679 à 1681," in Pierre Margry, ed., *Découvertes et établissements des français dans l'ouest et dans le sud de l'Amérique septentrionale. Mémoires et documents originaux,* 6 vols. (Paris, 1876–1886), 2: 277–278.

17. On La Salle see Céline Dupré, "René-Robert, Cavelier de La Salle," *Dictionary of Canadian Biography* (Toronto, 1966), 1: 172–184; Margry, ed., *Découvertes et établissements.* See also the biography of La Salle's lieutenant, Edmund Robert Murphy, *Henry de Tonty: Fur Trader of the Mississippi* (Baltimore, 1941); and Collections of the Illinois State Historical Library, First Series, vol. 1: *The French Foundations, 1680–1693,* ed. Theodore C. Pease and Raymond C. Werner (Springfield, 1934).

18. Lamothe Cadillac, appointed governor of Louisiana in May 1710, had no illusions about his assignment: "One can say," he wrote of his subjects, "that they are a heap of the dregs of Canada, jailbirds without subordination for religion and for government, addicted to vice principally with the Indian women whom they prefer to French women." Cadillac to Pontchartrain, October 26, 1713, in *Mississippi Provincial Archives 1701–1729: French Dominion,* ed. Dunbar Rowland and Albert G. Sanders (Jackson, Miss., 1929), 2: 167.

On the early years of the Louisiana colony, see Patricia Dillon Woods, *French–Indian Relations on the Southern Frontier, 1699–1762* (Ann Arbor, Mich., 1980). This valuable history unites a narrative from the French point of view with a sensitivity to Indian motives; it provides the most satisfactory single account of French–Natchez relations. Cf. the economic and political narrative in Marcel Giraud, *A History of French Louisiana* (Baton Rouge, La., 1974–1987). A rich local history, based on extensive primary research, which conveys the atmosphere of the early years of the Louisiana colony is Jay Higginbotham, *Old Mobile: Fort Louis de la Louisiane, 1702–1711* (Mobile, Ala., 1977).

holders accusing Bienville of corruption. One M. Hubert, the company's commissary, reported after his arrival in 1717 on rampant disorder and corruption, the state of affairs preferred by disobedient officers, seditious soldiers, and licentious settlers.[19] Frustrating official plans for economic control by duly constituted authority, Louisiana's European settlers, African slaves, and Indians developed an illicit network of trapping and trading.[20] One Sieur Dronôt de Valdeterre complained that if the authorities could not get a grip on things, the only colonists left would be "godless and lawless republicans, vagabonds, wanderers, mutineers, and libertines," who would unite with the surrounding Indians and overthrow the company.[21] At last, on March 15, 1727, a new governor, Étienne de Périer, arrived in New Orleans. A man of probity and determination, he worked with some success to improve the economy and public works. The locals resisted the reform efforts of this intruder, however, and the colony struggled along, as unruly and unprofitable as before.

When the rulers of the Louisiana colony looked for ways to expand beyond their first outpost in Mobile Bay, one of the places to attract them was the region settled by the Natchez Indians (in the same area as the town of Natchez today). Elevated above the Mississippi, it had well-drained soil suitable for tobacco farming and a healthful climate; the presence of native people, too, who could trade with Europeans and teach them about the area, was an inducement to settlement. Work began in 1716 on Fort Rosalie, a military outpost near the Natchez villages. There were fewer than 200 settlers in 1723, including a free, indentured, and slave population; by 1729 there were more than 400 whites and 280 black slaves.[22] As for the Natchez, by the time La Salle met them in 1682, they had probably already succumbed to epidemic diseases indirectly transmitted from Europeans and numbered perhaps 3,500; contact with the French after 1700 led to more disease and a halving of their population again by the mid-1720s. They were a people with memories of a greater past, struggling against demographic disaster but not readily intimidated by the Europeans who, during the 1720s, began crowding into their

19. [Hubert] to Conseil de Marine, Archives Nationales Colonies C[13a] 1: 47–48. (Microfilm copy.)
20. See Daniel H. Usner, *Indians, Settlers, and Slaves in a Frontier Exchange Economy: The Lower Mississippi Valley Before 1783* (Chapel Hill, N.C., and London, 1992).
21. "Il n'y restera que des habitans republicains sans foy, sans loy, vagabonds, errands, mutins, et libertins, lesquels venant à s'incorporer avec les nations indiennes tenteront indubitalement à se rendre les Maitres absolus du pays et par la suite à secouer le joug de la Direction, ce qu'est d'une consequence infinie a prévoir." Sr. Dronôt de Valdeterre, "Instruction sommaire . . .," (Louisiana, 1721 or 1722), Archives Nationales Colonies C[13a] 6: 371. (Microfilm copy.)
22. Giraud, *A History of French Louisiana*, 5: 388, 390.

area in growing numbers.[23] Close contact between settlers and natives led to mutual reliance, with Indians supplying game and fish in exchange for French goods and Indian women sometimes helping the French with domestic tasks.

The administrators in New Orleans and their partners in Paris dealt with the Natchez country as a promising if sometimes troublesome outpost. Settlement led to trade and friendly contacts but also to violent incidents. In the years after the creation of Fort Rosalie, the Natchez complained of arrogance and assaults, while settlers countered with accusations of horse stealing. Detchéparré, the commander of Fort Rosalie beginning in 1728, alternately drank with the Natchez and tyrannized them. When he declared his intention of seizing a piece of land belonging to a village chief, the Natchez leaders decided that the moment had come to expel the invaders.[24]

Natchez warriors visited Fort Rosalie on November 28, 1729, pretending to be a hunting party and even asking to borrow some rifles for their outing. When they then turned on the unprepared settlers, more than 200 were killed, although most of the women and slaves were spared.[25] News of the attack created panic in New Orleans. Étienne de Périer, the governor, could count on no more than a handful of reliable troops. He had his Indian allies burn a Natchez woman at the stake; she mocked her tormentors for using a torture properly reserved for men.[26] To impress the Indian peoples of the region, Périer ordered the massacre of innocent Indians living along the river bank below the town.[27] The survival of the colony depended largely on the courage of its African slaves and Choctaw Indian allies. After reinforcements arrived from France, Périer had trouble finding the Natchez, who continued to attack European settlements as late as 1732. They succumbed not to the French but to disease. The survivors took refuge among the Chickasaw Indians.

After the Natchez war, the French confronted a colony in ruins. Even an anonymous dispatch written in defense of Périer had to speak of Louisiana as "that colony whose name is so hideous to those who don't know it. . . ."[28] An

23. See Ian W. Brown, "An Archaeological Study of Culture Contact and Change in the Natchez Bluffs Region," in Patricia K. Galloway, *La Salle and His Legacy: Frenchmen and Indians in the Lower Mississippi Valley* (Jackson, Miss., 1982), 178–179; and Usner, *Indians, Settlers, and Slaves*, 66.
24. Giraud, *History of French Louisiana* 5: 395–397.
25. Ibid., 5: 398.
26. Anonymous sender to anonymous recipient, March 1730, Archives Nationales Colonies F³ 24: 187–187ᵛ, photocopy in Illinois Historical Survey, University of Illinois Library (Urbana-Champaign).
27. Périer to Maurepas, abstract of a letter of March 18, 1730, *Mississippi Provincial Archives* 1: 71, 73.
28. "cette colonie dont le nom est si hideux à ceux qui ne la connoissent point . . ." Anonymous sender to anonymous recipient, undated, Archives Nationales Colonies C¹³ᶜ 1: 375. (Microfilm copy.)

internal memoir written a few years later tallied up all the errors that had taken place before coming to the worst problem, the low character of the colonists and soldiers:

> One can say that even some of the commanding officers and soldiers have degenerated in this country, with terror universal among them since the Natchez attack. . . .The inhabitants who have served in this war have not been better behaved than the soldiers and there is reason to believe that the general discontent which reigns among the troops and the inhabitants is the cause of all this disaster, together with carelessness in the choice of officers and recruits. . . .[29]

For administrators in the metropolis or the colony, the Natchez were not an object of awe or legend, as they would become for later storytellers, but a tactical issue. The conflict with them had no clear message for French policy-makers, who alternated between neglecting the southern hinge of their empire and experimenting with new means of securing it. To the end of the French era, Louisiana remained an intractable dilemma.

The dilemma preoccupied Chateaubriand too. However much he poetized, he was also a politician who upheld France's traditions of military and colonial grandeur. At the end of the preface to the first edition of *Atala* he wrote: "If, as the result of a plan at the very highest level of policy-making, the French Government should dream one day of demanding Canada back from England, my description of New France would take on a new interest."[30] On the next page the story's opening lines sounded a long, mournful French horn of nostalgia for the lost American empire: "La France possédoit autrefois, dans l'Amérique septentrionale, une vaste empire, qui s'éntendoit depuis le Labrador jusqu'aux Florides, et depuis les rivages de l'Atlantique jusqu'aux lacs les plus reculés du haut Canada." ("In days gone by, France possessed a vast empire in North America, extending from Labrador to the Floridas and from the shores of the Atlantic to the most remote lakes of Upper Canada.")[31] Decades later, when he was ambassador to England, his thoughts still turned back to the lost empire. "Let us say," he recalled,

29. "On peut même dire qu'une partie des officiers qui les commandent et ces soldats, ont dégénéré dans ce pays, la terreur ayant esté universelle parmy eux après le coup des Natchez. . . . Les habitans qui ont servy dans cette guerre n'ont pas esté plus braves que les soldats et il y a eu de croire que le mécontentement général qui règne parmy les troupes et les habitans est cause de tout ce désastre, joint au peu d'attention que l'on a eu dans le choix des officiers et des recrües. . . ." Anonymous, no date, Archives Nationales Colonies C[13C] 1: 180–180[v]. (Microfilm copy.)
30. François-René de Chateaubriand, *Atala, ou les Amours de deux sauvages dans le désert* (Dresden, 1801), 14.
31. Ibid., 15. Cf. *Atala/René*, trans. Putter, 17.

to the honor of our country and the glory of our religion, that the Indians were strongly attached to us; that they have never stopped missing us, and that a Black Robe (a missionary) is still venerated in the forests of North America. The savage still loves us beneath the tree where we were his first guests, on the soil that we turned, and where we have left him guardian of our graves.[32]

Memories like these suppressed Louisiana's reputation as an inferno of prostitutes and thieves. Instead, in the propaganda tradition going back to La Salle, Chateaubriand lingered over the dream of a Mississippi Eden.

If the Natchez were a political nuisance to administrators, they were a religious provocation to missionaries. When Father Jacques Gravier voyaged down the Mississippi and reached the Natchez villages in February 1701, he made it his business to debunk the stories of fabulous Natchez wealth. After sniffing around the tribe's temple, he was satisfied that it contained "neither the gold, nor the silver, nor the precious stones, nor the Riches, nor the nine brasses of fine pearls" supposedly attributed to them.[33] The chiefs of the Natchez were cruel despots who ruled by mystifying their people. The temple only housed the bones of former chiefs, "whom they revere as divinities."[34] Gravier could not condone the Natchez practice of human sacrifice.[35] And tribal sexual mores excited even stronger condemnation: "They are polygamous, thievish, and very depraved – the girls and women being even more so than the men and boys, among whom a great reformation must be effected before anything can be expected from them."[36] Their open lewdness was in shocking contrast to the modest dress and behavior of the women among their neighbors, the Tonicas, whom Gravier had just visited.[37] "Everything," he observed tartly, "depends upon the Commission of the Chiefs, who have too much Interest in passing among their people for Spirits to embrace Christian humility very soon." Decades later, at the time of the Natchez war, their temple and religious cult were still intact.[38]

The Natchez massacre of the French at Fort Rosalie provided material for

32. Chateaubriand, *Mémoires d'outre-tombe*, 1: 249.
33. Jacques Gravier to Jacques de Lamberville, February 16, 1701, in *The Jesuit Relations and Allied Documents: Travels and Explorations of the Jesuit Missionaries in New France, 1610–1791*, ed. Reuben G. Thwaites, 65: *Lower Canada, Mississippi Valley (1696–1702)*, (Cleveland, 1900), 141 (hereinafter cited as *Jesuit Relations*). Gravier refers to the account falsely attributed to Henry de Tonty. The pseudonymous account mentions pearls, but none of the other wonders he ascribed to it. See *Dernières découvertes dans l'Amérique septentrionale de M. de La Salle* (Paris, 1697), 185–186.
34. Gravier to Lamberville, *Jesuit Relations* 65: 141.   35. Ibid., 141–143.
36. Ibid., 135.   37. Ibid., 130–131.   38. Ibid., 145.
    Cf. the later judgment of Father le Petit to Father d'Avaugour, July 12, 1730: "Their Religion in certain points is very similar to that of the ancient Romans." *Jesuit Relations* 68: *Lower Canada, Crees, Louisiana, 1720–1736* (Cleveland, 1900), 123.

an important genre of New World religious chronicles: martyrology. After the massacre, Mathurin le Petit wrote a report that began with a factual description of the Natchez before going on to relate the horrifying events of Natchez betrayal of the French settlers in and around nearby Fort Rosalie. The "barbarians," he wrote, had gone on a rampage of murder and atrocities, ripping out the bellies of pregnant women, making other women slaves, leaving the bodies of their dead victims as carrion for dogs and buzzards, and, while their captured brandy held out, abandoning themselves to drinking, dancing, and insulting the French. The loss Le Petit naturally dwelled on with special sadness was the murder of two missionaries – young men in their midthirties who were dedicated to their work and had already made good progress in learning native languages. Yet he and his correspondent knew that this was the inevitable danger of their work, part of the age-old history of martyrdom for the sake of their mission:

> But nothing has happened to these two excellent Missionaries for which we should mourn, or for which they were not prepared when they devoted themselves to the savage Missions in this Colony. This disposition alone, independent of everything else, has without doubt placed a great difference in the eyes of God between their death and that of the others, who have fallen martyrs to the French name. But I am well persuaded that the fear of a similar fate will not in the least diminish the zeal of those of our fathers who had thought of following them, neither will it deter our Superior from responding to the holy desires they may have of sharing our labors.[39]

The specific nature of the Natchez and their crimes, real or imagined, faded before the task of inserting the fallen missionaries into the annals of sacred history; Le Petit was unbroken at a moment of continued danger to the colony, unyielding in his determination to persist despite all the disappointments of New World missionary work.

Chateaubriand, too, takes up the theme of tragic heroism, but his approach is anthropological and comparative. Atala demonstrates her saintly character throughout the story as she risks her life again and again for higher ideals. For the sake of her lover, Chactas, she defies her father, renounces her status as an

---

39. Ibid., 185. Charlevoix, the great traveler and chronicler of the Jesuit mission to North America, passed through the Natchez country in 1722. The Natchez impressed Charlevoix at the time as good neighbors. See Pierre François Xavier de Charlevoix, *Histoire et description générale de la Nouvelle France, avec le journal historique d'un voyage fait par ordre du roi dans l'Amérique septentrionnale* [sic] (Paris, 1744), 6: 176. His subsequent history of Louisiana, however, turned them into mischief makers who tried at every turn to make trouble for the French. A little more firmness and caution, he thought, would have kept them from ever thinking of attacking. Ibid., 4: 233–236, 244–248.

Indian princess, and risks her life by rescuing Chactas.[40] This is but the worldly stage of Atala's heroism, which gives way to a higher quest. Out of faithfulness to her vow to her mother she renounces her mortal life, committing suicide in order to retain her Christian purity. Atala has only imperfectly understood the teaching of the new religion, having grasped its letter of asceticism but not its spirit of mercy that could have permitted her to marry; with a little more education, she would have realized that vows must make room for human weaknesses, that the Church would bless her desire for union with Chactas. Yet if Atala's grasp of the new religion is limited, it is not dull; the account of her behavior is anything but demeaning. Her relentless embarkation on a spiritual quest almost shatters the Christian framework of the story, for her suicide is the mark of a pagan heroic will.

Atala and her acts of sacrifice are not isolated; they have a European counterpart in the figure of Amélie, to whom she is linked by alliteration and trisyllabic name. Self-immolation is a sign that Amélie, too, is a being of highest nobility. At the beginning of the ceremony of initiation into her order "Amélie took her place beneath a canopy, and the sacrifice began by the light of torches amid flowers and aromas which lent their charm to this great renunciation." The priest administers the "sacrifice," and when it is over, despite the convulsion of sibling desire, René learns, on awakening from fainting, that "the sacrifice had been consummated."[41] Like Atala she has chosen a violent rupture of her ties to this world, in a form spiritual rather than physical, but hardly less horrifying for the narrator. Her exit from this world, like Atala's, is a tragic but elevating practice, the fulfillment of the imperative of *noblesse oblige,* obedience to a higher law than personal or even social interest, simultaneously loss of self and act of witness to a transcendent order.[42]

The most famous memoir on Louisiana (and a work that Chateaubriand knew well) was the three-volume *History of Louisiana* by Antoine Simon Le Page du Pratz, published in 1758. It takes the French experience out of the realm of colonial cliché and into the villages of the Natchez. Le Page, a former soldier, went to the colony in 1718 in the service of the Company of the Indies – the mercantile corporation charged with running Louisiana and turning a profit – and lived from 1720 to 1728 in Natchez country.[43] There he

---

40. Chateaubriand, *Atala/René,* trans. Putter, 38.
41. Ibid., 106–108. I have changed the translator's "Amelia" back to "Amélie."
42. See Boon, *Affinities and Extremes,* 56–57.
43. For biographical background see Joseph G. Treagle, Jr., "Le Page du Pratz: Memoir of the Natchez Indians," in *The Colonial Legacy,* ed. Lawrence W. Leder (New York, 1973), 3–4: 59–64. See also the article by the French geographer Jean-Baptist-Benoît Eyriès, "Pratz (Le

developed friendships with his Indian neighbors that make them come alive as fellow human beings. In contrast to most of the official correspondence and missionary missives, Le Page du Pratz evokes a human drama of a people whose world was destroyed by the misdeeds of the French.[44]

His memoir traces the steps that led beyond the typical prejudices of a French settler. A member of the opposite sex was his guide. She was also his slave, whom he bought shortly after arriving, a young woman captured in a conflict between the French and the Chitimacha Indians.[45] On one of their first nights out together, neither could speak the other's language, but when an interloper joined them, they managed to communicate. An alligator approached their cabin; she silently pointed it out, and then, while Le Page slunk away to get his gun, she clubbed it to death.[46] It wasn't far from there to mutual accommodation, perhaps even mutual tenderness: "I had the good fortune to find in her an excellent subject; I treated her with a great deal of gentleness, she became attached to me, and lost the habit of living and going out almost naked as in her country."[47] She advised him to leave his first property and move north to the Natchez country. It was beautiful and had ample game, she explained, and besides, her parents were settled there and could help them.[48] Le Page followed her advice, and they arrived at Fort Rosalie on January 5, 1720. From the local Indians, Le Page purchased a domain that already had a native cabin, some cleared ground, tobacco, and water.[49] With the help of the Chitimacha woman, he had found his way to an idyllic country.

Page Du)," in *Biographie universelle, ancienne et moderne* (Michaud), nouvelle édition (Paris, 1843–1865), 34: 295. Cf. the biographical entries "Pratz" in *Nouvelle biographie générale* (Hoefer) (Paris, 1852–1866), 40: cols. 986–987; and Sonya Lipsett, "Le Page du Pratz," in *A Dictionary of Louisiana Biography,* ed. Glenn R. Conrad (New Orleans, 1988), 1: 504.

44. Le Page du Pratz's memoir should be compared with the memoir of another soldier, Dumont dit Montigny. Dumont was an army lieutenant and engineer who also witnessed the crisis years of the 1720s and early 1730s in the colony. Unlike Le Page du Pratz, he had equal hatred for the French regime and the Natchez, who he thought were treacherous and perverse. He specifically wrote his memoir as a reply to Le Page du Pratz's sympathetic and at times gullible account of the Natchez. Dumont dit [de] Montigny, *Mémoires historiques sur la Louisiane, contenant ce qui y est arrivé de plus mémorable depuis l'année 1687 jusqu'à présent; avec l'établissement de la colonie françoise dans cette province de l'Amérique septentrionale sous la direction de la Compagnie des Indes; le climat, la nature & les productions de ce pays; l'origine & la religion des sauvages qui l'habitent; leur moeurs & leurs coutumes, &c.* (Paris, 1753), 1: ix, 134–135.

45. Le Page du Pratz, *Histoire de la Louisiane contenant la découverte de ce vaste pays; sa description géographique; un voyage dan les terres; l'histoire naturelle; les moeurs, coutumes & religion des naturels, avec leurs origines; deux voyages dans le nord du Nouveau Mexique, dont un jusqu'à la mer du sud; ornée de deux cartes & de 40 planches en tailles douces* (Paris, 1758), 1: 82–83.

46. Ibid., 84–85.   47. Ibid., 115.   48. Ibid., 90–91.   49. Ibid., 126–127.

After arriving contemptuous of the natives – and being warned by Bienville that he would change his mind if he got to know them better – Le Page learned to admire the Natchez. When he made a tour of the interior of Louisiana in September 1724, he refused to take along any Frenchmen and instead went with ten natives (including the Chitimacha woman).[50] The book abounds in instances of native wisdom and skill. His own physician failed to relieve an eye ailment; a Natchez physician set to work on it and cured it.[51] A marriage was proposed between Le Page and a Natchez princess; his demurral was accepted with good grace.[52] Again and again, his narrative counters French prejudice by presenting the Natchez as reasonable people.

If a traveler's interests determine his field of vision, then it is not surprising that Le Page, playing the role of seigneur on his Louisiana estate, was fascinated by the Natchez's social hierarchy. It consisted of a monarch called the Great Sun, three elevated ranks, and the common people. The powers and demeanor of the upper ranks were aristocratic; yet social mobility was possible within the Natchez system, with valor in battle rewarded by advance in rank.[53] They had a matrilinear nobility and a common people; the nobility were divided into descending groups of suns, nobles, and men of rank. Merit balanced inequality: descendants automatically lost rank but could raise themselves through acts of heroism.[54] Love balanced parental authority: "By an admirable harmony," wrote Le Page du Pratz, "very worthy of our imitation, they only marry those who love one another, and those who love one another are only married when their parents agree to it."[55] Especially appealing to Le Page was the Natchez's monarchy.

50. Ibid., 216–217.
51. Le Page du Pratz, *The History of Louisiana, or of the Western Parts of Virginia and Carolina; Containing a Description of the Countries That Lie on Both Sides of the Mississippi; With an Account of the Settlements, Inhabitants, Soil, Climate, and Products*, 2 vols. (London, 1763), 1: 79.
52. Ibid., 2: 206.
53. The Natchez kinship system has stimulated an extensive discussion among anthropologists, who have tried to explain a paradox in the early French reports: the elevation of commoners into noble ranks would have depleted the number of commoners over time and swelled the number of nobles. For historians not interested in structural-functionalist theory, these discussions confirm that the Natchez social hierarchy was highly unusual, although not without parallels among their neighbors, in particular the Chitimacha Indians. See Jeffrey P. Brain, "The Natchez 'Paradox'," *Ethnology* 10 (1971): 215–222; Douglas R. White, George P. Murdock, and Richard Scaglion, "Natchez Class and Rank Reconsidered," ibid., 369–388; and Vernon James Knight, Jr., "Social Organization and the Evolution of Hierarchy in Southeastern Chiefdoms," *Journal of Anthropological Research* 46 (1990): 1–23. See also the description of Natchez social organization in John R. Swanton, *Indian Tribes Of the Lower Mississippi and Adjacent Coast of the Gulf of Mexico*, Smithsonian Institution, Bureau of American Ethnology *Bulletin* 43 (Washington, D.C., 1911), 100–108.
54. Le Page du Pratz, *History of Louisiana*, 2: 202–203.
55. Ibid., 199.

The *Natches* are brought up in a most perfect submission to their sovereign; the authority which their prince exercises over them is absolutely despotic, and can be compared to nothing but that of the first *Ottoman* emperors. . . . But he has this singular advantage over the *Ottoman* princes, that he has no occasion to fear any seditious tumults, or any conspiracy against his person . . . the order of the sovereign is executed on the spot, and nobody murmurs. But however absolute the authority of the *Great Sun* may be, and altho' a number of warriors and others attach themselves to him, to serve him, to follow him wherever he goes, and to hunt for him, yet he raises no stated impositions; and what he receives from those people appears given, not so much as a right due, as a voluntary homage, and a testimony of their love and gratitude.[56]

Whether in their marriage practices or in their politics, the Natchez fulfilled the social ideal of old regime conservatives, in which paternalism and deference were the cement of the social order. The nobles following their monarch were like children obeying their parents, or for that matter like the Chitimacha woman, "excellent subject" that she was, helping her master.

Le Page cultivated the friendship of the Natchez leaders. One of his best informants was the guardian of the Natchez temple. He, in turn, introduced Le Page to the Great Sun and the Great Sun's brother, Stung Serpent.[57] Le Page soon faced painful choices between obedience and friendship. In response to news of quarrels between the Natchez and the French, in September 1723 Governor Bienville arrived at the settlement, backed by 500 men, and attacked the Natchez for four days until they sued for peace.[58] Le Page was ordered to march at the front of this French force. Thereafter the natives no longer came, an economic hardship for the settlers.[59] When Stung Serpent one day walked by his house without stopping, the Frenchman asked him why he had become so aloof. Stung Serpent replied by asking him to explain his behavior during Bienville's visit, to which Le Page replied that, like a Natchez warrior, he had to obey his superior. Stung Serpent was not satisfied; he went on to pose questions about the French right to invade the Natchez country and act as if it were their own. There was plenty of land, he pointed out, for both the French and the Natchez, and he and his people had at first hoped that they could live together in harmony. The French were to blame for disturbing the peace by taking more than their due. It is hard to

56. Ibid., 184–185.
57. Le Page du Pratz, *Histoire de la Louisiane*, 2: 322; on his role in introducing Pratz to the Great Sun and Stung Serpent, see ibid., 323.
58. Six hundred, according to Woods, who gives a different account of this incident. She writes that Bienville was careful to attack only one Natchez village while keeping the majority of the Natchez on his side. Woods, *French–Indian Relations*, 75–78.
59. Le Page du Pratz, *History of Louisiana*, 1: 72.

know whether we hear the distant echo of the Natchez leader's voice or an insertion of French frustration with absolute monarchy in the culminating lines of his speech: "Before the arrival of the *French* we lived like men who can be satisfied with what they have; whereas at this day we are like slaves, who are not suffered to do as they please."[60] Le Page was able to restore his friend's personal confidence with the present of a calumet. He could not, however, repair the larger injuries to Natchez self-esteem.

The final Natchez uprising was only a logical continuation of the same refusal to submit to foreign tyranny. When Detchéparré commanded one of the Suns to leave his ancestral land, his words only roused the spirit of opposition, for "he knew not, that the natives of *Louisiana* are such enemies to a state of slavery, that they prefer death itself thereto; above all, the *Suns*, accustomed to govern despotically, have still a greater aversion to it."[61] When the Sun explained his reluctance to obey by stating that his ancestors had long lived in the village, what could appear more noble to French readers than this seigneur's attachment to the soil? When the commandant replied with more threats, the Sun made the final case for a partnership of mutual respect: "When the *French* came to ask us for lands to settle on, they told us, there was land enough still unoccupied which they might take; the same sun would enlighten them all, and all would walk in the same path."[62] After Detchéparré interrupted him, he calmly withdrew to hold a council on the French demands. According to Le Page, the eldest warrior railed against the French, accusing them of preparing to reduce them to a state of slavery.[63] It was a nobility's defense of freedom versus foreign despotism that triggered the war.

Le Page thus introduced the theme of native nobility that would be so important for Chateaubriand. Yet Stung Serpent and his peers were but one panel of a panorama that included everything useful that Le Page could cram into three volumes: a history of Louisiana, information on flora and fauna, his personal woes and triumphs, the story of his trip through the countryside, and tips on good plantation management. His aim – at a moment when France needed to decide how much to invest in the American theater of the Seven Years' War – was to weigh in on the side of the Louisiana colonial experiment; he wanted to show that the colony had rich natural resources (including its natives) and only required better management in order to turn a profit. In the larger scheme of his book, to portray the Natchez sympathetically was to point out that Indians were not demons, but dignified warriors who would respond reasonably to respectful French behavior.

Chateaubriand took up the theme of native nobility at a very different his-

60. Ibid., 75.   61. Ibid., 135–136.   62. Ibid., 136.   63. Ibid., 140–141.

torical moment: four decades after Le Page published his book, nobility in France itself was under a physical and intellectual threat of execution. With Revolutionary ideology omnipresent, the story of the Natchez turned into something new: a medium for reinventing noble values. Chateaubriand made an equation between savage and noble that did not yet exist for Le Page. The colonial administrator kept his distance from the Natchez no matter how close his physical proximity was; René, figment of an author who probably never came within a thousand miles of the Lower Mississippi, merged into their history. Following the trail of René, future French travelers visited North American Indians in order to revitalize their own aristocratic identity.

The choice of the Natchez suggests in its own right how Chateaubriand altered the image of American Indians. The philosophes of the eighteenth century preferred peoples like the Iroquois and Hurons, whose consensus politics satisfied their search for examples of social equality. While this use of Indians imposed a European ideology on them, it also recognized that their societies contained elements of meritocracy at odds with the hierarchical and hereditary organization of Western and Central European societies. Chateaubriand bypassed the philosophes and their theory of natural equality by turning to a people famed for their social hierarchy. The Natchez, as he portrayed them, behaved with the corporate consciousness of European nobility. The preface to *Atala* even proclaimed that the Natchez uprising was part of a general Indian uprising, attempting to overthrow centuries of European oppression! The assertion was historically absurd, but it gave them the stature of like-minded patriots and guardians of ancient freedoms.

Chateaubriand was not simply nostalgic for the bygone era of free nobilities, however. A digression in *The Natchez* makes clear his wish to rework noble values in order to bring them into the modern era. Chactas is captured and enslaved by the French, taken in chains to Marseilles and Toulon, and personally pardoned by Louis XIV. The "savage" then has a chance to comment on all the defects of European civilization. Such use of the "savage" as critic of civilization was a familiar literary device of the Enlightenment, but Chateaubriand filled it with new meaning. Chactas is not primarily a man of natural reason like Voltaire's Huron, pointing out the irrationality of European behavior; rather, he has an ethos of independence and discovers that the French are a nation of slaves. The great men of the age and the splendor of France disappoint him on his visit to Versailles, for he recognizes that dependence on monarchy has created a service – and servile – aristocracy. Yet he cannot return home secure in his belief in the superiority of his old way of life. Modern society and state will encompass the world and divest primitive no less than European nobles of their ancient freedoms. His people will not always be able to live from hunting, Chactas learns, and will need to find new forms of dignity and happiness compatible with modern society.[64]

Chactas's lesson would haunt the younger generations of French travelers who came to the United States after Chateaubriand. By the time they arrived, it was even harder to recognize it as the onetime land of Atala and René: Romantic forests were yielding to the settlers' open fields, and the misty ambiguities of settler – native meetings were giving way to the clear outline of a commercial civilization. The poetry of the New World was remote. Instead, the confrontation with the United States after 1815 stimulated a different kind of writing, in its own way as imaginative and original: the sociology of modern democracy.

---

64. Chateaubriand, "Les Natchez," 270–271. Cf. Chateaubriand's remarks on archaic and modern freedom in the memoir on the United States he published as part of the 1827 edition of his works, *Travels in America,* trans. Richard Switzer (Lexington, Ky., 1969), 191.

PART II

Ending a Tradition: The French
Romantic Travelers, 1815–1848

3

◁ ══ ▷

Critics and Nostalgics

The year 1815 marks a great divide in European politics: the end of the Congress of Vienna and with it the establishment of an era of conservative rule in Western and Central Europe. In France, the Bourbon monarchy was restored to the throne. Its return signaled a slowing down of the revolutionary dynamic of European society and the beginning of an era of renewed prestige for the country's traditional elites. At the same time, neither the Congress of Vienna nor Louis XVIII, the newly installed king, attempted to bring back the privileged legal order of the old regime. Rulers throughout Europe were well aware that theirs was an age of accommodation in which they could best maintain political control by acting in partnership with the newly emancipated bourgeois classes.

This balance between the old and the new – the return of pre-Revolutionary political classes and the emergence of modern society – created a new standpoint for French evaluations of the United States. Most of the post-1815 French accounts of travel to America continued to come from elite authors. The elite they belonged to was different, however, from the one that had existed before the French Revolution, for the transformation of French politics had changed the meaning of its social status. French society was supposed to be founded on the principle of legal equality, abolishing the status distinctions that had existed for centuries. The social reality was more complicated, however; during the era from the end of the Napoleonic wars to the Revolution of 1848, a handful of bourgeois and noble families continued to enjoy exceptional political influence and economic opportunities. The overlap of old and new families led to the formation of a distinctive social type, which the French historian André-Jean Tudesq has named the "notable."[1] With luck

1. See André-Jean Tudesq, *Les Grands notables en France (1840–1849): Étude historique d'une psychologie sociale*, 2 vols. (Paris, 1964). Cf. David Higgs, *Nobles in Nineteenth-Century France: The Practice of Inegalitarianism* (Baltimore, 1987), which draws valuable distinctions

and skill, young men from the right background could rise rapidly to positions of power and wealth during these years. They and their families inhabited a mixed society characterized by juxtapositions. It was neither quite of the old regime nor of the new; the titled and the untitled jostled side by side, uncomfortable with one another, not yet marrying or meeting in salons without acute awareness of their different origins. The nobility could still look back to the days when they enjoyed unquestioned legal superiority, but they could no longer ignore the money and ambition of their inferiors; social climbers might behave with greater assertiveness, but they assimilated the tastes of their social superiors. Despite their unease, together they formed a class that strove to revive an aristocratic culture.

Membership in this elite circumscribed the stories that early-nineteenth-century travelers told about the United States. Diplomats consorted with American political and social leaders; Jesuit missionaries spread across the land once more; scientists gathered flora and fauna; politicians studied American republican institutions; refugees dreamed of a return to France; men of leisure continued the grand tour tradition of the eighteenth century. These travelers could go from one French-speaking house to another, if they chose, without much need to speak English.[2] America as a land of social opportunity had no direct appeal for them. No mass immigration from France to America, no ordinary interest in jobs and farming on the part of their countrymen, balanced their political and philosophical concerns. And they traveled before the age of the tourist, alone or with one companion, attracting notice as genteel Europeans, reciting meetings with members of the American social elite and recounting their impressions with the self-assurance that such things had not been said too often.

Their travels were a way of asserting social status. As in the old regime, going abroad was an experience that helped prepare the young for positions of authority in polite society, the arts, and politics. The nature of the experience depended on the traveler's destination. To go to Italy was to participate in a ritual that annulled the forward movement of time: it meant repeating the itinerary of earlier humanist generations, taking in the monuments and

between the different subgroups of the nineteenth-century elite and delineates the distinctive ethos of the nobility; and François Furet, *Revolutionary France, 1770–1880,* trans. Antonia Nevill (Oxford, 1988), which pays considerable attention to the role of liberal notables in politics.

2. "Le théâtre de New-Yorck," noted Édouard de Montulé after a visit of November 1816, "est beau; mais ne sachant point encore l'anglais, je ne puis jouir du spectacle." See his *Voyage en Amérique, en Italie, en Sicile et en Égypte, pendant les années 1816, 1817, 1818 et 1819* (Paris, 1821), 1: 23.

atmosphere of classical antiquity that were the unchanging models of human excellence. To go to America in the early nineteenth century had an altogether different significance: it put the traveler in touch with historical progress. The visitor could see, firsthand, the transformation of a continent from a wilderness to a civilization. French travelers, like other Europeans, experienced America as a place of political innovation and of a distinctively modern relationship to nature.

There was, however, a special reckoning with the past for post-1815 visitors from France: they came to a site of colonial ruins. The French empire in North America may have collapsed in the late eighteenth century, but it continued to inhabit the imagination of visitors from the metropolis, who followed the trail of former French glory from New Orleans to St. Louis, from the battlefields of upstate New York to the towns and villages of Canada, dreaming of a New France that had but recently flourished, its remnants still scattered across the gray skies and vast forests of the interior. They warmed their imaginations on the dwindling embers of the former empire, now fated either to disappear or to endure as an isolated minority culture. To be sure, the nostalgic tradition reached back into the previous century. It was at least as old as France's defeat in the Seven Years' War, from then on combining sympathy for American Indians with resentment toward the successful British and their English-speaking colonists. The nineteenth century added a deeper register of regret to visitors' memories of empires past, however. In the aftermath of the French Revolution and Napoleon, the vanished grandeur of New France mingled with the irretrievable sweetness of life before the Revolution in a powerfully united mood of melancholy.

Yet nostalgia was only one side of their experience. Fascination with money and all that it could do, habitual expectation of novelty, and curiosity about a completely democratic society drew travelers to America too. After the generation-long interruption of contact during the Napoleonic years, post-1815 travelers encountered political surprises. Earlier generations could view America, however fancifully, as a patrician republic ruled by wealthy and landed gentlemen who belonged to the same kind of civilization as themselves. With every passing year after 1815, this vision of an idealized republic became more at odds with the realities of a modern, democratic settler society. In part the change was political. The populist politics of Andrew Jackson vanquished the older patrician leadership and challenged French visitors to rethink their own understanding of democracy. Travelers also responded to day-to-day encounters with American business-mindedness, democratic manners, and expansion across the continent. They had to decide whether American society was sinking into disorder or stood for a new system of social organization.[3]

Finally, there was the nature of North America: a distinctly romantic setting for the traveler. At the end of an upstate New York tour came the most important natural wonder, Niagara Falls. Writers tried to describe the experience of standing on the edge. It was a peek into hell, a reminder of the majesty of man's Maker, an experience beyond words. The clouds and tumult of the giant cataract put them in touch with a higher power, demonic or divine[4] (Fig. 5). No less important were the North American forests. Awesome in their vastness, they were seemingly untouched since the creation; all the more jarring, by comparison, was the pace of movement across the continent as settlers cut down trees, built roads, and linked fields and houses and towns to the coasts and the wider world. Some compared themselves to Romans watching the civilization of a Gallic or Teutonic wilderness; but there was an unpleasantly modern speed to the transformation, jolting them out of this classical reverie. The American felling of the forests was brutal and quick, and it replaced the stillness of ancient groves with the din of modern commerce. Nowhere more than in their contemplation of nature could visitors take a measure of the acceleration of historical change.[5]

The United States after 1815 challenged French visitors to come to terms with democratic politics and society. The successive waves of émigrés responded to American populism attentively. Reactionary monarchists, constitutional monarchists, liberal aristocrats, liberal revolutionaries, Bonapartists, anti-Bonapartists, and technocrats considered the New World against a French background of revolution, terror, imperial glory and dictatorship, legitimate monarchy, and liberal monarchy. For these visitors the United States was a place to consider democracy with a certain degree of distance. Had Ameri-

---

3. On the transition in French opinion from admiration for a neoclassical republic to dislike of a plebeian democracy, see René Rémond, *Les États-Unis devant l'opinion française, 1815–1852* (Paris, 1962).
4. Francis de La Porte Castelnau, "Les Chutes de Niagara," in *Vues et souvenirs de l'Amérique du Nord* (Paris, 1842), 74–78; Montulé, *Voyage en Amérique,* 284; Hyde de Neuville, *Mémoires et souvenirs* (Paris, 1888–1892), 1: 461; Jacques Milbert, *Itinéraire pittoresque du fleuve Hudson et des parties latérales de l'Amérique du Nord, d'après les dessins originaux pris sur les lieux* (Paris, 1828–1829), 1: 198.

On Niagara and early-nineteenth-century travelers, see William Irwin, *The New Niagara: Tourism, Technology, and the Landscape of Niagara Falls, 1776–1917* (University Park, Pa., 1996), chap. 1.
5. See Milbert, *Itinéraire pittoresque,* 1: xx–xi; and Alexis de Tocqueville, "A Fortnight in the Wilds," in *Journey to America,* trans. George Lawrence and ed. J. P. Mayer with A. P. Kerr (Garden City, N.Y., 1971), 399–400.

5. *Horse Shoe of Niagara, from the Canada side.* From Jacques Milbert, *Itinéraire pittoresque du fleuve Hudson et des parties latérales de l'Amérique du Nord, d'après les dessins originaux pris sur les lieux*, 2 vols. and atlas (Paris, 1828–1829), atlas plate no. 34. Courtesy of Yale Center for British Art, Paul Mellon Collection, Yale University.

cans made a different and better revolution than the French, or were they descending into chaos? Was their country a place of cultural barbarism or human dignity? French visitors debated these alternatives, and indeed were attracted to both of them, registering disappointment and admiration of the young republic.

Even though politics was never far from their minds, the United States also stimulated the *sociological* imagination of French visitors. This was the founding era of sociological theory in France itself, the period in which Auguste Comte promulgated the arrival of the age of society in world history, succeeding the theological and military epochs. Comte was one of a generation of utopian socialists and thinkers from across the political spectrum who tried to understand the civil society that had emerged from the ruins of the old regime. The rapid succession of French governments, the personal misfortunes and opportunities of a turbulent age, and well-developed habits of sociological speculation fermented in French theorizing after 1815.[6] The United States, contemporaries knew, offered special opportunities for observing the workings of a modern society far less disturbed than its European counterparts by the crosscurrents of premodern institutions. Throughout their writings, travelers scattered insights that Tocqueville and others would make part of the century's lasting sociological legacy.

A gifted satirist, Baron Montlezun, traveled down the East Coast and through the South as far as New Orleans in the years 1815 to 1817. Montlezun was a royalist who came to the United States and the Caribbean in order to recoup his lost fortunes (although he does not spell out what he had once owned or how he expected to prosper). The hustling commercial society all around him only enhanced his personal bitterness and mordant witticisms. American crudeness began with the hotel meals, where badly cooked ham and boiled corn passed for delicacies and where the other guests deserted the table after bolting down their food, leaving the stranger alone and astonished.[7] The comic effect of his writing comes from his inexhaustible amazement over the untutored behavior of a nation of upstarts.

Protest against the democratic leveling of hierarchies was the motive underlying his observations. In an alphabetical guide to Philadelphia, Montlezun returned several times to the free manner of American women.

---

6. See Frank Manuel, *The Prophets of Paris: Turgot, Condorcet, Saint-Simon, Fourier, and Comte* (New York, 1965).
7. [Baron de Montlezun], *Voyage fait dans les années 1816 et 1817, de New-Yorck à la Nouvelle-Orléans, et de l'Orénoque au Mississipi* . . . (Paris, 1818), 1: 6–7. This was sequel to another work published the same year, M. [Baron de Montlezun], *Souvenirs des Antilles: Voyage en 1815 et 1816, aux États-Unis, et dans l'archipel Caraïbe* (Paris, 1818).

Under "demoiselles" he wrote: "[They] leave freely and alone at any time of day. . . . Custom permits them to touch the hand of men in their society as a sign of mutual courtesy. They affect masculine manners, gait, and airs. It is rare, especially in the Northern and Middle states, to see any with small feet and delicate hands."[8] American women did in fact enjoy a degree of independence that contrasted with the control of women by male heads of households in France. Tocqueville too noticed and commented at length on the unusual freedom of American women, which he considered one of the most admirable features of American democracy.[9] For Montlezun, however, elevating the status of women was another name for upsetting the natural order of things. His descriptions of the appearance of American women – their masculine air, their forward behavior – captured his revulsion toward a democratic relationship between the sexes.

The baron's remarks on Americans' commercial mentality hover on the verge of sociological insights taken up by later, more systematic thinkers. Wealthy American merchants seemed to live for nothing but making money, he observed in Baltimore. Charles Street, he wrote, was the residence of businessmen who had made their fortunes but refused to give up commerce, although they could live in great comfort:

The impulse is fixed, the habit is formed, the love of gain internalized; it would be impossible for them to keep busy with anything but mercantile affairs and speculation and to lose sight of lovely perspectives on lucre. The commercial towns offer little nourishment for curiosity; they are ordinarily the grave of talent and letters.[10]

Like Tocqueville and (at the beginning of the twentieth century) Max Weber, he observed America as a foreigner, not just because he came from a different continent, but because capitalism visibly clashed in his home society with European conceptions of status. The *meaning* of accumulation of wealth already surfaced here as a puzzle: it did not make sense from the utilitarian viewpoint that otherwise seemed to be the highest value of American society. To grasp the underlying motives, however, required a deeper psychological interpretation of the kind Weber furnished in *The Protestant Ethic and the Spirit of Capitalism*. For Montlezun, such observations remained scattered insights. Their only larger purpose was to justify a social snobbery contrast-

8. Under "Women" he added: "Point belles . . . Sortent seules, même le soir, d'un pas déterminé." Montlezun, *Souvenirs des Antilles*, 54–55, 64–65.
9. See Alexis de Tocqueville, *Democracy in America*, trans. George Lawrence, ed. J. P. Mayer, (Garden City, N.Y., 1969), 590–603. On the status of American women, cf. Christine Stansell, *City of Women: Sex and Class in New York, 1789–1860* (New York, 1986).
10. Montlezun, *Voyage*, 1: 17.

ing an ancient civilization, inherited wealth, and noble lineage to the deficiencies of new money.[11]

An aristocratic woman left behind a briefer but no less stinging portrait of American democracy. Countess Maria de las Mercedes Merlin, daughter of one of the first families of Madrid, was married to a Napoleonic general who continued to reap offices and honors in the Restoration and the July Monarchy. Famed for her salon and her talent as a singer, she made a brief visit to the United States from May 3 to May 25, 1840. The most telling moment in her account was her visit to the theater in New York. Here she observed the indifference to rank of streetwise New Yorkers:

The performance hall is attractive and well lit, but the principle of equality, intolerable slavery, requires that the seats be unreserved, to the extent that most of the time daughter is separated from mother, husband from wife; everyone is seated, or rather thrown in place, by chance.

Disorder reaches its height as one leaves the theater. There are no guards lest the freedom of the people, who trample on the infirm, be restrained; there are no servants – this aristocratic device would be too much of a shock for the masses who furnish without having them; there are no doormen who, for a tip, hail a cab. No American is permitted to put himself in the service of another.[12]

The countess does not mention whether she had read Tocqueville – one suspects not – but with or without his guidance, she put her finger on the fundamental principle of American society: equality. She was able to convey to her readers how the effects of democratization went beyond questions of political representation to pervade the tiniest crevices of public life, down to the way people jostled after a performance. Her remarks belong to a tradition reaching back to antiquity of viewing the theater as a microcosm of larger social relations; here it put on display the chaos of American society. Merlin's nightmare of a world without seat assignments or servants was particularly appropriate to New York of the early nineteenth century, where the theater was in fact a central institution of a self-consciously democratic culture, its audiences exulting in the rough and tumble that dismayed the upper classes.[13] The well-lit

11. Ibid., 154–156. Very similar in their strengths and weaknesses (though without the same biting wit) are the observations of Adolphe Fourier de Bacourt, who served as French ambassador to the United States between 1840 and 1842. Like Montlezun, he was struck by the inability of wealthy businessmen to find any aim in life apart from making money. "These retired merchants," he wrote, "die from neglect and loneliness, and from want of something to do in the midst of the stir and activity of every one around them." Adolphe Fourier de Bacourt, *Souvenirs of a Diplomat: Private Letters from America during the Administrations of Presidents Van Buren, Harrison, and Tyler*, introd. Comtesse de Mirabeau (New York, 1885), 178.

12. Maria de las Mercedes Merlin, *La Havane* (Paris, 1844), 1: 80–81.

13. On working-class republican culture and the theater, see Sean Wilentz, *Chants Democratic: New York and the Rise of the American Working Class, 1788–1850* (New York, 1984), 257–259, 358–359.

building, representing the technical proficiency of American society, only illuminated the disorder of the public space. In the eyes of this beholder, democratic freedom was another name for "intolerable slavery."

Let us linger for a moment over the comparison between democracy and slavery. It was not a casual one at a time of rising debate over slavery in Europe as well as in the United States. Travelers' reactions depended on their general views of democracy. For defenders of hierarchy, slavery was not an offense against human dignity but a well-constituted bottom rung of society. Not everyone was willing to say so as shamelessly as Bernard-Adolphe Granier de Cassagnac, but then he was an unusually expressive Romantic. Born in Toulouse in 1803, he went to Paris an enthusiast for Victor Hugo; the poet helped him make his debut in the literary journals of the capital. Even by the standards of a combative age he was querulous, landing in court again and again over duels and literary disputes.[14]

On a visit to the Antilles, Granier married a creole and became a fanatical partisan of slavery. His account of his voyage sets out to prove "that the colonial regime has morally elevated the African race" and that "the Africans of the Antilles, prematurely left to themselves according to the principles of the philanthropists, would regress toward barbarism and lose all of the advantages of the progress already under way...."[15] His feelings faltered, he confessed, when he first heard the crack of the overseer's whip summoning slaves to prayer. But after learning to what extent their bondage was softened by "the goodness, the humanity, the affection, the generosity of the masters," he regained his confidence.[16] Granier was almost a caricature of the counterrevolutionary: feudalism, the subordination of industrial workers, the authority of the Catholic Church, and Jesuit pedagogy were among his other favorite causes. He was also a political opportunist who jumped successfully from regime to regime, first as a journalistic partisan of Louis-Philippe, then as a legislator under Napoleon III and – surviving the third great change of regimes in his lifetime – in the early years of the Third Republic. The tone of his travel account reveals his political shrewdness, for he adapts it to the discourse of the post-Revolutionary era. Slavery is no longer part of a stable society of orders, unchanging over eons of time. Instead it enjoys a place in the history of progress as a tutelary institution.

14. See the biographical entries "Granier de Cassagnac" in *Biographie universelle, ancienne et moderne* (Michaud), nouvelle édition (Paris, 1843–1865), 21: cols. 685–688, which I have in part paraphrased, and in *Dictionnaire de parlementaires français*, vol. 3 (Paris, 1889–1891), 240–242.

15. Adolphe Granier de Cassagnac, *Voyage aux Antilles: Françaises, Anglaises, Danoises, Espagnoles; À Saint-Domingue et aux États-Unis D'Amérique*, 2 vols. (Paris, 1842), 1: vii.

16. Ibid., 2: 394–395.

Not all titled visitors were so illiberal. Jean-Guillaume Hyde de Neuville was a combative royalist who was traumatized in his early years by the trial of Louis XIV and intrigued ceaselessly thereafter for the restoration of the monarchy. His exile in the United States from 1807 to 1814 (followed by the role of Envoy Extraordinary and Minister Plenipotentiary from France to the United States from 1816 to 1821) did not turn him into an uncritical admirer of his place of refuge. As a man of inherited high status, he wrote with little patience for the supreme value of a class society: "Americans love money too much. They don't say about a man: 'what good points does he have?,' but 'how much is he worth?,' and they classify him according to this ridiculous scale of cupidity; profit is their grand preoccupation and the only thing that matters."[17] Yet he also valued the simplicity and directness of American social forms. Unlike Montlezun, he appreciated American women's freedom from affectation: "Women are flirtatious only to the point necessary to be attractive; beyond this, there is no iniquity and no mystery. Girls love openly and without constraint, and married women do not look beyond the conjugal union."[18] The turmoil of the Revolutionary era had a maturing effect on this stolid but principled conservative. Hyde de Neuville was able to appreciate the American achievement of creating a stable political order, opposed though it was to all the principles he stood for in his own country:

If one thinks of all the difficulties of constituting a state across the immense extent of a continent whose population has little internal homogeneity, and where until now colonial interests have predominated, one asks what will has been energetic enough, which man virtuous enough, to establish liberties without license, power without tyranny.[19]

The question was born of years of observing political misfortune and awareness of the fragility of freedom. Hyde de Neuville anticipated Tocqueville in his combination of distance toward America's culture and admiration for the wisdom of its political system.

Another aristocratic admirer of America, Édouard de Montulé, was stimulated by his boyhood reading of voyage accounts to seek for himself the great monuments of nature and history.[20] A traveler in the grand tour tradi-

17. Jean-Guillaume Hyde de Neuville, *Mémoires et souvenirs*, 1: 453.
    For biographical background on Hyde de Neuville, see the biographical entries "Hyde de Neuville" in *Dictionnaire de parlementaires français*, 3: 379–380, and in *Biographie universelle*, 20: 239–245. There is also a brief biographical sketch of Hyde de Neuville and his wife in Frank Monaghan, "The American Drawings of Baroness Hyde de Neuville," *The Franco-American Review* 1 (Spring 1938): 217–220.
18. Hyde de Neuville, *Mémoires et souvenirs*, 1: 453.
19. Ibid., 2: 199–200.   20. Montulé, *Voyage en Amérique*, 1: vi.

tion, he visited Italy, Sicily, and Egypt, as well as the United States from 1816 to 1819. After landing in New York on November 16 of the former year and visiting Philadelphia, he departed by boat for the West Indies, arrived at New Orleans in April 1817, ascended the Mississippi by steamboat as far as St. Louis, traveled on the Ohio River to Pittsburgh, crossed the Alleghanies, and passed through Buffalo before returning to Europe. Well born enough to assume antidemocratic prejudices if he had so chosen – he attended a military school, he tells us, and letters of recommendation carried him from house to house of French merchants in the United States – Montulé exuded frankness, self-assurance, and spontaneous enjoyment of all that a new continent had to offer. He savored the boutiques and beautiful women of Broadway, declaring New York's main thoroughfare to be perhaps the most brilliant street in the world.[21] He had no less admiration for Philadelphia, which he called the most beautiful city in the United States, with special praise for its orderly street plan.[22] Not for him the racial hatred of a Granier: distancing himself from status anxieties, he protested the barbarism of slaveholding in the West Indies and New Orleans and regretted the persistence of prejudice toward free blacks in Pennsylvania.[23] His assessments of American character are remarkable for their freedom from both American and European prejudice. The national vanity of the Americans amused him; their stiffness in social relations with a stranger annoyed him. He looked deeper than these frictions of conversation, however, to reflect on the practical intelligence of the Americans:

To know how to *do* something, you have to *do* something (*Pour savoir faire, il faut faire*); otherwise, you have no reputation and no fortune: which explains why so many people with only pretentions abruptly leave America. . . . Latin is little cultivated; that's why so many Europeans, who think they have a good education because they have learned that language, think Americans are ignorant. It seems to me that one has to judge them completely differently.[24]

This was a no-nonsense observer: in contrast to the insularity of Merlin and Montlezun, Montulé recognized that a consistent logic, non-European but with its own dignity, underlay this incessant activity. Though they did not yet have a name, he sensed the emerging habits of American pragmatism.

European fans of modernization could come to the United States to study technical and economic innovation on a continent less encumbered by memories of privilege. One of the best known was Michel Chevalier, an engineer, journalist, and politician.[25] Adolphe Thiers, then Minister of the Interior, sent

---

21. Ibid., 11, 18, 20.   22. Ibid., 29.   23. Ibid., 33–34, 151.   24. Ibid., 313–314.
25. For biographical background see *Dictionnaire des parlementaires français*, 2: 90–91.

him in November 1832 to study the railways and other means of transporta-
tion in the United States. His professional interests provided him with a starting point for appreciating American society's technical achievements. So, too,
did his youthful admiration for Henri de Saint-Simon, the famous aristocrat
turned prophet of a new age of technocracy, who attracted a sectarian cluster
of admirers, some of whom went on to brilliant careers in business and politics. Chevalier publicized his views at the time through a series of reports to
the *Journal des Débats,* subsequently published as *Lettres sur L'Amérique du
Nord,* and in a separate study of liberty in the United States.[26] Not a democratic leveler, he praised America for successfully raising the skills of its masses
while preserving elite leadership. The Yankee, he thought, had hitherto played
the dominant role in settling the country and shaping its culture, but in the
future the more aristocratic Virginian would grow in influence, with the two
types merging in a third character, the Westerner.[27] Against Europeans who
feared that freedom in America shaded over into chaos, he emphasized how
the austere morality of the Americans permitted their leaders to dispense with
the external constraints of bureaucracy and to enjoy a high degree of freedom
of movement, occupation, and industrial association.[28] A booster of industrial
expansion, Chevalier held up America as a practical alternative to France's traditional and bureaucratic constraints on entrepreneurship.

A well-defined debate emerges from the accounts of early-nineteenth-
century French travelers: friendly observers like Chevalier and Montulé, as
well as unfriendly observers like Montlezun and Merlin, introduce their readers to a dramatic contrast between France's hierarchical civilization and
American egalitarianism. The tension between monarchy and democracy in
France made them acute observers of the democratic revolution across the
Atlantic and its pervasive effects on all aspects of American life. Even the
more friendly upper-class observers tended to be critical as well as admiring,
but precisely this mixture enriched their observations; they were genuinely
inquiring, examining issues from all sides as they tried to sort out the unfamiliar qualities of a new kind of society. The challenges of American democracy gave their writings at best a brio and freshness of insight that had few
precedents. Aristocratic writers like Hyde de Neuville and Montulé turned
their social distance into an advantage, maintaining a critical perspective yet
urging on their readers a deeper understanding of the New World.

26. Michel Chevalier, *Lettres sur L'Amérique du Nord,* 2 vols. (Paris, 1836), trans. T. G. Bradford
    as *Society, Manners and Politics in the United States: Being a Series of Letters on North Amer-
    ica* (Boston, 1839); idem., *La Liberté aux États-Unis* (Paris, 1849).
27. Chevalier, *Lettres,* 1: 161–185; cf. his admiring discussion of the Yankee in *La Liberté aux
    États-Unis,* 45–47.
28. Chevalier, *La Liberté aux États-Unis,* esp. chap. 3 and the concluding remarks on 55.

America was the land of the democratic future, yet it also contained hidden byways into the past. New France already had an archaic quality: it represented a late age of French heroism, and even though it was just over a half century old, it lay on the other side of the Revolutionary watershed. One could only read about the Middle Ages, or at most make pilgrimages to its churches and castles, but travelers could seek out villages that still spoke the language of New France and take up with the Indians who had been France's colonial partners.

One sign of enduring regret for the lost empire was French admiration for the novels of James Fenimore Cooper. *The Last of the Mohicans* (translated in the year of its American publication, 1826) turned Cooper into a celebrity. Review after review praised the author who seemed to be the poet-historian of a continent that hitherto had lacked a literature. Cooper stayed in Paris from mid-1826 to 1828 and returned from 1830 to 1833. Lafayette was his friend and protector; he presented Cooper to the court of Charles X, the last Bourbon to sit on the French throne, and after 1830 to the court of Louis-Philippe, the so-called bourgeois monarch from the Orléans dynasty who ruled in alliance with the upper middle class. The relationship between Cooper and his French hosts soured during the 1830s as the fad for his novels passed and Cooper published several works critical of his old-world hosts. Yet his writings haunted the Romantic imagination: Balzac, George Sand, and the elder Alexandre Dumas were among his admirers. These Europeans took up his *Leatherstocking Tales* as an authentic American witness to a charming and mysterious world.[29]

The Last of the Mohicans is a many-layered book with different messages for different audiences. For American readers it continued the genre of the captivity narrative, the stories, reaching back to Puritan autobiographies, of Europeans kidnapped and held by Indian peoples.[30] Set during the French and Indian War, it tells the tale of two sisters, Cora and Alice, daughters of a British general, who are captured by Hurons. A father-and-son pair of good Indians (the Mohicans of the title), a backwoodsman named Natty Bumpo, and a young British officer pursue them. In the end the sisters are freed, but

29. On the reception of Cooper in France, see Georgette Bosset, *Fenimore Cooper et le roman d'aventure en France vers 1830* (Paris, 1928); Margaret Murray Gibb, *Le Roman de Bas-De-Cuir. Étude de Fenimore Cooper et son influence en France* (Paris, 1927); and George D. Morris, *Fenimore Cooper et Edgar Poe d'après la critique française du 19. siècle* (Paris, 1912).
30. On captivity narratives, see two works that in exemplary fashion examine the meanings of captivity from multiple points of view: Pauline Turner Strong, "Captivity in White and Red: Convergent Practice and Colonial Representation on the British-Amerindian Frontier, 1606–1736," in Daniel Segal, ed., *Crossing Cultures: Essays in the Displacement of Western Civilization* (Tucson and London, 1992), 33–104; and John Demos, *The Unredeemed Captive: A Family Story From Early America* (New York, 1994).

only after the death of the young Mohican, Chingachgook. His death symbolizes the end of an era of Indian nobility. All that remains is either "women" Indians – Delawares who have given up their warrior birthright – or demonic Hurons who have lost their claims on human compassion. After the extinction of the Mohicans, Anglo-America may feel justified in pushing the remaining, ignoble savages aside as it expands westward.[31]

While at one level the story is a straightforward allegory of conquest, at another it recalls the chivalric quest. The Mohican characters are nobles in a completely European (and non-Indian) sense who attempt to reclaim their throne as monarchs of the Delawares, the larger "nation" of which they are the royal house. Their nobility is tested and found true through their dedication to rescuing the maidens in distress. If they are wiped out in their attempt to fulfill their mission, then it is not they who are at fault, but an age that no longer has room for chivalry. A European parallel strengthens this theme: the sisters' father, Munro, retains the special identity of a Scotsman who blasts England as a commercial-imperial nation. He is descended from a "primitive" nobility in contrast to the pseudoaristocrats of England (who have turned into tradesmen) and France (their legitimacy lessened by the monarchy's practice of selling titles). *The Last of the Mohicans* calls up a larger-than-life place of courage and honor in conflict with evil, about to vanish before the progress of British enterprise. Its evocation of an archaic American past could set off uncanny resonances in the imagination of French readers inhabiting an anachronistic Restoration.[32]

Another sign of ongoing French fascination with the American past was the continued popularity of Chateaubriand's Natchez cycle. Editions of *Atala* and *René* continued to appear throughout the period. The rediscovery of *Les Natchez* and publication of it in 1826–1827 opened up Chateaubriand's vision of the American past, hitherto available only in the tantalizing fragments of the novellas, on a full epic scale. Chateaubriand was convinced that the market for Americana was not yet saturated, for in 1827 he also brought out a volume of memoirs and reflections, *Travels in America*. Minor sculptors and painters gave lasting Romantic features to Atala and Chactas, though none of their art could compare to Delacroix's masterpiece of 1824–1835, *Les Natchez*, which shuns melodramatic portrayal of the two lovers and instead turns to the novella's epilogue to depict a forlorn couple and their infant, the last of their race. Chateaubriand, it will be remembered, compares the fate of

---

31. See Richard Slotkin's interpretation in his introduction to James Fenimore Cooper, *The Last of the Mohicans* (New York, 1986).
32. Cooper himself came from a family with strong gentry pretensions. See the biography of his father, Alan Taylor, *William Cooper's Town: Power and Persuasion on the Frontier of the Early American Republic* (New York, 1996).

6. *Les Natchez.* Eugène Delacroix, 1824–1835. Courtesy of The Metropolitan Museum of Art, Purchase, Gifts of George N. and Helen M. Richard and Mr. and Mrs. Charles S. McVeigh and Bequest of Emma A Sheafer, by exchange, 1989 (1989.328).

these exiles to his own, and the picture no less powerfully evokes our compassion[33] (Fig. 6).

The sympathies of French visitors were stirred by more than just memories of the past, however. United States policy toward Indians provoked widespread controversy in the late 1820s and early 1830s. Anglo-Americans themselves were divided over the policy of expulsion finally adopted by Andrew Jackson.[34] French observers did not have any material interests to qualify their judgment of the treaties, legislative proceedings, and other legal forms that were used to dispossess Indians of their homes. Coming as they did from a highly politicized culture, in which public debate was intense and

33. On the iconography of Chateaubriand's tales and the Delacroix painting, see Hugh Honour, *The New Golden Land: European Images of America from the Discoveries to the Present Time* (New York, 1975), 220–227.
34. See the concise yet nuanced account by Anthony F. Wallace, *The Long, Bitter Trail: Andrew Jackson and the Indians* (New York, 1993).

the hypocrisy of governments was well known, they were rarely deceived by official proclamations of good faith. The major French newspaper in the United States, *Le Courrier des États-Unis,* followed the events leading up to the expulsion with sympathy for the Cherokees, Chickasaws, and other Indians of the Southeast who were at the center of the conflict. It let its readers compare government statements with a Cherokee newspaper's protest against "the bitter brew prepared for us by a republican and religious government."[35] This was an urbane newspaper, generally a booster of the technological and political movements of the age, and its pro-Indian stance was testimony to how jarring French observers found this particular piece of Jacksonian policy.

French visitors, then, could view America as a palimpsest. On top was the scribble of contemporary America – the bustling, the building, the radiating out from the coasts to the interior that impressed even hostile observers. Closer scrutiny revealed traces of Cooper's forests, historic scenes of backwoods heroism, and partnership with native peoples. In between were scenes like the epilogue to *Atala,* the "bitter brew" of exile served up to native peoples before travelers' very eyes. It was a troublesome mixture of messages for travelers to decipher.

The attempt at a revival of former grandeur was nowhere more ambitious than in the return of the nineteenth-century Jesuits to North America. The order was dissolved in France and its colonies in 1764 (part of a general movement of abolition of the order culminating in a papal decree of 1773). While Enlightenment writers created a general atmosphere of suspicion toward the Jesuits, some European monarchs disliked them because their high degree of loyalty to the pope was thought to make them an uncontrollable political force. The suppression was never completely carried out, however, and former members and friends of the order quietly worked to prepare for an eventual restoration.[36] The turmoil of the French Revolution created an atmosphere newly favorable to the order, which was officially reestablished on August 7, 1814. The quasi-military discipline of the Jesuits and their talent as educators recommended them to secular authorities in search of allies. The early members who trickled back into the order carried with them a collective experience of persecution and suffering during the Revolutionary and Napoleonic years. Hostility did not end after the order's revival; during the 1820s its members were hated as agents of couterrevolution. The story of the

35. *Courrier des États-Unis,* vol. 3 (June 19, 1830), 195. See also ibid., 107, 118, 231, 243, and 290.
36. See J. F. Broderick, "Jesuits," in *The New Catholic Encyclopedia* (New York, 1967–1979), 7: 906.

Jesuits in North America, then, fits into the larger pattern of elite early-nineteenth-century travelers. Like their secular counterparts, they brought with them nightmarish memories of the Revolutionary era. Their experiences prepared them to view Anglo-American democracy with suspicion and Native America with a sympathy born of nostalgic memory and solidarity with the victims of the democratic era.

A dedicated group of religious émigrés prepared the way for the renewal of the Jesuit mission in North America. During the 1790s religious exiles, like political exiles, found refuge from the French Revolution in the United States. John Carroll, a former Jesuit, was able to provide them with a haven in Baltimore, and in 1806 he opened the first college of the order, Georgetown, which in 1815 received the title and privileges of a university. A Belgian missionary living in the United States, Charles Nerinckx, who had fled the Revolutionary authorities in Louvain in 1804, made a first return visit to his native country in 1817 and came back with five novices. On a second visit in 1821 he picked up nine more students at the seminary at Malines, who left secretly, without notifying their families, to pursue a missionary life across the Atlantic. Tiny though these early groups were, they included young men who had imbibed the historic spirit of the order and brought its famous conquering zeal to new missions on the North American continent.[37]

The most famous of these missionaries was Pierre-Jean De Smet. From a moderately prosperous family in the Belgian village of Termonde, De Smet grew up in a family tradition of resistance to the French Revolution. In 1792 his father was supporter of the traditional Belgian constitution and an opponent of assimilation into the French Republic. The oldest son became a priest and an active opponent of the Revolution; condemned to deportation to Guyana, he managed to hide at first in his parish, but was arrested and held until his father was able to buy his release. As for Jean-Pierre De Smet, he was notable as a child mainly for his unusual physical strength.[38] Born in 1801, he spent his early years listening to stories about Napoleon and returning veterans' bragging about their adventures across Europe. "The glory of the conqueror," wrote his biographer, "haunted his childhood."[39] And indeed, he lived a life as ambitious and errant as that of any general. He and the other novices brought over by Nerinckx first continued their education at Whitemarsh, a plantation set aside for novices. After finishing his studies, he began his lifelong work of missionizing among the Indians of the American West, using St. Louis as the base to which he returned again and again

37. On the return of the Jesuits to North America, see E. Laveille, *Le P. De Smet, Apôtre des Peaux-Rouges (1801–1873)*, 4th ed. (Louvain, 1928), 13–30.
38. Ibid., 4–7.   39. Ibid., 9.

from trips that took him as far as the North Pacific coast. Working in the Upper Missouri, the Rocky Mountains, and present-day Oregon, he criss-crossed the American interior as no other educated traveler of his generation was willing or able to do. De Smet was a grand entrepreneur, a founder who did not stay long to build but looked for new tribes to proselytize. In addition to his Western travels, he crossed the Atlantic nineteen times, wrote book after book glorifying the success of the mission, and pleaded for money and men to further the revived Jesuit empire.

A missionary encounter that seemed guided by divine light was his meeting with the interior Salish ("Flathead") Indians of present-day western Montana. They numbered perhaps 4,000 to 15,000 people before the arrival of European disease but shrank terribly in size as a result of repeated smallpox epidemics beginning in the late eighteenth century. The fur company representatives who met them in the late eighteenth and early nineteenth centuries found them distinctly courteous and interested in trapping and trading. Lewis and Clark, too, were welcomed by the Salish in 1805.[40] In contrast to dangerous Plains warriors like the Sioux, they offered an oasis of hospitality.

In 1831 a delegation of Nez Percé and Salish Indians arrived in St. Louis seeking teachers to instruct them in the Christian religion. They specifically wanted "black robes," as the Jesuits were called, not "short robes," or Protestant missionaries. At a moment when the first Jesuits were still being trained for missionary work in North America and communications were slow between the frontier and the cities of the East Coast and Europe, however, Catholic Church leaders had no missionaries to send out in response to this remarkable request. More delegations came, and in 1833 a petition went out from Baltimore to Rome for missionaries, a request approved in 1834. It was not until 1840, however, that De Smet was chosen to lead a mission to these peoples so eager to receive a religious education. When De Smet and his party finally arrived in their country, the Salish seemed to receive them with real joy. The Jesuits for their part were pleased by these earnest people, who longed so openly for a higher ethical and religious life. "Our meeting," he recalled, "was not that of strangers, but of friends; they were like children who had run out to meet their father after a long absence. I cried with joy to embrace them, and they too, tears in their eyes, welcomed me with the most tender expressions."[41] After a long march through the desert, De Smet and his companions had entered a religious land of milk and honey. There seemed to

---

40. John Fahey, *The Flathead Indians* (Norman, Okla., 1974), 27–35.
41. Pierre-Jean De Smet, *Voyages aux Montagnes Rocheuses, chez les tribus du vaste territoire de l'Orégon dépendant des États-Unis d'Amérique*, 6th ed. (Lille and Paris, 1875), 32.

be something truly providential about this encounter of natives and the bearers of European religious civilization. After the Jesuits' "long absence," they had returned to reclaim their rightful kingdom.[42]

The Salish search for Christian leaders may have been a gamble to strengthen their own position in the rapidly changing, dangerous conditions of trade and warfare on the Great Plains. Their traditional enemies, the Blackfeet, were enjoying a moment of high military and economic success, and terrorized the Salish when they roamed the Plains in search of food and furs. Iroquois Christians who had followed the trade routes west and joined the Salish seem to have introduced them to Christianity and persuaded them that the Jesuits possessed powerful magic that could help them bolster their fortunes.[43] Cultural peculiarities made the Salish and the Jesuits a natural match: although they were capable warriors and hunters, the Salish placed a high value on peacemaking that was compatible with Christian teachings. The Catholic and Jesuit emphasis on making religious life visible was compatible with the Salish emphasis on personal vision in the search for a guardian spirit. Even though Belgium and Montana were worlds apart, they also contained moments of religious rapprochement.[44]

Not yet corrupted by Western culture, the Salish as De Smet described them had a pure natural religion: they recognized the existence of a supreme being, the immortality of the soul, and a future life in which people were rewarded or punished according to their merits.[45] To be sure, they did some gambling when De Smet got there, but once he explained to them that it was contrary to divine will, they put a stop to it. Otherwise they came ready-made for the Beatitudes: "They are polite, always of a jovial humor, very hospitable, and take care of one another's needs. Their lodges are always open to the whole world. . . . Often I asked myself: are these the peoples whom civilized folk dare to call by the name of savages?"[46] De Smet's question may

---

42. Fahey, *The Flathead Indians,* 71–75.
43. Ibid., 75–76. On the Blackfeet, see Howard L. Harrod, *Mission Among the Blackfeet* (Norman, Okla., 1971). Harrod's study is especially valuable for its comparison of Catholic and Protestant missions.
44. See the sensitive exploration of this meeting of alien religious traditions in Jacqueline Peterson with Laura Peers, *Sacred Encounters: Father De Smet and the Indians of the Rocky Mountain West* (Norman, Okla., 1993). On the culture of the Salish and their neighbors, see Verne F. Ray, *Cultural Relations in the Plateau of Northwestern America* (Los Angeles, 1939).
45. "[E]n général, les sauvages des montagnes admettent l'existence d'un Être suprême, le Grand-Esprit, créateur de toutes choses; l'immortalité de l'âme, et une vie future où l'homme est récompensé ou puni d'après ses mérites. Ce sont les points principaux de leur croyance." De Smet, *Voyages aux Montagnes Rocheuses,* 47.
46. Ibid., 39–40.

seem like a repetition of generations of missionary propaganda designed to impress donors and potential missionaries back home. And yet we may wonder whether De Smet was not trying to express his personal surprise over these people, who were unique among the many he encountered on his travels. The traveler lacks an adequate language to capture novel experiences and falls back on the standardized language that is available to him; this was De Smet's way of trying to convey to his European audience his sense of wonder over Salish–Jesuit affinity.

De Smet quickly moved on to other business and left the mission in the hands of Gregory Mengarini, a Roman aristocrat moved by a mixture of religious zeal and romanticism to live among the Indians of North America. Mengarini was a highly conscientious missionary who arrived with De Smet in 1841. In the Jesuit tradition, he became an ethnographer recording his knowledge of the Salish for the benefit of future missionaries. His memoir captures the conditions that made his task a frustrating one despite the native virtues described by De Smet. Above all he condemned the hunt for its disruptive effect on the routines of a religious life. "It is not an exaggeration," he wrote, "but rather from the experience of many years that I claim that this single factor is enough to render completely useless and without fruit all the efforts of a missionary to train their souls and to civilize them."[47] The wandering life of the hunters threw them back on the habits of an earlier way of life, removed them from the social controls of a settlement, and allowed no time for learning, even if a missionary went with them. When they returned home, the missionary had to start all over again, he concluded, "as if it were the first day of instruction."[48] The same errant life admired by secular aristocrats as the shaper of warrior skills was the insurmountable barrier to Christianization. Isolated and overwhelmed, Mengarini reluctantly closed the mission in 1850 and went to Santa Clara, California, to assist in the founding there of a missionary college.

As for the Salish, they were forced onto reservations that afforded little protection as white settlers entered the area and coveted their land, while missionaries and government officials corroded their traditional culture without providing them with adequate means for Anglo-American agriculture or education. By the turn of the century the Salish were a demoralized community, not without remaining reserves of spirituality and moral authority, but with a profound consciousness of having lost a way of life. Like their eigh-

47. Gregory Mengarini, *Recollections of the Flathead Mission: Containing Brief Observations both Ancient and Contemporary Concerning this Particular Nation*, trans. and ed. with a biogr. introd. by Gloria Ricci Lothrop (Glendale, Calif., 1977).
48. Ibid., 211.

teenth-century predecessors, the Jesuit missionaries to the Salish were remarkable for their ambition, yet were unable to shape a peaceful relationship between the Native and Euroamerican worlds.[49]

Secular no less than religious travelers stepped into scenes of former French glory, no one more self-consciously so than the naturalist and artist Jacques-Gérard Milbert. Born in 1766, he became professor of drawing at France's School of Mines in 1795 and went on official government trips to make sketches in the Pyrenees, in the Alps, and along the Rhône River.[50] Five years later he joined the Pacific expedition of Nicholas Baudin; because of poor health, he disembarked at Mauritius and stayed there for two years before returning to France. With the end of the Napoleonic wars he was eager to go to North America, inspired, like many travelers of his generation, by the example of Alexander von Humboldt's journey through the Americas. Arriving in New York on October 20, 1815, he seized an opportunity that unexpectedly came his way to take part in the initial preparations for the Erie Canal, a project commissioned by the State of New York. For six months he persevered through the heat of summer across forests, mountains, and swamps. His labors permitted him to fulfill his dream of immersing himself in the natural history of the region and making a pictorial atlas of the Hudson Valley. On returning to New York City he met with Hyde de Neuville, who communicated his interests to the professors of the Royal Botanical Garden in Paris. They commissioned him to gather and ship to France all of the objects of interest to natural history that he could find on the American continent.[51] From 1817 to 1821 Milbert threw himself into his task, sending back more than 50 species of mammals, 49 live animals (including a cougar, an Appalachian bear, a male and female moose, and a male and female bison), 70 live birds, 26 live reptiles, 200 quadrupeds skinned or in alcohol, 2,000 birds, 600 reptiles, 1,200 fish, 1,000 insects, some 600 live trees, and 700 rocks. In all he sent back some 7,869 animal, vegetable, and mineral items.[52] Widely admired in both the United States and France, he returned home in 1825 and published his illustrated travel account three years later.

---

49. D'Arcy McNickle's novel, *The Surrounded* (1936; Albuquerque, 1978), dramatizes this later history. It is especially notable for its insights into traditional religion and into the good and evil wrought by Catholic missionaries. Cf. Dorothy R. Parker, *Singing an Indian Song: A Biography of D'Arcy McNickle* (Lincoln, Neb., and London, 1992). Another valuable literary work is *Mourning Dove: A Salishan Autobiography*, ed. Jay Miller (Lincoln, Neb., and London, 1990). Even though Mourning Dove belonged to the coastal Salish (a linguistically and ethnically related people with their own distinctive history), she offers a subtle picture of the way in which a Native people could blend Catholic and traditional religiosity.
50. *Appleton's Cyclopedia of American Biography* (New York, 1888), 4: 320–321.
51. Jacques Milbert, *Itinéraire pittoresque*, 1: i–x.   52. Ibid., 3–11.

Milbert treated his voyage through the Hudson Valley as a nostalgia tour. Leaving Glens Falls for Caldwell and Lake George, he sought the spot where Montcalm's troops had battled the English forces of Colonel Ephraim Williams – and where, after their defeat, the French dead were thrown into Lake George. First, he recalled the tragedy that had taken place there and then ascended a hillside for a "magical" view of the spot[53] (Fig. 7). There were special attractions for Cooper buffs: at one point he discovered just the kind of place where Indians would hide behind a waterfall, planning one of their ambushes. Nature and natural man melded here, as in Cooper's novels, into a single tableau of hidden terror and beauty.[54]

Crossing over into Canada at Niagara, Milbert felt the magic of a kind of legendary, fairy-tale France. As soon as he set foot there he felt himself to be breathing a European atmosphere again, entirely different from the one he had left behind. The construction of the houses and the arrangement of the fields transported him to Normandy, and the illusion of being home was heightened by the sound of his native language. These descendants of ancient compatriots were usually well built; the women were pretty and in many cases beautiful. Their clothing, he added, was almost the same as their mothers' in the era of French domination. This was a traveler's dream: the discovery of a lost kingdom, a place out of time, away from the modern world, abandoned and forgotten by the mother country.[55]

Indians past were not absent from the North America evoked by Milbert. During the short visit to Canada his mind returned to "all the awesome deeds and unbelievable labors of these intrepid Canadians who, at a time when this vast continent was still almost entirely unknown, crossed through it in every direction, and extending over eighteen hundred miles taught thousands of savages to know and respect above all the name of France."[56] Compare this French partnership with the results of American conquest. In the town of Manlius, in the courtyard of his inn, he met some Oneida and Mohican Indians. After several minutes of conversation with them, their expressions of

---

53. Ibid., 124.   54. Ibid., 104.
55. Later in the nineteenth century Gabriel Paul Othenin de Cléron, Vicomte d'Haussonville, came as part of a French delegation celebrating the centennial of the victory at Yorktown. In imitation of Tocqueville and other literary predecessors, he ascended the Hudson Valley and visited the Mississippi Valley in search of the former sites of French grandeur. Nostalgia for a lost empire mingled once again with the aristocratic faith that the French had an ethos apart from Anglo-American utilitarianism: "Pendant cette éclipse momentanée de ton astre," he prayed to his country, "demeure au moins fidèle à ton génie en n'essayant pas de devenir un peuple positif, calculateur et pratique!" Vicomte d'Haussonville, *À travers les États-Unis: Notes et impressions* (Paris, 1883), 396.
56. Milbert, *Itinéraire pittoresque,* 1: 188.

7. *Lake George and the Village of Caldwell.* From Milbert, *Itinéraire pittoresque*, atlas plate 24. Courtesy of Yale Center for British Art, Paul Mellon Collection, Yale University.

defiance relaxed, and he took a closer look at the women – not unattractive, he thought, with their magnificent black hair and small hands.[57] He recalled their past as a nation of conquerors and the dignity of councils that had had no equal since the assemblies of ancient Greece.[58] So much irretrievable greatness, so much contemporary ruin. "Every day," he wrote, "furthers the decline of this race, once so numerous and so powerful; and soon, following the example of so many other nations, there will be nothing left of them on the very soil they once inhabited but a name and memories."[59] While Anglo-Americans might celebrate the advance of their own civilization and their triumph over "savages," Milbert longed for the classical dignity that only a few years ago had dwelt along the Hudson.

As a participant in the building of the Erie Canal, Milbert was in the forefront of the very forces of improvement that were eradicating the traces of an earlier America. He was not unusual in occupying this double role, simultaneously furthering the advance of civilization and regretting its destructive consequences. Just this ambiguity was typical of Romantic travelers, who were unable to imagine an alternative to progress even as they anticipated its most terrible effects.

Another ambivalent observer of Native America was Francis de La Porte Castelnau. From childhood on, his imagination was stimulated by travel literature, and as soon as he could, he set out on his own. Traveling from 1837 to 1841, he traversed a great arc from Mackinac Island and Green Bay to upstate New York and from there to Florida (and, he claimed, as far west as Texas). Castelnau's travels never stopped. From 1843 to 1847 he led a government-sponsored scientific expedition from Rio de Janeiro to Lima, the results of which were published in a multivolume work. In later years he specialized in ichthyology while going on to serve in the French consulates of Bahia, the Cape Colony, Singapore, and Melbourne, where he died as consulate-general at age sixty-eight.[60]

Castelnau's account of North America was a compilation of his scientific and literary writings from the journey. The first essay, "Des États-Unis et de leurs habitants," attempted a racial description of the "three races" in Amer-

57. Ibid., 162.   58. Ibid., 180.   59. Ibid., 183.
60. See the biographical entry, "Castelnau (Francis de La Porte, dit comte de)," in *Dictionnaire de biographie française*, (Paris, 1933), 7: 1377; and Castelnau's autobiographical remarks in *Expédition dans les parties centrales de l'Amérique du Sud, de Rio de Janeiro à Lima, et de Lima au Para; exécutée sous la direction de Francis de Castelnau. Histoire du voyage* (Paris, 1850), vol. 1, part 1:3–7. For a sample of Castelnau's later work that shed the romanticism of his early travel accounts for strictly factual classification, see Castelnau, "Researches on the fishes of Australia," part 7, no. 2, in Victoria, Australia, Commission, Philadelphia Exhibition of 1876, *Official Record* (Melbourne, 1875).

ica. The title suggests a racialist reply to Tocqueville's socioeconomic interpretation of "race" in the similarly named chapter of *Democracy in America,* which had already appeared. It began with the physical characteristics of "pure" races, went on to "mixed" races, and continued with generalizations about language, family, social life, agriculture, and manufacturing. Castelnau sought out American Indians wherever he went and claimed to have seen Seminoles, Creeks, Iroquois, Ottawas, Winnebagos, Menimonees, Delawares, Sioux, Chippewas, and Hurons. His admiration for them contrasted with his contemptuous later description of South American Indians. The peoples of the tropics represented lassitude and social atomization, he later wrote, while in the North he discovered peoples whose primitive hardiness and energy mirrored the qualities he admired in Northern Europeans[61] (Fig. 8).

The elective affinity between French explorers and a "savage" continent was rarely attested to more lyrically than by Castelnau. The very harshness of the rivers and woods, he wrote, exerted an irresistible magnetism on their longing for adventure.[62] After fighting for months to ascend the St. Lawrence River and reach Quebec, their real travels would begin, he imagined, as they contemplated the dark woods into which they would disappear – the place where they would confront eerie beings from another world: Iroquois, Hurons, Algonquins,

sons of the primeval forests, whose bodies (painted in the most brilliant colors and decorated with the bizarre finery of the woods), whose horrible war cry, fatal arrow and bloody tomahawk were the only things that could deliver something of those delicious sensations of combat that had faded among them. . . .[63]

America, as Castelnau recalled it here, was a voyage from tepid Europe to a land of primeval virility. His attempt to imagine – almost to relive in his imagination – the extremes of pain and ecstasy from the early days of French exploration reads like an anticipation of Arthur Rimbaud's "The Drunken Boat." In the poem's opening lines, Indians take aim at traders and nail them naked to totem poles; the act of violence arrests the movement of commerce and frees the boat to take a hallucinatory voyage around the world. The traveler, however, does not share the poet's aim of a radical departure from bourgeois Europe. Rimbaud seeks the breakthrough to a new world through a fantastic invocation of "Indian" violence; Castelnau pulls back from this merging into the "Indian" and reasserts his superiority as the man of civiliza-

---

61. On the Indians of South America and Castelnau's reflections on the influence of climate on race, see *Expédition dans les parties centrales de l'Amérique du Sud,* vol. 1, part 1: 6–7.
62. Castelnau, *Vues et souvenirs,* 74–75.   63. Ibid., 75.

8. *Wissigong, Indien Chippeway.* From Francis de Castelnau, *Vues et souvenirs de l'Amérique du Nord* (Paris, 1842), plate 15. Courtesy of Dechert Collection, Van Pelt-Dietrich Library, University of Pennsylvania Libraries.

tion. His ambivalence, and ultimate assertion of European aristocratic superiority, is typical of elite Romantic travelers, while Rimbaud points the way to the Fauves' and Expressionists' later mood of total revolt.[64]

Unlike the traders of Rimbaud's poem, Castelnau traveled by steamboat. At Green Bay, Wisconsin, Menominees gathered to watch the arrival of the monstrous machine. These Indians were no strangers:

> Their clothing consisted mainly of a great cloak which, draped graciously around their bodies, recalled the Roman toga; their long black hair was adorned with feathers or tufts of scarlet; I saw with pleasure how many of them comprehended French and how some spoke our language without the least foreign accent. . . .[65]

The education to empire through the classics pervades this passage, which compresses several layers of history into a single scene. Castelnau visiting the Menimonees is like a Roman gentleman of antiquity visiting a half-assimilated people at the empire's edge. The Indians preserve signs of their native culture but have adopted Roman garb, as if only this would be a form of dress corresponding to their innate nobility. At the same time, they have thoroughly absorbed the essence of civilization, the language of the conqueror. The fantasy of Frenchman-as-Roman sustained an attitude of imperial self-assurance even in the aftermath of actual empire. Throughout the trip, his consolation was his belief that Indians preferred the French to the English or the Anglo-Americans.[66]

Castelnau wavered between admiration and a conviction that Indians were heading toward extinction. He laid out the elements of a tragedy, attributing intelligence and nobility to American Indians only to predict their doom. The Americans would surround them on all sides, he wrote, until the last Indians were pushed into the Pacific and the "red race" would cease to exist.[67] But what was the right tone for their epitaph? At one point he imagined the fictive last red man dying calmly, content that he had preserved the traditions of his fathers.[68] Elsewhere, however, he took on the role of pitiless judge of a race surpassed. Despite their high intelligence Indians were hopelessly wedded to the world of their fathers: "It is that religion of remembering that makes the rapprochement of these races impossible. . . . Their forced emigration to the west of the Mississippi was therefore a barbaric political decision,

---

64. Arthur Rimbaud, "Le Bateau Ivre," in *Poésies complètes,* ed. Pascal Pia and introd. Paul Claudel (Paris, 1963), 72.
65. Castelnau, *Vues et souvenirs,* 94–95.
66. Ibid., 99. This scene again contrasts with Rimbaud, who in his memoir "Un saison en enfer" describes himself as a Gaul – hence a pagan, a savage, a member of a conquered race. See Rimbaud, *Poésies complètes,* 108–109.
67. Castelnau, *Vues et souvenirs,* 93–94.   68. Ibid., 94.

perhaps, but a necessary one."[69] Romantic enchantment coexisted in Castelnau's book with acceptance of policies of expropriation and extermination. In the end, Castelnau's nostalgia gave way to a ruthless affirmation of historical necessity. Despite his enjoyment of shared memories of the old days with the Menimonees, he separated their fate from his own.[70]

Other travelers played out variations of this divided relationship to Indians. Theodore Pavie made long journeys through South America and Southeast Asia as well as the United States. From 1852 to 1859 he taught languages and literature at the Sorbonne, and he contributed articles to the widely read *Revue des Deux Mondes*, as well as to more specialized journals like the bulletin of France's geographic society. In 1829, at age eighteen, he came to the United States and traveled along the East Coast, the Ohio Valley, the lower Mississippi, and Texas, if we may believe his later testimony. Like many travelers of the period, he reacted to the sight of Iroquois with disappointment: "Those who hoped to retrieve some poetry from the degenerate descendants of the Oneidas," he wrote, "will lose their illusions in the midst of these Indians; I myself felt a strange sense of surprise seeing them stretched out in the shade or gathered in groups, arguing among themselves over the last drops of a bottle of whiskey."[71] For the traveler passing through, the casual spectacle did not live up to the childhood fantasies that had first stirred his desire to see America.[72]

Another roving intellectual who expressed the Romantic ambivalence toward American Indians was Frédéric Gaillardet. After making a noisy start as a playwright in Paris (and getting involved in a lawsuit with the elder Alexandre Dumas over a play they had written together), he emigrated to the United States in 1837. Gaillardet traveled widely – he originally joined two brothers in New Orleans – before becoming publisher and editor of the *Courrier des États-Unis* in New York. At the same time, he kept up his connections to French literary circles and traveled back and forth between New York and Paris. In a book written near the end of his life, *L'Aristocratie en Amérique*, he confessed his ambivalence toward Indians. There was, he wrote, something "Homeric" and "Biblical" about them, a kind of "Oriental and primitive grandeur."[73] The Indian lived according to man's nature and the

69. Ibid., 4.   70. Ibid., 100.
71. Theodore Pavie, *Souvenirs atlantiques. Voyage aux États-Unis et au Canada* (Anger, 1833), 49–50. On Pavie see Frank Monaghan, *French Travellers in the United States, 1765–1932* (New York, 1933), 75; and *Nouvelle biographie générale* (Hoefer) (Paris, 1862), 39: 422.
72. Pavie, *Souvenirs atlantiques*, v.
73. Frédéric Gaillardet, *L'aristocratie en Amérique* (Paris, 1883), 269–270.

will of God's creation. But contact with civilization was inevitable and fatal. After predicting their total extermination, he added, "It's a slightly embarrassing fate for humanity, this elimination of the strong by the weak . . . but it is the law. *Dura lex, sed lex.*" ("A harsh law, but the law.")[74] By the time he published his memories in 1883, the "law" of extermination had turned into a Social Darwinist truism, part of the history of the evolution of the species.

During the Romantic era itself, however, French opinion was more deeply divided. Confidence in the right to European domination still alternated with memories of the world turned upside down during the decade after 1789 and protest against the victors' version of history. This mood of ambivalence, of traumatic memory contending with triumphant anticipation, found its fullest expression in the writings of Tocqueville.

74. Ibid., 267.

4

Tocqueville and the Sociology of Native Aristocrats

Alexis de Tocqueville wrote as a self-conscious successor to the liberal aristocrats of the eighteenth century. *Democracy in America* has the lofty tone of a Montesquieu or a Rochefoucauld, an aristocratic observer who surveys the teeming forms of social life from the heights above. Yet Tocqueville broadened this aristocratic perspective to include the religious life of Protestant society, the folk character of the Anglo-Americans, the pristine nature of the North American forests, and historic memories of New France. Compared to his fellow travelers of the early nineteenth century, his distinction lies not so much in the originality of his opinions as in his ability to organize them around the notion of democracy as the governing principle of American society, to balance sympathy and criticism, and to express his views with the finality of a great stylist. Tocqueville's contemporaries immediately acknowledged the superiority of *Democracy in America* as a work that captured widely felt European responses to the United States.

With Chateaubriand and Cooper as his literary guides, one of Tocqueville's keenest ambitions when he arrived in America was to see its native inhabitants. Yet more than just an impulse to savor the exotic motivated Tocqueville, who took out two weeks from his tight schedule to catch glimpses of them on the frontier. A mature comparative thinker at an early age, he sought to grasp the underlying principles of their way of life and understand how it conflicted with the demands of Anglo-American settlement. He also thought across greater reaches of time and asked about the relationship between American Indians and nobility in Europe. Tocqueville's sociological imagination, then, simultaneously worked Indians into the central themes of *Democracy in America* and the political preoccupations of an aristocrat in a democratizing France.

The mood of Tocqueville's family was darkened by memories of terror. His mother, Louise-Madeleine Le Peletier de Rosanbo, was the granddaughter of Malesherbes. The friend of the philosophes and patron of Chateaubriand was executed after aiding the defense of Louis XVI. There were closer family memories to come to terms with, too: the execution of his mother's father, of her sister Aline-Thérèse, and of her brother-in-law Jean-Baptiste de Chateaubriand (the poet's older brother); and most immediate, the victimization of his own parents, who were imprisoned for several months in 1794. The old regime's comfortable, cultivated way of life, with its prospects of wealth and honor, suddenly gave way to humiliation and violence. Tocqueville's father struggled for years – successfully, in the end – to reclaim family property and gain a position of political responsibility. After 1804 he served as a mayor and after 1814 as a government prefect. Later successes could not expunge the trauma of 1794, however; Tocqueville's mother turned into a depressed and withdrawn woman unable to provide her offspring with emotional nurturing.[1]

These family ghosts troubled Alexis too. The danger of a renewed attack on the aristocracy was never far from his thoughts. During a visit to England in the 1830s, between his American voyage and the completion of his book about it, a polite worker's speech was enough to trigger his worst fears: "In him I saw the precursor of those revolutionaries who will have the calling, at a not very distant point in time, to change the face of England."[2] Lords and rich proprietors, he predicted, would not subdue such workers much longer.[3] When he saw popular refusal to accept elite political leadership in Europe – whether in industrializing England or in France during the Revolution of 1848 – he feared a wave of social leveling.

There were many sources for Tocqueville's liberal aristocratic heritage. Montesquieu was the most fruitful for his conception of social science; his use of typologies and his attention to geography and institutions foreshadow the methodology of *Democracy in America.*[4] Tocqueville did not have to look further than his own family for a liberal aristocratic intellectual lineage: Malesherbes exemplified how one could blend aristocratic tradition and lib-

1. On Tocqueville's family and the Revolution, see André Jardin, *Tocqueville: A Biography,* trans. Lydia Davis with Robert Hemenway (New York, 1988), 3–12. My interpretation of Tocqueville has profited greatly from Jardin's study.
2. Alexis de Tocqueville, *Oeuvres complètes,* vol. 5, part 2: *Voyages en Angleterre, Irlande, Suisse et Algérie,* ed. J.-P. Mayer and André Jardin (Paris, 1958), 16.
3. Cf. Jardin, *Tocqueville,* 125, which mentions comparable fears occasioned by Tocqueville's American and Sicilian travel experiences.
4. See the remarks on Tocqueville and Montesquieu in Jean-Claude Lamberti, *Tocqueville et les deux Démocraties* (Paris, 1983), 19.

eralism, defense of the privileged order and sympathy for the Enlightenment.[5] His love of freedom, identification of it with the old aristocracy's defense of inherited privilege, and openness nonetheless to American democratic institutions were not at odds with the family example.

For Tocqueville's views on America – and specifically on American Indians – Chateaubriand stands out as a forerunner. They were related through the Le Peletier family: Tocqueville's mother was the sister of Chateaubriand's sister-in-law. The tragedies of the French Revolution strengthened the relationship between the Tocqueville and Chateaubriand families, for Hervé de Tocqueville, Alexis's father, became the guardian of the two orphaned children of Jean-Baptiste de Chateaubriand.[6] The author of *Atala* later mentioned watching Alexis grow up in the company of his nephews.[7] As for Tocqueville, he visited America – and sought out American Indians – fully conscious of the writings of his famous relative.[8] In later years, both men eagerly testified to their spiritual affinity. Chateaubriand helped open the doors of Paris literary life to his relative, drew on his ideas in the final version of his late reflections on America, and mentioned him in his memoirs.[9] In his recollections of the Revolution of 1848, Tocqueville used the death of Chateaubriand in the midst of the turmoil of that year to symbolize the passing of the aristocratic era.[10] It was one proof of the strength of his intellectual character that he was able to withstand the danger of being overwhelmed by a monumental predecessor and to absorb Chateaubriand's insights into his own original vision of American society.

Tocqueville grew up between worlds. Born in 1805, he experienced the end of the Napoleonic regime before coming to maturity in the Restoration. His lycée education opened him up to the ideas of the Enlightenment, and he listened to the university lectures of the liberal historian and politician François Guizot, who gave him a clear model for thinking of history as a story of universal progress. How could Tocqueville reconcile his urge to affirm the technical and political progress of the age with his loyalty to the ethos of the aristocracy? This was a fruitful dilemma, central to his writings on America and

5. On Tocqueville's relationship to Malesherbes, see the genealogical chart in Grosclaude, *Malesherbes, témoin et interprète de son temps* (Paris, 1961), 22.
6. Jardin, *Tocqueville*, 9.
7. Chateaubriand, *Mémoires d'outre tombe* (1849; Paris, 1951), 1: 576.
8. See Tocqueville's reference to *Atala* in his letter from New York, October 10, 1831, to his distant cousin Eugénie de Cordoue, Comtesse de Grancey, in *Oeuvres complètes* vol. 7: *Nouvelle correspondance entièrement inédite* (Paris, 1866), 75.
9. See Jardin, *Tocqueville*, 104–105 and passim.
10. See Alexi de Tocqueville, *Oeuvres complètes*, vol. 12: *Souvenirs*, ed. Luc Monnier (Paris, 1964), 177–178.

on the origins of the French Revolution. He responded by accepting the historical inevitability of middle-class triumph but insisting on the lasting importance of the aristocracy's love of freedom. Indeed, Guizot provided a valuable clue, for he had already insisted that archaic stages of history were not merely surpassed, but could offer enduring values to later generations.[11] It was his attempt to mediate between these two affirmations – to persuade his aristocratic readers that they needed to work for the success of modern democracy and to educate his middle-class readers about the inheritance that they could ignore only at the cost of their own mediocrity – that gave his analyses their special richness.[12]

The conflict of privilege and progress threatened to block his career just when he was ready to enter public life. Tocqueville was a marked man: the Revolutionaries had singled out his parents' generation as enemies, and after 1815 the restored monarchy rewarded his father for his loyalty by making him a prefect. To be tied so closely to the Bourbon monarchy, however, was to expose oneself to all the shifting currents of French politics. The reinstatement of the Jesuit order, savage laws punishing religious sacrilege, and the suppression of freedom of speech and the press set off fears of a punitive attempt to undo the work of the Revolutionary and Napoleonic eras. The regime relied on such a narrow coterie of supporters that even the wealthy and professional upper middle class was ready to desert it. Rarely has a regime crumbled so quickly as the Bourbon monarchy when Charles X was chased out in 1830 and replaced by Louis Philippe of the neighboring Orléans line.

Even though the Orléans were cousins of the royal family, a vast gulf separated them, for Louis Philippe was by his own choice a gentleman of the nineteenth century – educated, moderate, devoted to the progress of science and government, ready to promote the interests of businessmen and financiers. For many members of the middle and working classes, the change seemed like peaceful progress. Indeed, it gave them a false sense of self-assurance, confirming their belief in an inevitable historical progress that no cabal of kings could hold back. For Tocqueville, however, the transition created painful choices. He reluctantly accepted the new regime. Whether the regime or the French public would accept him was another question, bur-

---

11. This was a more general insight of Restoration liberalism. Hegel sketched a comparable vision of contemporary politics as a synthesis of traditional forms of social organization (family and monarchy) and the free movement of modern civil society in *Hegel's Philosophy of Right*, trans. T. M. Knox (1821; Oxford and New York, 1957).
12. For the preceding interpretation of Guizot's influence on Tocqueville, see Edward T. Gargan, *Alexis de Tocqueville: The Critical Years, 1848–1851* (Washington, D.C., 1955), xi, 4–8. Gargan's book remains one of the most incisive analyses of Tocqueville's development.

dened as he was with a family name tied to the defeated dynasty. His ambition of a career in politics seemed cut off by the victory of the liberal monarchy.[13]

Together with a friend and fellow aristocrat, Gustave de Beaumont, Tocqueville averted this impasse by traveling to America. The two friends stayed from May 1831 to February 1832. They visited the cities of the East Coast (New York, Philadelphia, Boston, Baltimore, and Washington), then went north to Michigan and Canada, and south as far as New Orleans.[14] The French point of departure stimulated comparison between inherited and contemporary values. The visit came just at the moment when Tocqueville could experience American democracy in its full first vigor. Tocqueville could look backward and, though he did not know the old regime, recall the culture he knew intimately from family and friends; he could look forward to the dynamic of a democratic society expanding across a continent; and he could consider the fate of France as a nation perched between extremes. It was precisely with those extremes of privilege and equality in mind, and with the fate of France caught in the middle, that he introduced the first volume of *Democracy in America* in 1835.[15]

Tocqueville's vision of American democracy was deeply divided. Like other travelers he could admire its energy but be put off by its rudeness, praise the American work ethic but recoil from the national obsession with money, and admire the courage of the pioneers but dislike their humorlessness. He raised this ambivalence to a novel level of insight, however, by presenting it in paradoxical form in Volume 1 of *Democracy in America*, simultaneously main-

13. For the preceding description of Tocqueville's situation before and after the Revolution of 1830, see Jardin, *Tocqueville,* pp. 73–89.
14. Ibid., chaps. 7–11.
15. See Alexis de Tocqueville, *Democracy in America,* trans. George Lawrence, ed. J. P. Mayer (1835–1840; New York, 1988), 9–18 (hereinafter cited as *Democracy in America*). Cf. Gargan, *Tocqueville,* x, and Jardin, *Tocqueville,* part 2. French references are from Tocqueville, *Oeuvres complètes,* vol. 1, part 1, *De la Démocratie en Amérique,* ed. J.-P. Mayer, introd. Harold J. Laski (Paris, 1961) (hereinafter cited as *Démocratie*).

    Readers who wish to explore Tocqueville's study of America in depth should turn to the excellent new critical and historical edition, *De la Démocratie en Amérique. Première édition historico-critique revue et augmentée,* ed. and introd. Éduardo Nolla, 2 vols. (Paris, 1990). They should also read Tocqueville's notes from his American journey, published as *Journey to America,* trans. George Lawrence, ed. J. P. Mayer (Garden City, N.Y., 1971).

    From the large Tocqueville literature I have also profited from James T. Schleifer, *The Making of Tocqueville's Democracy in America* (Chapel Hill, N.C., 1980), especially the discussion of Tocqueville's skepticism toward racial theories, 45–46 and 65–69; Francine Ninane de Martinoir, "Aristocrates et royalistes à l'époque de Tocqueville" in *Analyses & réflexions sur . . . Tocqueville, De la Démocratie en Amérique* (Paris, 1985), 29–36; and George Pierson, *Tocqueville and Democracy in America* (New York, 1938).

taining an aristocratic distance and acknowledging the historical necessity of democracy.[16]

The introduction to Volume 1 confronts the reader with a dramatic opposition of aristocracy and democracy. Like other leading social thinkers born in the early years of the nineteenth century – his slightly younger contemporaries John Stuart Mill and Karl Marx, for example – Tocqueville was convinced that his was an age of historical transition.[17] "A great democratic revolution is taking place in our midst; everybody sees it, but by no means everybody judges it in the same way."[18] The origin of this revolution is not material, as it is later for Marx, but providential; to oppose democracy "appears as a fight against God Himself, and nations have no alternative but to acquiesce in the social state imposed by Providence."[19] The old social state is gone and the new has not yet fully come, leaving precisely the noblest minds caught in vain struggles to defend antiquated ideals, while the meanest take up the causes of the new age:

Men of religion fight against freedom, and lovers of liberty attack religions; noble and generous spirits praise slavery, while low, servile minds preach independence; honest and enlightened citizens are the enemies of all progress, while men without patriotism or morals make themselves the apostles of civilization and enlightenment![20]

Tocqueville asks France to turn to America for political lessons. Without expecting slavish imitation, he seeks to show how spirituality and freedom can flourish on democratic grounds. The Puritan love of freedom has created a starting point different from the conflict of aristocracy and absolutism in Continental Europe. American local government provides a substitute for the provincial loyalties of an ancient landed society; the constitution, the independent court system, and the conservatism of the legal profession balance the tyranny of the majority; American voluntary associations are a wellspring of public-mindedness. Everywhere Tocqueville discerns dangers to freedom and institutions that counteract them, giving his book a dramatic rhythm that captures the adventurous spirit of American democracy itself.[21] The second volume appeared five years later; it is a different kind of work, as is often remarked, which moves from concrete analysis of a single country to general philosophical reflection on democratic versus aristocratic cultures.[22] The

---

16. Cf. Gargan, *Tocqueville*, 13.
17. See Mill's description of his time as "an era of transition in opinion," *Autobiography*, ed. Jack Stillinger (1873; New York, 1969), 100.
18. Tocqueville, *Democracy in America*, 9.   19. Ibid., 12.   20. Ibid., 17.
21. On the opposition of democracy and aristocracy, see Lamberti, *Tocqueville et les deux Démocraties*, 40 ff.
22. Cf. Gargan, *Tocqueville*, 13.

dangers of cultural mediocrity and political tyranny temper Tocqueville's admiration for America. Yet here, too, he stops short of wishing for a return to an earlier era and urges appreciation of aristocratic values as a check on the errors of egalitarian societies.

The two volumes of *Democracy in America* alternate between confidence and alarm as they contemplate the fate of freedom in the modern era. Near the end of the second volume Tocqueville writes: "I believe that it is easier to establish an absolute and despotic government among a people whose social conditions are equal than among any other."[23] The leveling of social differences leaves little guarantee that central authority and social conformity will not overwhelm individual freedom of action and expression. At the same time, the aristocrat confronting the dangers of equality goes on to disavow any dreams of returning to a regime based on social privilege. Rather, his position between aristocracy and democracy points to a difficult question: if the present is full of danger and the past is irrecoverable, how can one find a means of rescuing human freedom? His answer is synthetic. While aristocracy in its original form of particular legal advantage cannot return, the principle of aristocratic independence can invigorate democratic politics. Local government and voluntary associations can create the personal ties and place-bound loyalties that will be strong enough to resist the intrusion of central authority. He writes:

I think that associations of plain citizens can compose very rich, influential, and powerful bodies, in other words, aristocratic bodies. . . . An association, be it political, industrial, commercial, or even literary or scientific, is an educated and powerful body of citizens which cannot be twisted to any man's will or quietly trodden down. . . .[24]

Countess Merlin clearly saw the dangers of a democracy, and indeed, the opinion that American egalitarianism trampled on those with the appearance of rising above their fellow citizens belonged to the truisms of nineteenth-century European travel. Chevalier and Montulé countered that America brought forth its own forms of human dignity and excellence. No one but Tocqueville, however, outlined so clearly the balance of forces for freedom and tyranny in America. He was uniquely able to articulate the originality of American democracy and its capacity to sustain novel and modern political institutions.[25]

---

23. Tocqueville, *Democracy in America*, 695.   24. Ibid., 697.
25. For yet another sample of aristocratic hostility toward the United States, see Jacques de Saint-Victor, *Lettres sur les États-Unis, écrites en 1832 et 1833, et addressées à M. le Comte O'Mahony*, 2 vols. (Paris, 1835). The account is particularly interesting because Saint-Victor's visit overlapped with Tocqueville's. Cf. the comments in Frank Monaghan, *French Travellers in the United States, 1765–1932* (New York, 1933), 84.

American Indians were a subject of special interest to Tocqueville. In part he shared the Romantic attraction to them as remnants of an archaic past. Yet, in this as in so many other respects, he took familiar perceptions and lifted them to a new level of insight. From his own experience as an aristocrat in a democratizing society, Tocqueville was used to comparing the representatives of past and present historical eras. Indians filled the function of aristocrats in America, providing a critical vantage point for understanding the strengths and weaknesses of the Anglo-American conquerors and for remembering aristocratic traditions that were guardians of freedom even after the end of the age of privilege. Not every non-European people filled this aristocratic role; later, when he visited Algeria, he did so with the eyes of a politician surveying the prospects for French conquest and cast the native society in the role of decadents awaiting the benefits of French civilization – a line of argument resembling the Anglo-American ideology that he had challenged. In Algeria Tocqueville came as conqueror, in America as a witness to a site of defeat, prepared to sympathize with natives as former allies who had suffered a fall from greatness.[26]

He developed the interpretation with the aid of two friends. One was his traveling companion, Beaumont. A long appendix to *Marie*, Beaumont's fictional critique of American race relations, drew on Le Page du Pratz, Lahontan, and Charlevoix, among other authors, for clear and radical conclusions:

At the moment when Europeans entered into contact with them, all the peoples who inhabited the East Coast of North America had an analogous social state: all lived particularly from hunting. While agriculture was not unknown to them, none of them had yet arrived at the point of deriving from the fruits of the earth their only or even their principle means of subsistence. All the travel accounts are in agreement on this point.[27]

A nation of hunters: their entire national character follows from their means of subsistence. The men are devoted to hunting and making war, according to Beaumont, and leave all other forms of work to women, children, and slaves. As hunter-warriors, they love their liberty and despise anyone who would dare diminish it. The Iroquois are the extreme of the extreme, more stoic than the heroes of antiquity in their indifference to pain. And in his own time? European trade has ruined their virtues and taught them unknown vices; Beaumont has seen the fallen Iroquois, the "last" of the once great nation, reduced to begging.

---

26. On Tocqueville and Algeria see Timothy Mitchell, *Colonising Egypt* (Cambridge, 1988), 57–58; and Jardin, *Tocqueville*, 316–342.
27. Gustave de Beaumont de la Bonnière, *Marie, ou l'esclavage aux États-Unis, tableau de moeurs américaines* (Paris, 1836), 2: 305–306. Beaumont cites his major sources on 304.

The other friend to influence Tocqueville's judgment was Ernest de Blosseville, who borrowed and translated from his copy of an important testimony of Indian life, the *Narrative of the Captivity and Adventures of John Tanner*.[28] The son of a Kentucky settler, Tanner was kidnapped at age nine in 1789 by Shawnees and sold to an Ottawa woman, who moved with him to the Ojibwa area of her husband in present-day Red River country, Manitoba, Canada. After moving to Sault Ste. Marie in 1828 and serving as an interpreter there, Tanner attracted the attention of Edwin James, a physician, who took down and edited his *Narrative*.[29] Tocqueville met him there and bought from him a copy of the autobiography.[30]

Tanner's story is one of terror and pain, of personal misfortune and crisis among Indian peoples. Bouts of starvation alternate with frenzied drinking, violence with kindness. Tanner himself emerges as a walker between worlds. He suffers beatings and mistreatment, but he also feels that even the sick and weak will be cared for by Indians, whereas white society abandons its unfortunate. Tocqueville was predictably impressed by the *Narrative's* recitation of the insatiable passion for hunting that made Indians resist a sedentary way of life.[31]

Blosseville, whose edition Tocqueville praised as the best introduction to the study of American Indians, discusses Tanner's story as a refutation of the "noble savage" ideology of the eighteenth century. "It is the most conclusive response to so many self-proclaimed moralists who have incessantly confused the state of nature with the savage state, as M. de Chateaubriand has so justifiably reproached them."[32] Blosseville thought that Tanner refuted the myth of Montesquieu, Buffon, Montaigne, Raynal, and above all Rousseau,

28. John Tanner, *A Narrative of the Captivity and Adventures of John Tanner (U.S. Interpreter at the Saut de Ste. Marie), during Thirty Years Residence Among the Indians in the Interior of North America* . . . (New York, 1830).
29. For biographical background, see George Woodcock, "Tanner, John," in *Dictionary of Canadian Biography* (Toronto, 1988), 7 (1836–1850): 844–845.
30. See the critical remarks on Tocqueville's view of Tanner in Pierrette Désy, introduction to *Trente ans de captivité chez les indiens Ojibwa. Récit de John Tanner. Recueilli par le docteur Edwin James. Présentation, traduction, bibliographie et analyse ethnohistorique* (Paris, 1983), xv.
31. *Démocratie*, 347, n. 18.
    Tocqueville's account was incomplete, lacking insight into the ritual and religious dimensions of hunting among Indians. It was unusual, however, that he interpreted it at all as a cultural activity. Missionaries and government agencies thought of hunting simply as a negative impulse that blocked the way to successful conversion or civilizing of Indians. Tocqueville understood it as a meaning-making activity that had satisfactions at least equal to the settlers' business and farming.
32. Ernest de Blosseville, introduction to John Tanner, *Mémoires de John Tanner, ou trente années dans les déserts de l'Amérique du Nord*, trans. and introd. Ernest de Blosseville (Paris, 1835), 1: xii.

of a happy state of nature in which "savages" were free from wants.[33] Instead, according to Blosseville, American Indians are similar to Gauls or Franks on the border of the Roman Empire. Their culture resembles that of the Germanic tribes described by Tacitus.[34]

This interpretation was not free of its own imposition of older ideals on primitive peoples. Since the Renaissance, Tacitus's *Germania* had enjoyed considerable favor among French and German scholars for its portrayal of Teutonic peoples as warriors and as defenders of their native freedom from state authority.[35] Yet Blosseville was doing more than just dressing up Plains peoples in Teutonic costumes; he had, after all, taken the trouble to make available to French readers an important document of contemporary Indian life. His work was both a translation and a contribution to contemporary political discussion. It was in this double spirit of social scientific inquiry and political appropriation that Tocqueville, too, made use of his friends' Indian–aristocratic comparisons.

A determination to see for oneself – no longer just to rely on eighteenth-century fables and older travel writers, but to meet close up the native peoples who had for so long intrigued the French imagination – motivated a miniature masterpiece of travel writing, Tocqueville's "Fourteen Days in the Wilderness." There is no better evidence of Tocqueville's genius than this occasional essay, jotted down while he was on a steamboat at the beginning of August 1831 and only lightly corrected. It has the freshness of field notes yet distills recurring French views of North America and its indigenous inhabitants.[36] He and Beaumont were intrigued, he writes, by the chance to visit some of those Indian tribes "who would rather flee into the most primitive wastelands *(les solitudes les plus sauvages)* than submit to what whites call the pleasures of civilization."[37] But it wasn't easy to find them. For a start, they traveled the 360 miles from New York City to Buffalo. Next, they boarded the steamboat *Ohio* on July 19, 1831, crossing Lake Erie to Detroit. Four days later, they rented two horses and set out on their way to the settle-

---

33. Ibid., xii–xiii.   34. Ibid., xv.
35. See Donald R. Kelley, "*Tacitus Noster:* The *Germania* in the Renaissance and Reformation," in T. J. Luce and A. J. Woodman, eds., *Tacitus and the Tacitean Tradition* (Princeton, N.J., 1993), 152–167.
36. Alexis de Tocqueville, "Quinze jours dans le désert. Ecrit sur le Steamboat 'The Superior' – Commencé le 1. août 1831," in *Oeuvres complètes*, vol. 5, part 1: *Voyages en Sicile et aux États-Unis*, ed. J. P. Mayer (Paris, 1957), 342–387 (hereinafter cited as "Quinze jours"). On the composition and publication of the essay, see the editor's note. Translated as Alexis de Tocqueville, "A Fortnight in the Wilds," in *Journey to America*, trans. George Lawrence, ed. J. P. Mayer, revised in collaboration with A. P. Kerr (Garden City, N.Y., 1971), 350–403 (hereinafter cited as "Fortnight in the Wilds").
37. "Quinze jours," 342.

ment of Pontiac. A friendly host there explained to them how to reach Saginaw. Renting two horses, on their first day out they made their way as far as Flint River, where they picked up two Indian guides who accompanied them the rest of the way.

In "Fourteen Days" Tocqueville compresses many of the typical experiences of the European – Indian romance. He gives a careful description of the half-civilized Indians he meets near Buffalo: they are short and ugly, their skin not the "copper" color he expected, but a "bronze" closer to that of mulattos. Their discomfort in their clothes, their combination of European dress and strange plumage, and their unpleasant movements and voices make them seem like beasts of the forest in human clothing. These are the last of the Iroquois. Tocqueville portrays them with a "physiognomic" eye, a description of external features that reveals internal psychological states. His writing is not free here of a tendency toward racial psychology, even though it ultimately recedes and gives way to social and economic explanations of psychological motivation.

The authentic savage surprises them on their ride from Pontiac to Flint River. Man and nature merge as they approach a savage place:

Always keeping on our way, we came to a district of a different aspect. The ground was no longer level, but cut by hills and valleys. Some of these hills have the wildest possible look (*l'aspect le plus sauvage*). It was in one of these picturesque spots, when we had suddenly turned round to admire the imposing sight behind us, that we saw to our great surprise close to our horses' cruppers an Indian who seemed to be following on our tracks. He was a man of about thirty, large and wonderfully well proportioned as they almost all are. . . . His face had all the characteristic traits that distinguish the Indian race from all others. In his black eyes shone that savage fire which still lights up the eyes of half-castes and is not lost until the second or third generation of white blood. . . . When he saw that we had no hostile feeling on our side, he began to smile; probably he saw that he had frightened us. That was the first time that I had seen how completely gaiety changes the physiognomy of these savage men.[38]

The Indian who appears out of nowhere is almost a god of the place, a spirit of the woods like a pagan sprite meeting an ancient traveler. This Indian is the opposite of the Iroquois, well proportioned without and ablaze within. Tocqueville uses the same technique of inserting typical Indians into typical surroundings in his description of the guides who take him and Beaumont on the last stretch of their journey to Saginaw. He is impressed by their complete ease in a landscape that disorients him and Beaumont; the visitors are the awkward ones, he knows, and the Indians are at home. Tocqueville's self-ironization here is unusual, one of the traits that sets him apart from almost all the other

38. "Fortnight in the Wilds," 372–373; "Quinze jours," 361–362.

travelers of the period. So is his observation of the native's transformation from a dumb "other" into a fellow human being capable of laughter.

One of the functions of Indians in Tocqueville's writings is to serve as a point of departure for criticism of Anglo-American hypocrisy. After seeing an Indian intoxicated and nearly dead by the side of the road, Tocqueville appeals to his Anglo-American hosts in Buffalo to come to the man's aid. He meets with a shrug of the shoulders. Their unspoken sentiment seems to be that Indian life is too worthless to worry about. Such inhumanity disgusts him: "In the midst of this society, so well-policed, so prudish, and so pedantic about morality and virtue, one comes across a complete insensibility, a sort of cold and implacable egotism where the natives of America are concerned."[39] Upstanding citizens furnish other examples of their double morality as well: they explain to him that the alcohol they sell is killing off the Indians and that the land belongs to those who know how to extract its riches – only to go to church the next day to hear the minister preach the Gospel of brotherly love![40] Along the way to Saginaw, Tocqueville gets a further exposure to American hypocrisy. A settler provides Tocqueville and Beaumont with two native guides. He takes two dollars intended for the guides and exchanges them for moccasins and a handkerchief not worth more than one, which he passes on to them. Tocqueville recalls his own vulnerability to such practices:

Besides, it is not only the Indians whom the pioneers make their dupes. We ourselves were daily victims of their extreme greediness for gain. It is true that they do not rob at all. They are too enlightened to do anything so imprudent, but otherwise I have never seen a hotel-keeper in a great city overcharge more impudently than these dwellers in the wilderness among whom I expected to find the primitive honesty and simplicity of a patriarchal way of life.[41]

In the space of a few lines, Tocqueville satirizes the myth of rustic American simplicity and points to a typical feature of American society: its formal legality. Americans are eager for gain but always with respect to a rational structure. Tocqueville implicitly contrasts this to a different, aristocratic conception of honor. This systematic extraction of every last dollar from the stranger is simply alien to persons of a different breed and either escapes or astonishes them. Indian and aristocrat share the distinction of being dupes of the democratic creed.

And Saginaw itself? What spectacle greets Tocqueville when he finally gets a chance to view American civilization in the very act of transforming nature

---

39. "Fortnight in the Wilds," 354; cf. "Quinze jours," 345.   40. Ibid.
41. "Fortnight in the Wilds," 380; cf. "Quinze jours," 367.

into culture, wilderness into habitable land? The journey ends in dystopia. The French, the Anglo-Americans, the Indians, and the *métis* of the little settlement, with six religions among them, reproduce all the hatreds of the civilization they have left behind. The habits that divide are stronger than the needs that join:

Several exiled members of the great human family have met together in the immensity of the forests, and their needs are all alike; they have to fight against the beasts of the forest, hunger, and hard weather. There are scarcely thirty of them in the midst of the wilds where everything resists their efforts, but they cast only looks of hatred and suspicion on one another. Colour of skin, poverty or affluence, ignorance or enlightenment have already built up indestructible classifications between them; national prejudices, and prejudices of education and birth divide and isolate them.

Where could one find a more complete picture of the wretchedness of our nature in a narrower frame?[42]

Tocqueville is sometimes portrayed as an admirer of the American melting pot. Yet here is another Tocqueville, whose errand into the wilderness strips away his hope for the creation of a newer, better humanity.[43]

The discussion of Indians in *Democracy in America* is no less bleak. It expands on the theme of Indians' nobility, with special attention to their love of liberty. "No famed republic of antiquity," writes Tocqueville, "could record firmer courage, prouder spirit, or more obstinate love of freedom than lies concealed in the forests of the New World."[44] He returns to this theme in the tenth and penultimate chapter on "The Three Races That Inhabit the Territory of the United States." It sets American Indians into a symmetrical scheme in which African-Americans occupy the extreme of slavery, Indians the extreme of freedom.[45]

The Indian, as Tocqueville portrays him in this chapter, is not merely free; he is a free aristocrat. Like his friends Beaumont and Blosseville, Tocqueville compares Indians to Tacitus's Germanic warriors. Yet he revises the familiar equation to give it a new sociological significance. "I cannot avoid the conclusion," he comments, "that in both hemispheres the same cause has pro-

---

42. "Fortnight in the Wilds," 395; cf. "Quinze jours," 380–381.
    A few decades later, a local historian reckoned that there were just enough Indians left (about 1,000, he believed) to form a picturesque background to a hike or picnic. See Truman B. Fox, *History of Saginaw Country, From the Year 1819 Down to the Present Time . . .* (East Saginaw, Mich., 1858), 70–71.
43. "Quinze jours," 381. Cf. the subtle analysis of Tocqueville's wilderness mood in Eva Doran, "Two Men and a Forest: Chateaubriand, Tocqueville and the American Wilderness," in *Essays in French Literature*, 13 (November 1976): 44–61.
44. *Democracy in America*, 29.   45. *Démocratie*, 333–334.

duced the same effects and that amid the apparent diversity of human affairs it is possible to discover a few pregnant facts from which all others derive."[46] The Indian–Teutonic comparison is an occasion for causal analysis. Tocqueville is not just content to recite what he sees; he employs it in the search for economic and social conditions. The crucial point of comparison between Germanic and Native American warriors is their means of subsistence, hunting, and its companion activity, warfare. The latter "thinks hunting and war the only cares worthy of a man. Therefore the Indian in the miserable depths of his forests cherishes the same idea and opinions as the medieval noble. . . ."[47] The life of the hunter is an errant, free life, and the Indian can imagine no other. Accustomed to wandering, he resists settlement in one place. Accustomed to making his own decisions, he resists hierarchy. As master over game and enemies, he refuses to heed the command of the foreigners to his continent. He regards regular, systematic manual labor as beneath his dignity. This is the ethos of the pure aristocrat. It emerges in Tocqueville's interpretation as an effect of economic needs.

A few words of commentary from today's scholarship may serve as reminders of the limitations of Tocqueville's reporting. The Ojibwas he met on the way to Saginaw were not "pure" Indians, nor did they inhabit a primitive wilderness, as Tocqueville imagined; change over time took place before European contact and, for over a century before his visit, had accelerated under the impact of European trade. Following a widespread French stereotype, Tocqueville imagined that Indian societies were atomistic and thus gave wide scope to individual freedom. Ojibwas seemed to confirm this; yet the small-scale social organization of their time may have been the successor to a more organized clan system that broke down under the impact of trade with Europeans. Far from enacting a timeless culture, the Ojibwas were experiencing economic crisis in the early 1830s. Traders drove these Indian partners to overexploit their territory for fur, and the entire fur trade of the Great Lakes region was about to collapse as land speculators moved in and the fur trade moved westward in search of less exhausted grounds. The Ojibwas had participated in and indeed flourished within a trade economy. Their way of life was on the verge of crisis not, as Tocqueville imagined, because of contact with Europeans, but because the pattern of that contact was changing.[48]

Tocqueville lacked insight into many areas of Indian life – social organiza-

46. *Democracy in America*, 328.   47. Ibid., 328.
48. See Harold Hickerson, *The Chippewa and Their Neighbors: A Study in Ethnohistory*, Foreword by Charles A. Bishop, Review Essay and Bibliographical Supplement by Jennifer S. H. Brown and Laura L. Peers (Prospect Heights, Ill., 1988), esp. 9, 37–41, 49–50, 102; Lyle M. Stone and Donald Chaput, "History of the Upper Great Lakes Area," in *Handbook of North American Indians*, ed. William C. Sturtevant, vol. 15: *Northeast*, ed. Bruce G. Trigger (Wash-

tion, ceremony, and religion, to name just a few. And his writing lacked specificity: just as he wrote about the American as a national type, so he looked for the typical Indian, exemplified by the individuals who happened to cross his path. His writings summarized and synthesized French stereotypes instead of moving toward an understanding of different native peoples. In its methodology, however, Tocqueville's account reaches for a more profound level of understanding. Although the title of his chapter speaks of three "races," we should not be misled by the term, which in the early nineteenth century did not yet have a clear definition. As Tocqueville understands it, "race" corresponds more closely to our use of "ethnic group" today: it is an outcome of historical circumstances. While his emphasis on hunting was one-sided and misleading, it was also a first approximation of a socioeconomic analysis. The alternative of a racial interpretation was already available to Castelnau, whose travel account looked forward to the ever more insistent and "scientific" racial theorizing of the later nineteenth century, powerfully reinforced by European technological superiority, world colonization, and evolutionary theorizing. Tocqueville's analysis instead pointed the way to modern social science. It asked how diverse groups of human beings were comparable despite their different appearances. The socioeconomic analysis of *Democracy in America* is of a piece with "Fourteen Days" and its vision of a humanity needlessly divided against itself. In both his systematic work and his travel writing, Tocqueville took as his subject a single, united humanity whose differences could be explained through social scientific analysis.

Like most of his contemporaries, Tocqueville was convinced that the conflict of races in North America would lead to extinction of Native peoples. He portrayed this fate with the controlled anger of the trained attorney. "With my own eyes," he wrote, ". . . I have witnessed afflictions beyond my powers to portray." He described this scene of Choctaws crossing the Mississippi in the midst of the winter of 1831–1832:

It was then the depths of winter, and that year the cold was exceptionally severe; the snow was hard on the ground, and huge masses of ice drifted on the river. The Indians brought their families with them; there were among them the wounded, the sick, newborn babies, and the old men on the point of death. They had neither tents nor wagons, but only some provisions and weapons. I saw them embark to cross the great river, and the sight will never fade from my memory. Neither sob nor complaint rose from that silent assembly.

ington, D.C., 1978), 602–609; and Robert E. Ritzenthaler, "Southwestern Chippewa," in ibid., 743–759. See also Helen H. Tanner, *The Ojibwas: A Critical Bibliography* (Bloomington and London, 1976).

Their afflictions were of long standing, and they felt them to be irremediable. All the Indians had already got into the boat that was to carry them across; their dogs were still on the bank; as soon as the animals finally realized that they were being left being forever, they all together raised a terrible howl and plunged into the icy waters of the Mississippi to swim after their masters.[49]

When he saw these exiles from Jacksonian democracy, did Tocqueville have in mind the fate of the aristocratic exiles of forty years before? Although he was not so explicit, he did believe that the persecution had a class character: the perpetrators represented a bourgeois democracy and employed specifically bourgeois means to achieve their ends. Not for the Anglo-Americans the irregular massacres of the Spaniards. "Nowadays," he continued, "the dispossession of the Indians is accomplished in a regular and, so to say, quite legal manner."[50] Drawing on congressional legislative documents, he described the gatherings at which Indian leaders ceded vast lands, such as the exchange of 48,000,000 acres by the Osages for a rent of $1,000, and the oath to the Quapaws in 1818, after they ceded 20,000,000 acres for $4,000, to reserve a territory of 1 million acres for them, a promise soon broken.[51] "It is impossible," he concluded, "to destroy men with more respect to the laws of humanity."[52]

How did this assessment of the executionary logic of manifest destiny compare with the views of Anglo-American commentators? A number of contemporary Anglo-Americans visited the Ojibwas – sometimes following the same steamboat route as Tocqueville across the Great Lakes. They offer divergent points of view, not (as Tocqueville himself implied about Anglo-Americans) a single chorus of opinion.

Some provide evidence of the heartlessness that appalled Tocqueville and other European visitors. The incomprehension of the conqueror marks the comments of William H. Keating in his narrative account of the Long expedition of 1823. Major Stephen H. Long was commissioned by John Calhoun, then Secretary of War, to survey the country bounded by the Missouri River, the Mississippi River, and the northwestern border of the United States. Like the Lewis and Clark expedition, this was to be a scientific enterprise. Long and his company were to survey and map the area; describe the animal, veg-

---

49. *Democracy in America*, 324.   50. Ibid.   51. Ibid., 325.
52. Ibid., 339; cf. *Démocratie*, 355.
   For a sample of the legalistic fashion – and paternalistic language – in which Indians were expelled from their land, see the letter from John Calhoun to John Lewis, delegate from the Ohio Shawnees, March 2, 1825, in National Archives, Michigan Superintendency, 1814–1851, microfilm no. 1, Letters received by the Superintendent, roll 28 (January–August 1831; 1814–1825), 397.

etable, and mineral resources; and inquire into the character and customs of the Indians.[53] The account of the Ojibwas was written in the dispassionate scientific tone that characterized the entire work. It described them as divided into small bands consisting of a few families each. Keating, who edited the official compilation gathered from the travelers' notes, suggested that this had to do with the ravages of smallpox, as well as the scarcity of game in an area at one time well stocked with beaver, otter, and other small animals now almost extinct as a result of the fur trade.[54] "The Chippewas," states his report, "appear at present to be in the lowest stage of advancement. They have no national councils; their dispersed condition and their excessive indulgence in spirituous liquors have destroyed their national character."[55] The Long expedition met very few Ojibwas; most of Keating's information about their religious and burial beliefs, subsistence on wild rice, supposed cannibalism, diseases, hospitality, high opinion of themselves, quarrelsomeness, high esteem of chastity, kinship rules, and wartime practices came from a single informant.[56] Indians did not take up much time from these scientific explorers intent on opening up the region to settlers.

Other American observers gave Indians more serious attention, though it was difficult to check one's satisfaction over the steady settlement of new lands. One of the era's best-known ethnographers of American Indians, Henry Schoolcraft, traveled over much of the same northwestern route as Tocqueville when he joined a scientific expedition that was to prepare the Great Lakes for white settlement.[57] Passing through upstate New York on the way to Detroit, he recalled that the Iroquois "had acquired a national pride, and a national character"; left alone for another century, they might have reached a high state of civilization.[58] This did not inhibit his pride that a land once in the hands of "semi-barbarians, is now smiling under the hand of agriculture, and checquered with towns, and villages, roads and canals, the seats of learning, and the temples of religion. Perhaps no country presents so remarkable an instance of the progress of human settlements, achieved in so

---

53. William H. Keating, *Narrative of an Expedition to the Source of St. Peter's River, Lake Winnepeek, Lake of the Woods, &c. performed in the year 1823, by order of the Hon. J.C. Calhoun, Secretary of War, under the Command of Stephen H. Long, U.S.T.E.,* compiled from the notes of Major Long, Messrs. Say, Keating & Colhoun (London, 1825), 1: xiii, 1–3 (paraphrased in part from 3).
54. Ibid., 2: 148–149 (paraphrased in part).   55. Ibid., 150.   56. Ibid., 148–169.
57. Henry R. Schoolcraft, *Narrative Journals of Travels from Detroit Northwest Through the Great Chain of American Lakes to the Sources of the Mississippi River in the Year 1820* (1821; n. pl., reprint).
    On Schoolcraft, see Brian W. Dippie, *Catlin and His Contemporaries: The Politics of Patronage* (Lincoln, Neb., and London, 1990).
58. Schoolcraft, *Narrative,* 24.

short a period of time."[59] The contrast grows sharper in Schoolcraft's report on Michigan. Lest anyone should be distracted by its natural beauty, he pointed out that the greater glory of Detroit was its location at the intersection of a network of lakes and riverways. "It is thus destined to be to the regions of the northwest," he wrote, "what St. Louis is rapidly becoming in the southwest, the seat of its commerce, the repository of its wealth, and the grand focus of its moral, political and physical energies. . . ."[60] Saginaw Bay could not compete with the commercial opportunites of Detroit, but the banks of the Saginaw River, where Ojibwas and Ottawas had once enjoyed an easy life of hunting and fishing, would soon attract "enterprising and industrious farmers and mechanics."[61] Whereas Tocqueville sank into Romantic regret over wilderness lost, Schoolcraft was thrilled by the prospect of a promising spot for settlement.

By 1824 Schoolcraft had begun a period of service as an Indian subagent, first at lonely Sault Ste. Marie and later at Michilimakinac. His official correspondence with Washington, D.C., reveals an able, conscientious administrator who compiled statistics on his Indian charges, complained about white encroachment on Indian territory, and was infuriated by the American Fur Company's practice of distributing alcohol among Indians.[62] Schoolcraft believed that missionary work among the Indians was the white man's duty, but a thankless one:

It is not so easy to transform the habits and manners of a whole people, as certain theorists may imagine. And of all people "under the sun," our North American tribes seem most firmly attached to practices and opinions, which constitute the distinctive traits of their character. They hate the very idea of labor, and do not separate the idea of a laborer from that of a slave. Freedom constitutes the *beau idéal* of their existence,

---

59. Ibid., 29.   60. Ibid., 64–65.   61. Ibid., 98.
62. See especially Schoolcraft to Cass, Sault Ste. Marie, June 22, 1824; Cass to Schoolcraft, Detroit, July 8, 1824; and Schoolcraft to Thomas McKenney, Sault Ste. Marie, August 4, 1824, in National Archives, Letters Received by the Office of Indian Affairs, 1824–1881, microfilm no. 234, Sault Ste. Marie Agency (1824–1852), roll no. 770 (1824–1841). The survey and statistics included with the latter letter are impressive evidence of Schoolcraft's energy and thoroughness. See also Schoolcraft to Elbert Herring, Saute Ste. Marie, March 2, 1833, in ibid., Mackinac Agency (1828–1880), roll no. 402 (1828–1838), for Schoolcraft's complaints about the American Fur Company's distribution of alchohol.

See also Schoolcraft to Lewis Cass, Sault Ste. Marie, June 3, 1823, in National Archives, Michigan Superintendency, 1814–1851, microfilm no. 1, Letters received by the Superintendent (1819–1835), roll 28 (January–August 1831; 1814–1825), 310: "The Indians have no distinct ideas of a *right* to use & occupy the land, while the *land* itself belongs to the U. States. This is beyond their power of comprehension. It is important that the reservations I have assigned to them to encamp upon should be strictly reserved. If they are not, and these lands continue to be encroached upon, as they already have been, by the military, it is in vain that I continue to assure them that the United States are just."

though it be that kind of freedom, which is enjoyed amidst poverty and wretchedness. Whatever enslaves the mind enslaves the body. This seems to be sufficiently understood among them, and is doubtless one cause of their repugnance to the principles of Christianity and the practices of civilization, which equally impose a system of moral discipline, and physical restraint, very formidable to the mind of a simple hunter.[63]

The wording closely anticipates passages of *Democracy in America,* as does the general theme of the hunter's love of freedom versus the physical and moral constraints of civilization. The propagandist for settlement and the European aristocrat have sharply different values in assessing white–Indian relations, however. Indian resistance to white civilization is a nuisance to the government agent, a tragedy to the European visitor.

Tocqueville, then, was reporting on a social reality when he complained about inhumane American attitudes toward Indians. Not all Americans were so insensitive, however. Others were as pained as Tocqueville and tried to reach the ears of their contemporaries with Romantic rhetoric. "The history of the American Indians," wrote Calvin Colton on visiting the Great Lakes in 1830, "is the *Romance of Fact.*"[64] On the way to Mackinac, his party encountered an Indian canoe, and he recorded a moment of grace in color and motion.

The singular costume of the Indians, with many and various coloured feathers, bending and waving on their heads; the exquisite beauty of their canoe; their paddles of the most glaring red, so far as they are immersed; the perfect time and admirable exactitude of their movements, as if they and their bark were only so many parts of a piece of mechanism; and the amazing celerity, with which they seemed to fly over the tops of the waves; – absolutely confounded all the ideas I had ever indulged of the Indian's skill and dexterity in this exercise.[65]

Linguistic and cultural barriers made it difficult for him to form more than a superficial impression of the people he observed, but the sight of the canoers suggested another world with a beauty all its own.

On the steamboat Colton met a young woman of mixed ancestry, her father Scotch (or Scotch-Irish) and her mother an Indian. "She was well educated," he writes, "and was on her return home from a visit at Detroit. She

63. [Henry Schoolcraft], "Civilization and Conversion of the Indians," *The North American Review* (April 1829): 367. Attributed to Schoolcraft by Robert E. Bieder in his introduction to Johann Georg Kohl, *Kitchi-Gami: Life Among the Lake Superior Ojibwa,* trans. Lascelles Wraxall, Ralf Neufang, and Ulrike Böcker (St. Paul, Minn., 1985), xxx.
64. C. [alvin] Colton, *Tour of the American Lakes, and Among the Indians of the North-West Territory, in 1830: Disclosing the Character and Prospects of the Indian Race,* 2 vols. (London, 1833), 1: xii.
65. Ibid., 71.

was even highly accomplished, and had been used to the best society."[66] When a second canoe pulled alongside the steamer and spoke to the eight Ojibwa warriors inside, he marveled at the tenderness and musicality of their language. "An Indian dialogue, (and among themselves there is no people more sociable) in connexion with the melody of their voice, and the tenderness of the intonations and inflexions of their speech, is one of the finest scenes of the kind in the world."[67] Descriptions like this served as prelude to Colton's plea for a paternalistic American policy toward Indians. They were, he explained, children of nature who had been exploited by the people who ought to have been educating them: "The rapid growth and rising prosperity of European colonies in America, and their political and social interests have operated to induce them to forget their parental and moral obligations to the Aborigines."[68] Indian character was not savage, but included admirable qualities of generosity, loyalty, and kindness. The young woman on the steamboat represented the transforming power of education, and her conversation with the men in the canoe exemplified the kind of dialogue that could uplift them too. In contrast to Tocqueville's bleak opposition of Indian and Anglo-American cultures, Colton envisioned a peaceful process of conversion.

Another American who pleaded for a constructive American Indian policy was Caleb Atwater, who visited Prairie du Chien (in present-day Wisconsin) as one of the government commissioners appointed to mediate a violent dispute between whites and Indians over land discovered to contain lead mines. The government representatives negotiated in the summer of 1829 with Ojibwas, Ottawas, Potawatomis, and Winnebagos for the sale of about 8 million acres of land. Not far from the scene of peaceful negotiation were 30 steamboats with cannon and 400 U.S. soldiers.[69] The patriarchal manners of these Indians, in Atwater's recollection, resemble those of "the people of the earliest ages of the world," with wives respecting their husbands, children their parents, and everyone the aged.[70] Their speechmaking thrills him:

Like the rays of light, brought to a focus, by a lens, their ideas being few, and with only a few words to express them, Byron would call them "ideas of fire." Unaccompanied by enthusiasm, genius produces only uninteresting works of art. Enthusiasm, is the secret spirit, which hovers over the eloquence of the Indian.[71]

Thus, at Prairie du Chien, Atwater experienced firsthand the folk source of poetry.

66. Ibid., 81.   67. Ibid., 86.   68. Ibid., 98.
69. See Caleb Atwater, *Remarks Made on a Tour to Prairie du Chien; Thence to Washington City in 1829* (Columbus, Ohio, 1831), 1–3, 70–71.
70. Ibid., paraphrased from 101; cf. 108–109.
71. Ibid., 119; cf. 120–121.

Atwater's views form a democratic reformer's counterpoint to Toc-queville's tragic aristocratic perspective on American Indians. Atwater too criticized the Indian-hating, "bordering on madness," which, he warned, if sanctioned by Congress might bring down the condemnation of the civilized world on the United States. Whereas Tocqueville portrayed ruthless treat-ment of Indians as the national norm, however, Atwater blamed it on a few bureaucratic bad guys and argued that on the whole Americans were inter-ested in respecting the principles of indemnification.[72] Like Tocqueville, Atwater feared a coming extermination of all Indians (despite Tocqueville's complaint of general Anglo-American indifference, Atwater was horrified by the sight of the beggars on the road from Buffalo to Utica). Unlike Toc-queville, however, he was an optimist who believed that Indians could be per-suaded to give up the chase, take up farming, and receive the conquerors' reli-gion, art, and science.[73]

Anglo-American writers no less than French aristocrats could regret a van-ishing era and a vanishing way of life; reformers were no less acute observers of settlers' behavior and government failings. The reformers had a different audience, however. They aimed at influencing public policy; they faced a political problem and tried to find the most practical means of reconciling Indian and white societies. For Tocqueville, Indians illustrated an unavoid-able conflict of modern history. Their unalloyed devotion to freedom, char-acteristic of the "barbarian" stage of the evolution of mankind, made them the inalterable opponents of bourgeois civilization. European aristocrats owed their love of freedom to the same historical epoch; they too were "barbarians" in this respect, with an underlying longing for the freedom of the hunt. "Their unconquerable prejudices, their indomitable passions, their vices, and per-haps still more their savage virtues delivered them to inevitable destruc-tion."[74] Tocqueville wrote these lines about the hunter-warriors of North America, but they could apply just as well to aristocrats at home. The lesson of the American experiment was conclusive: to avoid destruction, Toc-queville's peers had to accept bourgeois routine.

72. Ibid., 140–141.   73. Ibid., 141–145.
74. *Democracy in America*, 30; cf. *Démocratie*, 25.

PART III

◁ ══════════════════════════ ▷

Founding a Tradition: The German Romantic Travelers

5

◁ ══════════════════════════════ ▷

Immigrants and Educated Observers

There was little reason for Germans to pay special attention to North America before the French Revolution. Maritime interest was restricted mainly to a few city-states like Bremen and Hamburg, which might have economic ambitions but not political visions of overseas empire. Unlike the French and the English, the larger German states had no imperial interest, past or present, in North America. Austria and Prussia were land powers, their attention fixed on intra-European conflicts. Prussia in particular was a poor state driven by ambitious rulers to play a great-power role within Europe that exhausted its means. It certainly could not afford the spendthrift game of imperial overseas ventures. Hence there were no colonial administrators to write American memoirs, no businessmen with ventures to investigate, no great enterprises to stimulate public pride. For the learned and privileged of Central Europe, North America remained a distant place.[1]

1. Among the most interesting eighteenth-century travel accounts are Frederike Charlotte Luise (von Massow), Freifrau von Riedesel, *Die Berufs-Reise nach Amerika. Briefe der Generalin von Riedesel auf dieser Reise und während ihres sechsjährigen Aufenthalts in America zur Zeit des dortigen Krieges in den Jahren 1776 bis 1783 nach Deutschland geschrieben,* introd. Carl Spener (Berlin, 1800); Johann David Schöpf, *Reise durch einige der mittlern und südlichen vereinigten nordamerikanischen Staaten nach Ost-Florida und den Bahama-Inseln unternommen in den Jahren 1783 und 1784,* 2 vols. (Erlangen, 1788); Dietrich von Bülow, *Der Freistaat von Nordamerika in seinem neuesten Zustand,* (Berlin, 1797). The most important of these is the work of Bülow, who visited the United States in 1791–1792 and again in 1795–1796. His disillusionment with the young republic and complaints about Americans' commercial mentality resemble French criticisms of the same period and anticipate the large chorus of similar German criticisms after 1815. See Bülow, *Der Freistaat von Nordamerika,* 1: 38ff. and 239.

  Even after 1815, German travelers did not write with an imperial consciousness. As late as the 1820s and 1830s, the proceedings of the German Geographic Society represent a rather modest organization compared to the wealth and ambition of the comparable French and English organizations. See especially the remarks by the chairman of the society, Carl Ritter, disclaiming any comparison between the German organization and its counterparts to the West in *Jährliche Übersicht der Thätigkeit der Gesellschaft für Erdkunde in Berlin* 1 (1834): 4.

A period of ferment was already beginning, however, that would change this relationship. Beginning in the late eighteenth century, local authorities lifted the previous restrictions on marriage, put in place to limit population growth. The pennywise mentality of princes and patricians gave way to an acceptance of the freedom – and with freedom, the dynamism – of modern society. In 1816 the population of Germany was 23.5 million. Over the next nine years it shot up 15 percent, the initial jolt in its rise to 38 million by 1865.[2] One of the effects of this population growth was the mass migration of Germans to the United States. The number of immigrants for the period 1816–1844 – some 303,000 – was not great compared to later figures.[3] To contemporaries, though, these departures signified a breakdown of order and stimulated a controversy about the United States.

Perspectives on the New World diverged along class lines. For peasants and craftsmen, America offered the promise of relief from hunger and sinking social status, especially in the heavily overcrowded Southwest. If the decision to cross the ocean meant a farewell to home towns and loved ones, it also brought opportunities for improving one's diet, owning land, and prospering in an old or a new trade. For Germany's educated and political elites, however, America was a more ambiguous destination. The deep-seated paternalism of noble and educated Germans led many to view the migration with dismay. One group of aristocrats formed a society in the 1840s to establish a German colony in Texas by buying up land and systematically settling immigrants there. Poor planning led to hardship for the immigrants and financial troubles for the planners, but the attempt shows how seriously they took their responsibility to provide for their social inferiors, who in the early years of the Restoration often experienced exploitation and neglect as immigrants.[4]

More than just paternalism moved German leaders to take an interest in the United States, however. The governments of Central Europe remained monarchies, and in contrast to France, the nobility retained many of its privileges after 1815. To the upholders of this anachronistic political order, a suc-

---

Two important works on German travelers have recently appeared: Peter J. Brenner, ed., *Der Reisebericht: Die Entwicklung einer Gattung in der deutschen Literatur* (Frankfurt am Main, 1989); and idem., *Reisen in die Neue Welt: Die Erfahrung Nordamerikas in deutschen Reise- und Auswandererberichten des 19. Jahrhunderts* (Tübingen, 1991).

2. Peter Marschalk, *Bevölkerungsgeschichte Deutschlands im 19. und 20. Jahrhundert* (Frankfurt am Main, 1984), 27. "Germany" refers here to the territories that comprised the later German Empire.

3. See Marschalk, *Bevölkerungsgeschichte*, 31–32, and Table 5.1 (177).

4. On the misery of the early immigrants, see James J. Sheehan, *German History, 1770–1866* (Oxford, 1989), 461–462. On the Verein zum Schutze deutscher Einwanderer in Texas (Society for the Protection of German Immigrants in Texas), see Rudolph L. Biesele, *The History of the German Settlements in Texas, 1831–1861* (Austin, 1930).

cessful republic was a provocation.[5] America unsettled Germans' sense of cultural legitimacy, too. Moritz von Fürstenwärther – sent by Heinrich von Gagern, minister to the German Bundestag, to visit America and report on the condition of German immigrants – was able to appreciate that the New World offered prosperity to immigrants who were able to survive the initial difficulties of getting settled in a new country. But high culture was missing: "People in this country have no notion, not the slightest suspicion, of a higher and finer life . . . they are notable for their unsociability, contemptuous pride, reserve and crudeness, and repel the European of education and feeling." Like their French contemporaries, educated and titled Germans disliked Americans' obsession with money, emphasis on practicality, and crude manners.[6]

American Indians were a frequent topic of German commentary in the travel accounts of the early nineteenth century. While not everyone mentioned them, they were clearly one of the items that teased German readers' curiosity. In contrast to France, where discussion of North America took place largely within the cultural elite, Germany developed a cross-class debate about the United States and its Native peoples. Discussion of Indians ran along two lines. Writers concerned with America as a political topic – a destination for immigrants, an alternative to monarchy – turned to Indians to advance their beliefs, whether friendly or hostile, about the worth of a settler republic. The second set of writers were aristocrats who could enjoy a West-

5. On the German nobility, see Werner Conze, "Adel," parts 1, 2.2 and 3, in Otto Brunner, Werner Conze, and Reinhart Koselleck, eds., *Geschichtliche Grundbegriffe. Historisches Lexikon zur politisch-sozialen Sprache in Deutschland* (Stuttgart, 1990), 1: 1–48; Robert M. Berdahl, *The Politics of the Prussian Nobility: The Development of a Conservative Ideology, 1770–1848* (Princeton, N.J., 1988), esp. 5–6, 14, 55, 75, 154–156, and 220–227; Jerome Blum, *The End of the Old Order in Rural Europe* (Princeton, N.J., 1978), chaps. 1 and 4, esp. 12–20; Hans-Ulrich Wehler, *Deutsche Gesellschaftsgeschichte*, vol. 2: *Von der Reformära bis zur industriellen und politischen "Deutschen Doppelrevolution" 1815–1845/49* (Munich, 1987), 145–161; Sheehan, *German History*, 271–272, 481–482, 504–508.
6. Moritz von Fürstenwärther, *Der Deutsche in Nord-Amerika* (Stuttgart and Tübingen, 1818), 46, 78–79, 85–86. Cf. Ludwig Gall's disappointment with republican government in *Meine Auswanderung nach den Vereinigten-Staaten in Nord-Amerika, im Frühjahr 1819 und meine Rückkehr nach der Heimath im Winter 1820*, vol. 1: *Meine Beweggründe und mein Wirken zur Erleichterung der Auswanderung nach den Vereinigten-Staaten und mein Reisetagebuch enthaltend* (Trier, 1822), 5. See also his discussion in the second volume of America's lack of civic virtue as the cause of its decline, 215ff., 307; and the repudiation of a land of chaos in Friedrich Schmidt, *Versuch über den politischen Zustand der Vereinigten Staaten von Nordamerika* (Stuttgart and Tübingen, 1822), 1: xi–xii.
   For other educated criticisms of the United States, see Wilhelm Grisson, *Beiträge zur Charakteristik der Vereinigten Staaten von Nord–Amerika* (Hamburg, 1844), 9; and Jonas Heinrich Gudehus, *Meine Auswanderung nach Amerika im Jahre 1822, und meine Rückkehr in die Heimath im Jahre 1825. Nebst Bemerkungen über den kirchlichen, ökonomischen und moralischen Zustand der dortigen Deutschen und Winke für Auswanderungslustige* (Hildesheim, 1829), 2: 25, 32.

ern adventure that included encounters with Indians. Their stories advertised
the warrior and leadership qualities that set them apart from farmers, craftsmen, and burghers.

Anyone expecting to find solidarity between the oppressed of the Old World
and the New will be disappointed by the written record. In writings from the
popular classes, Indians make their appearance as a past or present menace.
"We are as safe from Indians here as in Europe" was the lapidary comment of
one anonymous letter writer on the State of Kentucky in 1831. Another
writer commented on the beautiful lands safely available in northern Illinois
now that the Indians had signed a contract to leave (a comforting assessment
disturbed a few years later by the Black Hawk War of 1832).[7] Others mentioned them to add an exotic touch to their story, drawing on either casual
glimpses or the writings of previous travelers.[8] Altogether, Indians had little
importance for immigrants preoccupied with their own problems of survival
as they moved from a Europe that could no longer feed them to a North
America full of dangers and opportunities.

Middle-class writers who sympathized with immigrants wrote advice literature to prepare them for the rigors of life in a new continent. The most spec-
tacular success in this genre was Gottfried Duden's account of his years in the
United States from 1824 to 1827.[9] Born in 1785, Duden was the son of an
apothecary, a modest but respectable profession; he received a classical education, studied law, and entered the Prussian civil service. He went to America
in part for health reasons but also out of a desire to study the conditions of
German immigrants in America. Arriving in St. Louis in October 1824, he
bought land in Missouri and led the life of a gentleman farmer. He described
Missouri as an ideal place for German immigrants, somehow ignoring the thin
topsoil there and the rich soil available in Illinois on the other side of
the Mississippi River. His book evoked a petit bourgeois idyll and described
the details of setting up a farm that would appeal to German craftsmen and
peasants hoping to buy land. Its encouragement of immigration corresponded

---

7. Briefe Deutscher Auswanderer, Edward E. Ayer Collection, Newberry Library, 7; Ferdinand
   Ernst, *Bemerkungen auf einer Reise durch das Innere der vereinigten Staaten von Nord-
   Amerika im Jahr 1819* . . . (Hildesheim, 1820), vii–viii.
8. See T. W. Lenz, *Reise nach Saint Louis am Mississippi* . . . (Weimar, 1838), 57–59; M. Buhle, ed.,
   Reisen durch die Vereinigten Staaten von Amerika, 2 vols. (Nuremberg, 1808), 1: 76ff. and 2:57
   ff.; and Anonymous, *Wanderungen eines jungen Norddeutschen durch Portugal, Spanien und
   Nord-Amerika. In den Jahren 1827–1831*, ed. Georg Lotz (Hamburg, 1834), 4: 103–105, 106.
9. The following biographical sketch and the overview of Duden's book are drawn from the editors' introduction to Gottfried Duden, *Report on a Journey to the Western States of North
   America and a Stay of Several Years Along the Missouri (During the Years 1824, '25, '26, and
   1827)*, ed. James W. Goodrich et al. (Columbia, Mo., and London, 1980), viiff.

all too well to what his listeners wanted to hear; after enjoying initial success, the book was bitterly attacked in the 1830s for its overly optimistic picture of American conditions.

Duden's famous account carefully set his readers' minds at ease about American–Indian relations. For a start, he assured them that no Indians had lived in his part of Missouri for about ten years, and the ones occasionally seen were harmless. There was no need to feel guilty about Anglo-American behavior toward them. Indians were habitually cruel toward whites and toward one other; they lacked the restraining influence of reason; they indulged in sexually aberrant behavior; their hunting life, with its bouts of famine, occasionally turned them into cannibals who ate their own children.[10] European do-gooders had no justification for their carping about American policy when in fact American treatment of Indians had been beneficent and fair-minded: "All evils that have resulted from associating with citizens of the United States must seem negligible in comparison with the good," he wrote.[11] And he scoffed at the notion of Indian rights to the land: "To speak of the rights of a few persons to the exclusive possession of large areas is just as ridiculous as to complain about the increasing numbers of whites."[12] The liberal publicist could not imagine setting any limits to settlers' rights.[13] In another work he attempted a more scholarly refutation of philanthropic sympathy. Many Europeans, he noted, compared the Indians to the ancient Teutons, and he admitted that there were important similarities, but these could lead to absurd conclusions:

The Indians have many traits in common with the ancient Teutons. They love drink like the Teutons, and just as passionately, gambling. Often they wager their dearest possessions. And the only occupation of both is war and hunting. But whoever wants to decide according to such criteria should look around to see whether there aren't quite a few Europeans, precisely from the higher social ranks, who belong to the category of Indian.[14]

Duden read here like an upside-down Tocqueville: precisely those qualities that the French aristocrat admired, especially the hunting and warrior skills, provoked his sarcasm. (Duden later felt himself to be in rivalry with Tocqueville and wrote a tract condemning the elite bias of *Democracy in America* and its educated admirers.)[15] His feelings were wholly on the side of the

10. Ibid., 87–89.   11. Ibid., 91.   12. Ibid.
13. Gottfried Duden, *Europa und Deutschland von Nordamerika aus betrachtet, oder: Die europäische Entwicklung im 19. Jahrhundert in Bezug auf die Lage der Deutschen, nach einer Prüfung im innern Nordamerika* (Bonn, 1833–1835), 1: 327ff.
14. Ibid., 327.
15. Duden added, in response to one of the critics of his book, that the educated were defending their own social superiority when they expressed their dissatisfaction with America: "Nun

peaceful farmer, far from the passion and the danger of American and European "Indians."

Friedrich von Raumer was another educated traveler who admired the United States. Professor of history at the University of Berlin, Raumer was for a time a member of the Stein–Hardenberg circle of reformers and after 1815 tended toward a strongly republican, indeed populist, view of politics. He mixed liberal ideology with a racialist view of society and history. In his well-received overview of life in the United States (which he visited in 1841), he viewed American expansion as a triumph of liberal principles and "the white race."[16] Indians, according to von Raumer, conformed to a single physical and cultural type: everywhere they looked the same, and their art showed the same lack of authentic feel for beauty. If their population was diminishing, this only demonstrated their insistence on clinging to a primitive level of culture and their refusal to learn from their civilized neighbors. Like Duden, von Raumer ridiculed the humanitarians who supposed that Indians had a legitimate right to the land, replying, "Savages and animals must rightfully retreat before peoples of culture. . . ."[17] In Raumer's language of 1845 we can hear the emerging tone of European high imperialism, un-self-conscious in its identification of European colonial expansion with historical progress.

Most other educated observers were shocked by the effects of American Indian policy.[18] Nicolaus Heinrich Julius, a physician and prominent prison reformer, who visited the United States from 1834 to 1836, admired the transformation of America into a civilized land and recommended it to German immigrants, but he also recounted three centuries of mistreatment of Indians culminating in Jackson's policy of expropriation.[19] Ludwig de Wette, a Basel physician, who visited in 1837, was saddened by the Indians he met on the

wird es aber eben durch die Auswanderung den Europäern erst recht kund, wie viele dieser Ungerathenen es unter den sogenannten Honoratioren gibt. Es ist nämlich mit ziemlicher Sicherheit zu erwarten, dass sobald es der letztern einem in Amerika nicht behagt, er seinen Tadel nicht bloss mündlich oder in Briefen an Verwandte und Bekannte, sondern um so mehr an das ganze Publicum zu richten strebt, je weniger er an sich selbst zu zweifeln gewöhnt ist." Gottfried Duden, *Die nordamerikanische Demokratie und das v. Tocqueville'sche Werk darüber, als Zeichen des Zustandes der theoretischen Politik . . .* (Bonn, 1837), 99–100.

16. Friedrich von Raumer, *Die Vereinigten Staaten von Nordamerika* (Leipzig, 1845), 1: 227.

17. Ibid., 283.

18. In addition to the figures discussed later, see Heinrich von Martels, *Briefe über die westlichen Theile der vereinigten Staaten von Nordamerika* (Osnabrück, 1834), which contrasts the noble Indians of the past and the ruined vestiges that have survived the onslaught of white civilization, 28–29, 75–76. See also Moritz Wagner and Carl Scherzer, *Reisen in Nordamerika in den Jahren 1852 und 1853* (Leipzig, 1854), 1: 13, and their sympathetic discussion of the demoralization of American Indians, 3: 63, 68–74.

19. N. H. Julius, *Nordamerikas sittliche Zustände. Nach eigenen Anschauungen in den Jahren 1834, 1835 und 1836* (Leipzig, 1839), 1: 328–350.

East Coast and in the South and gave an affecting portrayal of a large encampment of Creeks near Mobile, Alabama, who treated him politely and entertained him with their skill at a ball game.[20] Joseph Salzbacher, a Catholic cleric from Vienna, stopped at a Seneca village near Utica, New York, and was impressed by the mild appearance and artisanal skill of the inhabitants, whom he compared to the Jews in Babylonian captivity.[21] Clara von Gerstner, who traveled in the United States from 1838 to 1840 with her husband (a railroad engineer), was alternately impressed by the dignity of the Indian diplomats she saw in Washington, D.C., and saddened by her conversation with the handful of Indians who escaped mass expulsion from Alabama.[22] These observers did not make a special case for Indians as part of a debate over Rousseau or a world-historical comparison of the kinds that enticed more politicized or theory-minded intellectuals; they also did not attempt to probe very far beyond the sights they observed on their travels; they simply bore witness to the condition of the refugees.

The most trenchant voice of disillusionment with American democracy – and, at the same time, of identification with Indians – was that of the poet Nicholas Lenau, the pen name of Nikolaus Franz Niembsch Edler von Strehlenau (1802–1850). The son of an aristocratic mother and an Austrian army officer, Lenau spent his early years rebelling against the stuffiness of Habsburg society and a family that expected him to follow a career in the army or civil service. Alternately cheered by the July Revolution and despondent over the failure of the Polish Revolution of 1831, he went to America in 1832 hoping for a new life of material ease, new subjects for his writing, and personal dignity. After arriving in Baltimore in October he made his way to Lisbon, Ohio, where he bought farmland.[23] Lenau wrote several letters from Lisbon in March 1833 that capture his disgust with his new surroundings. America was a continent in which stunted external growth was the outward expression of a lack of inner soul:

How do I like it in America? . . . As you know, there is no nightingale here, altogether no real songbirds. This seems to me to be a poetic curse on the land, and of deep significance. Nature here is never so joyful or sad that it must sing. It has no soul and no imagination and therefore can give nothing of the kind to its creatures. It is quite sad, the sight of these burnt-out men in their burnt-out woods. The German immigrants

20. Ludwig de Wette, *Reise in den Vereinigten Staaten und Canada im Jahr 1837* (Leipzig, 1838), 181–186 and 345–346.
21. Joseph Salzbacher, *Meine Reise nach Nord-Amerika im Jahre 1842* (Vienna, 1845), 263–264.
22. Clara von Gerstner, *Beschreibung einer Reise durch die Vereinigten Staaten von Nordamerica in den Jahren 1838 bis 1840* (Leipzig, 1842), 225–227, 320–322.
23. Biographical background is from the introduction by Reiner Schlichting to Nikolaus Lenau, *Lenaus Werke*, ed. Walter Dietze (Berlin and Weimar, 1970), viiiff.

make an especially deadly impression on me. After they have been here for several years all the fire that they brought from home has disappeared to the last spark.[24]

Not since De Pauw's *Recherches philosophique* of 1771 had anyone given such full force to the educated European's sense of horror over America as a place of degenerate nature. De Pauw had been a mere philosophe writing from afar, but Lenau had witnessed with his own senses a land of egoism. Degeneration spread from nature to the practical education of the American – an artificial, mechanical intelligence that was on the verge of collapse.[25]

Lenau got very little poetic material out of his American journey. Among the poems he did publish, however, were two from 1833 about Indians. One, "Der Indianerzug," describes a procession of Indians crossing the Susquehanna River on their march westward, while the other, "Die Drei Indianer," observes three Indians at Niagara Falls. In both poems, the Indians stand for an authentic life nurtured by nature; fire, the element lacking in the soul of their oppressors, is their metaphorical element, and they are also at one with the purifying waters of river and cataract. Though they are being driven to their death, they depart with their pride unbroken and leave a curse upon their successors.[26] The Indians embody Lenau's own hatred for the new nation that breaks the bond between man and nature. European and Native American aristocrats are allied against the decadence of Anglo-American civilization.

Lenau's remarks were extreme, but for just this reason they articulate a distinctive Central European notion of culture with great clarity. There was a conflict of class ideals between Lenau and the populist spokesman Duden. Both were Romantics, but from different ends of the social scale. Duden's utopia was a Romantic idyll of the little man, quietly sitting in his newly built farm home and enjoying a peaceful life of communion with nature. Lenau was in quest of a heroic way of life, which he found completely lacking in the same Midwestern cultural terrain.

At almost the same moment that Lenau was trying to settle in Ohio, another young nobleman was making a tour that took him to the Oklahoma Territory. Count Albert Pourtalès went in the company of his English tutor, a Hartford insurance executive, and the writer Washington Irving. It was a motley group, and their inexperience lent a comic flavor to their misadven-

24. Lenau to Emilie and Georg von Reinbeck, Lisbon, Ohio, March 5, 1833, in Nikolaus Lenau, *Werke und Briefe*, vol. 5: *Briefe 1812–1837*, part 1: *Text*, ed. Hartmut Steinecke and András Vizkelety et al. (Vienna, 1989), 235–236.
25. Lenau to Joseph Klemm, Lisbon, Ohio, March 6, 1833, in ibid., 244.
26. "Der Indianerzug" and "Die Drei Indianer" in Lenau, *Lenaus Werke*, 102–107.

tures on the frontier. All four wrote down their impressions of the visit. With strong personalities and dislikes for one another that resulted in unusually frank testimony, they permit us to compare American, English, and Continental attitudes toward Indians in a single time and place.

Pourtalès's biography demonstrates the difficulty of pinning a national label on aristocrats whose identities were sometimes intensely local, sometimes cosmopolitan. He was born in Paris in 1812.[27] His father, Count Friedrich Pourtalès, was the grandchild of a Huguenot refugee who emigrated from southern France to Neuchâtel in 1720 and in 1751 was elevated by Frederick the Great to the nobility. He saw service first in the Prussian and later in the Napoleonic army, and in 1810 was made a count of the Napoleonic Empire; the next year he married Marie de Castellane-Norante, a lady-in-waiting of the empress, whose parents had lost their lives in the French Revolution. After 1814 the family returned to Prussia; in later years, from 1840 to 1853, the father served as master of ceremonies to the Berlin court. An aristocratic family, to be sure, but an agile one that rose by steering its loyalties to its best advantage. "Nobility" signified not just ancestry, but also the prize for survival skills throughout the Revolutionary and Napoleonic years.

Albert was educated in Geneva, then in Berlin; he entered the diplomatic service, serving in England beginning in 1838, in Constantinople, and in Naples. While serving in Constantinople he made the most of his exotic post, riding by horseback to the farthest provinces of the Ottoman Empire. Back in Germany from 1844 to 1848, he married a daughter of the distinguished Bethmann-Hollweg family, and transformed himself from a rake into a pious Christian. In Berlin at the time of the Revolution of 1848, he disguised himself as a coachman, drove the royal couple out of the castle, and then served as official companion to the Prussian prince on his flight to England. He was rewarded with the appointment of ambassador to France. Later he opposed Bismarck (also in diplomatic service at the time) over Prussian policy in the Crimean War, with Bismarck a supporter of Russia, Pourtalès on the side of France and England. The rivalry was as much personal as political between the two men, who were the leading contenders for conservative leadership. The conflict between them came to an end only with Pourtalès's premature death from a heart attack; Bismarck was his successor in Paris.[28]

Between his schooling and his years in diplomatic service, Albert took time

---

27. The biographical description is drawn from the introduction by Hermann Oncken to Albert von Mutius, ed., *Graf Albert Pourtalès. Ein preussisch- deutscher Staatsmann* (Berlin, 1933), 9ff.
28. On the Pourtalès–Bismarck rivalry see ibid., 41.

out for a two-year tour of America. His companion was Charles Joseph Latrobe, an Englishman, who later entered the British diplomatic corps and served in the West Indies and Australia.[29] Two chance meetings led to an opportunity to go to the Oklahoma Territory. When Pourtalès and Latrobe departed from France in May 1832, one of their shipboard companions was Washington Irving, returning to America after years abroad. The three men did some touring in New England and New York together and struck up a friendship on a steamboat with Henry Leavitt Ellsworth, an insurance executive from Hartford, Connecticut, recently appointed one of three commissioners to the Indians in the Oklahoma Territory. Ellsworth invited the three young men to go with him on a trip to Oklahoma; they took up the offer and traveled via Cincinnati and Louisville to St. Louis, where they visited with William Clark and saw the recently captured Sauk and Fox leader Black Hawk before continuing south to Fort Gibson, Oklahoma.[30]

Ellsworth's mission was the difficult one of judging how to create peace among the different Indian peoples forced into the area by settler pressure and American policy. Under pressure from the Chouteau family (which dominated the Midwestern fur trade from its home in St. Louis) and the American government, Osages began moving into and came into conflict with the Cherokees; Delawares and Cherokees had already settled there; after the Indian Removal Act of May 1830, other immigrant groups too began streaming in.[31] Ellsworth and the two other commissioners were supposed to adjudicate among the existing tribes and prepare the way for more waves of exiles, easing the competition for resources that the federal government itself had created.

To prepare for the Oklahoma adventure, Pourtalès had himself outfitted in buckskin in St. Louis. He wrote from there to his mother that he was "overjoyed at the prospect of realizing all I have hoped for on this trip: visiting the Indians, seeing them in their meetings and assemblies, watching them dance, joining them in buffalo hunts, killing bears with a carbine. I am about to die of excitement."[32] Hunting, of course, was one of the chief attraction of the trip. He imagined the easy kills of the hunter's paradise:

The Indians are perfectly willing to welcome us with all the festivities imaginable: one of their ceremonies consists of a hunt. They surround a field, and buffalo, bear, deer,

29. For biographical details, see the editor's introduction to Albert-Alexandre de Pourtalès, *On the Western Tour with Washington Irving. The Journal and Letters of Count de Pourtalès*, ed. George F. Spaulding, trans. Seymour Feiler (Norman, Okla., 1968), 4ff.
30. Editor's introduction, ibid., 4–12.
31. See Brad Agnew, *Fort Gibson: Terminal on the Trail of Tears* (Norman, Okla., 1980).
32. Pourtalès, letter to his mother, September 14, 1832, *Western Tour*, 21.

moose, hares, rabbit, wildcat, and wolves are driven out in front of us "diplomats." We shall be able to kill them with no danger to ourselves. My mouth watered when I heard the agents and Governor Clarke [sic] of Missouri describe their magnificent hunts.[33]

Early in the expedition, Pourtalès and Latrobe branched off from the main party and tried to ride out to catch up with a party of Osages on their way to the fall buffalo hunt. The rangers warned them of the dangers of losing the trail and of running into hostile Pawnees, but the count was not to be stopped, and his guardian felt obliged to go with him. A few hours later they came back, unable to find their way alone. At one point Pourtalès saw a flock of birds, misfired, and swore so loud that he frightened the birds away. Fortunately, one of his servants had gone out on his own and brought down a deer, which the hungry group was able to eat "with joy, happiness, pleasure, and voluptuousness."[34]

Real Indians did not disappoint him. The Osages were nearing the end of an extraordinary era of commercial and territorial empire building. In the early seventeenth century, Osages had moved from the forests of the lower Ohio River to the prairies and plains of the Mississippi Valley, Oklahoma, and Arkansas.[35] There they became aggressive commercial hunters and traders, serving as especially successful suppliers to the French.[36] A resilient clan organization and a competitive warrior culture allowed them to balance personal dynamism and political cohesion.

After a group of Osage horsemen joined their party, Pourtalès wrote: "The latter, with whom we are going hunting, are really the best people in the world. They are hospitable, generous and love the whites with all their hearts. I have eagerly begun to learn their language. I am assured that I shall be able to understand it and even speak it within two weeks."[37] Pourtalès's fondness for them did not lessen over the course of the trip. A way of life without the baggage of civilization (it escaped his notice that they were dependent on a cash economy) elated him, as did the hunter's alternation between feast and famine.[38] He dreamed of settling among them and uniting with them against the Americans, "those commercial Thebans of the New World," while gently civilizing them by teaching them the arts of agriculture and winning them to Catholicism, "a necessary bridge between barbarism and the civilized state in

33. Ibid., 21–22.
34. Pourtalès, journal of October 16, 1832, ibid., 54.
35. Willard H. Rollings, *The Osage: An Ethnohistorical Study of Hegemony on the Prairie-Plains* (Columbia and London, 1992), 1ff.
36. Rollings, *The Osage*, 5–10.
37. Pourtalès, letter to his mother, Oct. 9, 1832, *Western Tour*, 37.
38. Pourtalès, journal of Oct. 17, 1832, *Western Tour*, 56.

which we find Europe today."[39] Afterward, aboard the steamboat *Cavalier* on the Missisippi below Memphis, Tennessee, he thought back nostalgically to his days of freedom:

Give me the Osages and the wilderness a thousand times rather than the inhabitants of the Mississippi. I miss my complete independence among the Indians and the constant interest aroused in me by their customs, which are so different from ours. I miss their great hospitality, which does not subject us to any of the annoying duties that civilization imposes upon us. I know of no more agreeable way for a young man to spend his time than to lead the solitary and adventurous life that I have had these last two months, and which I am impatient to resume next year.[40]

While Oklahoma was a place of freedom for Pourtalès, it placed insuperable constraints on the Osages. After vastly expanding their territory and their political and economic influence, they were now buffeted between the immigrants thrust into the region. Their prosperity faltered and their political organization disintegrated as the United States forced them in a series of treaties to give up their lands. Smallpox, cholera, and other epidemic diseases further weakened them in the 1830s.[41] Pourtalès was an unknowing witness to a moment of historical tragedy as the Osages fell from mastery of the Plains to reservation confinement.

As for Ellsworth – forty-one at the time, a Yale man and the son of a judge – he took his responsibilities seriously, and he took a serious view of Pourtalès's wild behavior. At the end of the tour he set down his reactions in a letter to his wife. When Pourtalès tried to join the Osage buffalo hunters, Ellsworth was beside himself over his recklessness but also a little relieved to think that he might not come back. The young aristocrat's behavior had already scandalized the commissioner:

After Pourteles [sic] had left us, I entered fully into the examination of his conduct, and told Mr. Irving that I rejoiced that he was not considered as Mr. Ellsworth ['s, eds.] party – His passions led him to great extreemes [sic] – His conduct at the Union mission was censureable in the highest degree – Stimulated by the example of Col Chouteau, he attempted to seduce an amiable young indian girl at that school – the mother had been won by presents, and went to talk with Mr. *Vail,* the wife of the superintendent, about the matter, & see whether the girl might go – what presumption! indignation and refusal, ought to have covered the Swiss gentleman [with?, eds.] shame – There were other instances of misconduct more gross, but I will not pollute my pages with a recital of them....[42]

39. Ibid., journal of Oct. 21, 1832, 62, 63.   40. Ibid., Dec. 6, 1832, 81–82.
41. Rollings, *The Osage,* 11ff., 220ff., 233ff, 267–268, 273–274, 279, 281.
42. Henry Leavitt Ellsworth, *Washington Irving on the Prairie: or, A Narrative of a Tour of the Southwest in the Year 1832,* ed., Stanley T. William and Barbara D. Simison (New York, 1937), 13–14. For biographical background, I have drawn on the editors' introduction, vii–xviii.

But this was not the end of girl trouble. Pourtalès returned, and later he connived with the servants to bring an Osage woman to his tent, over Ellsworth's warning to the servants that "they should not act as imps" (in the end, all Pourtalès got was three Osage bowls and a buffalo skin).[43] Ellsworth didn't lack a sense of humor when the antics were less offensive. One evening three Osages sang and drummed on their bellies for them, a performance the count then imitated: "[W]e laughed heartily, and Mr. Pourteles began to pra [c]tice – and ever and anon, he would strike up an Indian song & rub, a dub, dub, on his belly – He even got so completely master of the art as to imitate the natives drum, with much accuracy. . . ."[44] Puzzled, amused, and angered, Ellsworth concluded that "his conduct cannot be justified, & he will later in life, look back upon his western follies (to say the least) with shame. . . ."[45]

Controlling Indians was no easier than taming an aristocrat. Of the Osage camp, where women, children, the elderly, and the weak stayed while the warriors were on the buffalo hunt, he wrote, "Never did I see such a *dirty disgusting* set of beings. . . ." The reaction probably had something to do with the reception they gave him:

There were many of them, naked – several little boys 13 years old came out before us, and when I was addressing them and urging them to peace & not to fight the pawnees, or steal horses, and provoke revenge; these little boys made water before all the women, and even *upon* some of them, laughing, heartily to show us how they could, wet the folks around by their jet. . . .[46]

"You should understand," commented Pourtalès on the same scene,

that the Lord Commissioner is one of those good old philanthropists, one of those peaceful and calm Yankee republicans who, devoted to his cause like a prophet of old, imagined that peace would follow immediately and that the Indians would shake hands, would establish Plato's Atlantis, the living Utopia, and would retrace the era of the Golden Age for corrupt man.[47]

Young though he was, the count had no trouble understanding that stopping warfare between the Osages and Pawnees would take more than pious speeches. Compared to Ellsworth, who completely failed in his business (he and the other two commissioners quarreled over their recommendations, and after two years the whole commission was dissolved without achieving any results), he already had the makings of a diplomat who could contend with difficult foreign posts.

Worldly wise Washington Irving published his impressions of the Oklahoma tour. His motives for going were different from Pourtalès's or Ellsworth's; after a long stay in Europe, he needed to ingratiate himself with the

43. Ibid., 21.   44. Ibid., 22.   45. Ibid., 67.   46. Ibid., 18.   47. Pourtalès, *Western Tour*, 46–47.

American public. He tried to entertain his readers with exotic imagery. The Osages "had fine Roman countenances, and broad deep chests; and, as they generally wore their blankets wrapped round their loins, so as to leave the bust and arms bare, they looked like so many noble bronze figures." What Irving admired in the Osages was their cultural purity. "They have not," he wrote, "yielded sufficiently, as yet, to the influence of civilization to lay by their simple Indian garb, or to lose the habits of the hunter and the warrior; and their poverty prevents their indulging in much luxury of apparel."[48] On the other hand, the sight of cultural mixture on the frontier left him disgusted: "There was a sprinkling of trappers, hunters, half-breeds, creoles, negroes of every hue; and all that other rabble rout of nondescript beings that keep about the frontiers, between civilized and savage life, as those equivocal birds, the bat, hover about the confines of light and darkness."[49] The party could not head out without hiring two of them, Antoine Deshetres and Pierre Billet, to serve as hunter and guide. One he called a "little vagabond" without a country, the other a member of the "uncertain and faithless race" of "half-breeds." (Actually, both, according to the editor of his narrative, probably came from fully French families.)[50] Irving detected, and resented, the native guide's sense of superiority to the dilettantes as they left the security of the fort; his urbanity gave way to annoyance as the powers of colonial master and servant were reversed.[51] Pourtalès may have been adolescent in his admiration for the Osages, but he showed a frank adventurousness, too, that contrasted with Irving's anxieties in a world that his fame and gentility did not suffice to bring under control. Pourtalès felt no affinity for white settlers; he enjoyed the Osages not because of their Roman countenances but because they were good hunting companions. His attitudes were those of a prenationalist conservative who was happy to ride with fellow aristocrats, whatever their local origin.

As for Latrobe, he had a saturnine view of both Indians and white settlers. The independence of the Osages and the civilized achievements of the Cherokees impressed him, but on the whole he thought Indian life was violent, disease-ridden, and unhappy, and had been so even before the time of Columbus. Europeans had brought even greater misery on them, however, and had shown bad faith since their first days in the New World. Current American policy seemed to him well intentioned, but it still added up to expatriation that sent Indians to destruction amid vicious agents and traders and naive missionaries. He captured the difficulty of Ellsworth's mission when he wrote that the federal government occasionally sent out men of character, but

---

48. Washington Irving, *A Tour on the Prairies,* ed. and introd. John F. McDermott (Norman, Okla., 1956), 22.
49. Ibid.   50. Ibid., 14, 23–25.   51. Ibid., 28.

they were personally inexperienced in Indian affairs and dependent on the very frontier people who were part of the problem.[52] Sober and analytical, Latrobe had the makings of a good colonial administrator without the dare-devil quality that carried his charge to a higher historical role.

Pourtalès's Western tour was not as frivolous as it appeared to Ellsworth. If other gentlemen cultivated an air of traditional refinement by going to Rome for their grand tour, he preferred to test his courage among the buf-faloes. His ardor for the hunt and his pooh-poohing of danger were the same qualities he would later put to good use in defending the monarchy. His was the derring-do of the nineteenth-century aristocrat who did not hesitate to beat back the movement of history that mere professors and businessmen thought inevitable in 1848. Pourtalès was not alone in his Romantic excesses: his rival Bismarck, too, cultivated a reputation as a wild Junker before under-going his own conversion experience and settling down with a pious wife. The Romantic high spirits of the two aristocrats carried over into the politi-cal confidence that steered Prussia and later Germany onto a conservative course.

While Pourtalès's tour had the appearance of a young man's romp through the West, other aristocrats made earnest scientific expeditions. One of the most ambitious was Duke Paul Wilhelm of Württemberg, a professional sol-dier and skilled naturalist, who made repeated tours of the Mississippi and Missouri valleys. Born in 1797, Paul Wilhelm was a nephew of King Friedrich I of Württemberg. This was a region almost synonymous with enlightened liberalism. Paul Wilhelm was trained for a military career, but he also received a broad education in the sciences and language.[53] After beginning a career in the army, he decided instead to follow his scientific interests. In 1822 he began his first voyage, traveling from Hamburg to New Orleans, where he arrived on December 20. After spending two weeks there he traveled to Cuba, then returned to New Orleans a month later and traveled up the Mississippi, departing from North America in 1824. In 1829, two years after marrying, he made a second voyage of three years to Mexico and the American West, and then remained at home to classify and arrange his specimens. From Septem-ber 1839 to August 1840 he took part in an Egyptian expedition sponsored by Mahomet Ali to explore the upper Nile. On a third American voyage begin-ning in 1849 he went from western Texas into Mexico, returned to New

52. Charles Joseph Latrobe, *The Rambler in North America: 1832–1833* (London, 1835), 1: 160–171.
53. This biographical sketch is drawn from Louis C. Butscher, "A Brief Biography of Prince Paul Wilhelm of Württemberg (1797–1860)," in *New Mexico Historical Review* 17 (1942): 181–225.

Orleans, went up the Mississippi, over to Mormon country, spent 1852 in the eastern United States, explored South America in 1853, returned to the United States in 1854 and 1855, and finally went back to Germany in 1856. In 1857 he visited the United States once more and in the following year set off for Australia, Ceylon, the Middle East, and Greece before returning to Stuttgart.[54] In his own lifetime, newspapers in New Orleans, which he used as his home during his crisscrossings of the North American continent, and in his native Württemberg regularly reported on his adventures. Scientific journals and newspapers took note of his achievements (in particular his collection of 8,000 bird skins) after his death in 1860.[55]

The first expedition of a lifetime traveler had the freshness of a *Bildungsreise* in which Paul Wilhelm cast off his attachment to the comforts of civilization and discovered his calling as a traveler. Paul Wilhelm was an admirer of Anglo-American expansion. Although critical of other settlers, he found the Kentuckians to be industrious, persistent, and excellent riflemen. "The inhabitants of Kentucky," he wrote, "still live in such intimate contact with their forest and the wilderness that one need not fear that this vigorous breed of men will lose their bold and attractive manly spirit."[56] General William Clark, Lewis's partner on the famous transcontinental expedition and Superintendent of Indian Affairs, struck him as the epitome of an enlightened administrator. On meeting him in 1823, Paul Wilhelm commented:

His entire effort aims at reconciling the aborigines with the new immigrants, and by a generous and sane behavior of the latter toward their often very unhappy red brothers, to blot out, as much as possible, that stain so sadly blemishing the history of former centuries and the occupation of America.[57]

At the end of his narrative, Paul Wilhelm thanked the people and government of the New World that had received him with generosity and friendship.[58]

Paul Wilhelm recorded many scenes of the fallen state of American Indians, contrasting them with their past prowess. Arriving in New Orleans in the fall of 1822, he wrote:

---

54. Ibid., 185–187; P. Stälin, "Paul," in *Allgemeine Deutsche Biographie* (1887; Berlin, 1970), 25: 243–244.

    For biographical background, see also the valuable introduction by Savoie Lottinville to Paul Wilhelm, Duke of Württemberg, *Travels in North America 1822–1824*, trans. W. Robert Nitske (Norman, Okla., 1973); and John Francis McDermott, "The Reconstruction of a 'Lost' Archive: The Diaries and Sketches of Prince Paul Wilhelm of Württemberg," in *Manuscripts* 30 (1978): 167–178.

55. On the contemporary reports on Paul Wilhelm, see the valuable unpublished biographical manuscript by Betty Alderton Spahn ("Foreword for Duke Paul's Trip from St. Louis to Ft. Laramie, 1851"), Research Collections, Southern Illinois University at Edwardsville, 2–3, 17.

56. Paul Wilhelm, *Travels*, 163.   57. Ibid., 181.   58. Ibid., 412–413.

Of the aborigines one sees only sad remnants in single families of Choctaws and Creeks wandering around town half-naked and ragged, selling trophies of the hung and woven mats and baskets. Reeking of filth, full of vermin and usually drunk, these repulsive survivors of once mighty tribes now exhibit scarcely any signs of their nationality except the color of their skin. So degraded have they become that the most careful and keenest observer strains in vain to discover anything of a national characteristic which might remind him of their powerful forefathers.[59]

Going up the Mississippi, he passed Natchez and recalled the war of extermination there. "This horrible lot," he commented, "was in no way deserved by the unfortunate Natchez, since they belonged to the better and the more civilized Indians on the North American continent, and since the most unheard-of act of cruelty had forced them into war against their oppressors."[60] On his continuing journey upstream, he observed yet another reminder of tragedy in May 1823 at the intersection of the Mississippi and Kaskaskia rivers. A Delaware Indian, "wrapped in rags and riding a wretched horse, brought a fallow deer, which he offered to sell."[61] He and his companion "revealed but little of a proud and warlike people which distinguished this mighty nation half a century ago."[62] The Indians at trading stations, too, he commented, would give travelers a false impression of native peoples.[63]

In Saint Louis he had a chance to begin closer observation of Indians. On the second day after his arrival, Clark told him that he was expecting a visit from Junaw-sche Wome (Stream of the Rock), a Potawatomi leader, and some of his most prominent warriors. The Potawatomis exemplified how much cultural mixing could take place between settlers and neighbors under favorable circumstances. During the eighteenth century, French and Potawatomis had been faithful allies and frequently intermarried; as late as the 1820s, Potawatomis continued to look to French traders as models of success. Anglo-American settlers poured into the Lower Great Lakes in the early nineteenth century and began driving them out of their homes; a steady process of treaty negotiations began in 1816 and culminated in the expulsion of the Potawatomis from their territories east of the Mississippi by the end of the 1830s. Although they showed a remarkable capacity for cultural borrowing and renewal in the later nineteenth century, Paul Wilhelm met them at a moment of demoralization.[64]

---

59. Ibid., 33.   60. Ibid., 135.   61. Ibid., 175.   62. Ibid.   63. Ibid., 184, 185.
64. See R. David Edmunds, "Potawatomi," in *Encyclopedia of North American Indians*, ed. Frederick E. Hoxie (New York and Boston, 1996), 506–508; and Edmunds, *The Potawatomis: Keepers of the Fire* (Norman, Okla., 1978). See also the discussions in Helen H. Tanner, ed., *Atlas of Great Lakes Indian History* (Norman, Okla., and London, 1987), esp. 138–139 and 178–179.

On learning that they were encamped outside the town, he hurried over to see them and found them dressing and making their preparations for their meeting the next day. He recorded mixed impressions of filth ("The Potawatomis belong to the dirtiest tribe that I have ever seen") and tasteful, finely worked decorations, of sinister facial expressions and great suffering.[65] The duke accompanied them as they walked through the streets of St. Louis to their meeting with General Clark, earnest and indifferent to the gawking crowd that followed them. During their interview they subdued their feelings:

> The Chief delivered a long and well composed speech concerning the sad condition of his tribe. Complaining especially bitterly about the decrease of game, their most important food supply, due to existing hunting privileges, he begged the General to take appropriate measures against the complete destruction of game and fish along the tributaries of the Illinois. Although the very life of the wild one was at stake, I could not, despite the closest scrutiny, observe the least trace of passion in his face. From the beginning to the end of his speech, the Chief did not pronounce a single word more emphatically than any other.[66]

The general promised to satisfy their demand as much as possible and the delegation left, apparently satisfied. Yet when Paul Wilhelm spoke to them afterward, they shared with him their despair. In contrast to his stolid behavior during the interview, Junaw-sche Wome was moved to tears as he described his people's impending ruin.[67] The Potawatomis were an impoverished group and received only modest gifts from the European settlers, in contrast to some Osages, who happened to be in town to purchase hunting supplies for the coming season. The Potawatomis, he noted, seem to be afraid of the Osages, and by nightfall all had crossed the Mississippi back to Illinois.[68]

In June 1823 Paul Wilhelm went to visit Osages near the river bearing their name. While not fully aware of the rapid modifications their culture had already undergone, he was sensitive to the current challenges to their way of life. European settlement was already encroaching on them, he noted, even though they still were prospering. Commenting on their victories over almost all the surrounding peoples, he wrote that the Osages "won their victories almost always in the open field. Endowed by nature with striking size and bodily strength, the Osages, mounted on their spirited horses, despised every kind of treacherous attack by which, especially in small wars, the cunning savage seeks to gain victory." He admired, too, their skills at social organization: "Obeying the authority of his chiefs and the counsels of his old men, he

---

65. Paul Wilhelm, *Travels,* 190–191.   66. Ibid., 192–193.   67. Ibid., 193–194.
68. Ibid., 194–195.

acquires with surprising ease the advantages which accrue to a regulated society, and it would not be easy to find an Indian nation to whom the bonds of social union are as dear and holy as to the Osages."[69] Not all of the native people he met won over Paul Wilhelm. He admired the Osages, however, as *Herrenmenschen* who shared the manly qualities that he himself asserted through the very act of traveling.

If we compare the overall shape of the French and German discussions of North America in the first half of the nineteenth century, national patterns emerge. The nostalgic tenor of French travel writing had no exact counterpart across the Rhine, for America was a former colony for the French, a site of contemporary immigration for the Germans. A debate developed in Central Europe between populist writers, who praised America's plentiful soil and freedom from Old World overlordship, and the educated writers who resented America's attractiveness to the masses and replied to the America boosters that material gain came at the cost of one's soul.

At the upper end of the social hierarchy, however, there was a convergence between French and German travel writers. Aristocrats of both countries turned the journey to America into a symbolic quest to test their own wild qualities through contact with the nature and natives of an untamed continent.

Chateaubriand daydreamed of throwing a bearskin over his shoulders and returning to his "Iroquois wigwam" even while serving as ambassador to Britain in 1822 and getting dressed to meet the king.[70] Tocqueville took out precious weeks of his American journey to see authentic natives. Pourtalès and Paul Wilhelm sought out the Osages.[71] Again and again, these incidents marked a mutual recognition of nobility in which European visitors demonstrated their ability to socialize with native leaders, to win their respect, and to receive gestures of kinship or acknowledgment of comparable social standing. The memory of such meetings could still inspire acts of showmanship in the early twentieth century. When Marshall Foch visited the United States in 1921, he made a stop at Crow Agency, Montana, where he was photographed with the Crow leader, Plenty Coups.[72] And on the German side, a colorful adventurer who had served as a naval captain in World War I and styled him-

69. Ibid., 238–239.
70. François-René de Chateaubriand, *Mémoires d'outre tombe* (1849; Paris, 1951), 1: 252–253.
71. See also Paul Wilhelm's description of the hospitality of Wakansare, a noted Kansa leader, who sought him out as a close brother of great chiefs across the great sea. Paul Wilhelm, *Travels*, 281.
72. See Frederick E. Hoxie, *Parading Through History: The Making of the Crow Nation in America, 1805–1935* (Cambridge and New York, 1995), 347. "The hero of World War I," comments Hoxie, "had come to see his friend and fellow warrior!"

self a count, Felix Graf von Luckner, recounted his meeting with an Indian and fellow warrior in Yosemite Park.[73] Such encounters dramatized travelers' martial qualities for European audiences.

These incidents remained fleeting gestures of mutual acknowledgment, asserting a shared aristocratic culture that crossed countries and continents. Few European travelers stayed long enough in one place for more serious knowledge of the peoples they met. One German did tarry, however, who had the patience, training, and ambition to make a serious study of native peoples. We turn next to Prince Maximilian of Wied, writer of the first scientific ethnography of Plains Indians.

73. Felix Graf von Luckner, *Seeteufel erobert Amerika* (Leipzig, 1928), 265–267.

6

⊲ ════════════════════════════════ ▷

Maximilian of Wied and the
Ethnography of Native Aristocrats

In the late eighteenth and early nineteenth centuries, Germans developed a distinctive tradition of scientific travel. This achievement belongs to the era's larger renaissance of German culture. As Friedrich Schlegel wrote in his essay on the world traveler Georg Forster (who had accompanied Captain Cook on his second world voyage), *Bildung*, or education, was undergoing a transformation in meaning from book learning to encounter with the world. When Schlegel urged the example of Forster on his contemporaries, he was advising what they were already practicing. Travel could follow familiar routes, such as Goethe's Italian journey, or it could strike out on exotic paths, such as Forster's voyage to Polynesia and Antarctica.[1]

An educator to generations of travelers was Johann Friedrich Blumenbach, professor of medicine at the University of Göttingen (like many early contributors to anthropology, he was a physician by training). He himself did not leave Europe, but he systematically read through all the travel literature available in the Göttingen library; he was also a collector who gathered artifacts (including part of the collection from the Cook voyages) and brought order into Göttingen's ethnographic collection. During the period of his greatest influence, from the 1780s to the 1800s, he was a leading figure in European science who met Sir Joseph Banks on a visit to London in 1791 and was welcomed by the scientific elite of Paris and by Napoleon himself during a visit of 1806. As a scientific entrepreneur, he linked the burgeoning interest in travel to university learning and powerful patrons.

1. Georg Forster, *Werke. Sämtliche Schriften, Tagebücher, Briefe*, ed. Gerhard Steiner, vol. 1: *A Voyage Round the World*, ed. Robert L. Kahn (Berlin, 1968); Goethe, *Italienische Reise*, 3 vols. (Frankfurt, 1976).

In Blumenbach's anthropological paradigm, mankind was a unified species but contained five distinctive races. The Caucasian was historically the original man and enjoyed, according to Blumenbach, "the most exemplary skull and facial form according to European conceptions of beauty."[2] The other races were degenerate forms that had fallen away from the European norm under the influence of climate and other environmental factors. This was an ambiguous theory that joined monogenism to justification for the superiority of Europeans to non-European peoples. Travelers could pursue either its racialist or its humanist implications. Students of American Indians, if they were looking for a justification for their work, could point to Blumenbach's view that they had not strayed far from the European norm.[3] One could view them as a distinctive type, interesting and worthy of respect.[4]

Blumenbach's most famous student was Alexander von Humboldt. His voyage through the Americas from 1799 to 1804 combined scientific discipline and Romantic appreciation of nature in a fashion that held a peculiar fascination for the imagination of the nineteenth century; there seemed to be something larger than life about his South American journey, giving him a stature for Germans that can only be compared to that of Captain Cook in the English-speaking world. Indeed, for Germans, he combined the roles of Cook and Sir Joseph Banks. Like Cook he was able to make an expedition through a strange and difficult part of the world, a task requiring character and scientific skill. Like Banks he was a master naturalist with an astonishingly wide range of knowledge of the sciences of his age; and just as Banks became head of the Royal Society in England, Humboldt was one of the great organizer-entrepreneurs of Continental science, first in Paris, where he lived for decades, and later in Berlin. Both in the field and in the metropolis, Humboldt exemplified an unprecedented scientific mastery of the world.[5]

2. Johann Friedrich Blumenbach, *Handbuch der Naturgeschichte,* 12th ed. (Göttingen, 1830), 56.
3. Blumenbach, *Handbuch der Naturgeschichte,* 58.
4. For example, an anonymous commentary from 1837 turned to Blumenbach in their defense: "Die Indianer sind die besten Repräsentanten der Menschenrace, welche Blumenbach die amerikanische nennt.... Sind die Indianer auch nicht den ritterlichen Helden der europäischen Vorzeit ähnlich, mit denen sie einige Schriftsteller vergleichen, oder die sentimentalen Naturkinder, für die sie andere ausgeben, so zeigen sie sich doch als ein interessantes und kräftiges Geschlecht, dessen Erhaltung und Ausbildung wir mit allen Menschenfreunden innigst wünschen." *Das Westland. Nordamerikanische Zeitschrift für Deutschland* (Heidelberg, 1837), 1: 173, 181.
5. For a recent appreciation of Humboldt's work that describes its scientific importance and political context, see Michael Dettelbach, "Global Physics and Aesthetic Empire: Humboldt's Physical Portrait of the Tropics," in David Philip Miller and Peter Hanns Reill, eds., *Visions of Empire: Voyages, Botany, and Representations of Nature* (Cambridge and New York, 1996), 258–292.

Humboldt's writings combined exact measurement with Romantic philosophy. The work that preceded the actual narrative of the voyage, and that perhaps in the end made the greater impact on his contemporaries, was a series of lectures, *Views of Nature (Ansichten der Natur)*. A mystical philosophy of organic connection between man and nature entered into Humboldt's writing as he tried to capture how the human soul mirrored the surrounding landscapes:

The things that give a landscape its character – the outline of the mountains, defining the horizon in the misty distance; the darkness of the fir forest; the forest stream raging as it falls over extended cliffs – all of them stand in an ancient, secret intercourse with the soul of man.[6]

He praised those authors such as Forster, Goethe, Buffon, Bernardin de St. Pierre, and Chateaubriand who had already linked nature and moral character in their writings. His work went beyond theirs by proposing typical landscapes that could, in turn, be viewed as the formative settings for cultures around the globe. A kind of geographic determinism, then, could guide the observer, helping him to grasp Southern and Northern cultures – indeed a finely graded variety of types, for Humboldt proposed sixteen climatic zones – as part of a global environmental schema.[7]

Humboldt wished the traveler to convey to his readers the total impression of a place. Yet the attempt to duplicate one's experience of a totality was frustrated by the fragmentary nature of language itself, for the diversity of nature could be captured only in a succession of linguistic moments.[8] The visual artist, believed Humboldt, could grasp more adequately the constellation of elements that one intuitively sensed to be Swiss nature or an Italian sky.[9] While art did not replace the work of scientific analysis, it provided an indispensable complement to it, crowning the succession of scientific observations with a unifying artistic vision.[10] Humboldt's personal heroism and international prestige merged with the scientific and aesthetic achievement of his writings to provide an inspiring example of travel as a vocation with its own method and mission.

The traveler who extended Blumenbach's theorizing and Humboldt's example of scientific travel to the interior of North America was Prince Alexander Philipp Maximilian of Wied-Neuwied (1782–1867). Following a route simi-

---

6. Alexander von Humboldt, *Ansichten der Natur, mit wissenschaftlichen Erläuterungen*, 3rd ed. (1807; Stuttgart and Tübingen, 1849), 252–253.
7. Ibid., 16, 18–20.   8. Ibid., viii–ix.   9. Ibid., 16–17, 26.
10. There are illuminating discussions of Humboldt's artistic and scientific synthesis in Bernard Smith, *European Vision and the South Pacific* (New Haven and London, 1985), 4, 202–212.

lar to that of Paul Wilhelm on his first visit, Maximilian traveled up the Missouri River and made an extended stay among the agricultural villages of the Upper Missouri in 1833–1834. His own account of the voyage has been almost overwhelmed by the splendid visual record of the artist he took along, Karl Bodmer, whose paintings and sketches, together with those of George Catlin and Alfred Jacob Miller, have done much to fix the modern image of Plains Indians. Yet Maximilian firmly shaped his artist's vision. As for his own writing, his rigorous and detailed empiricism may at first seem flat, yet on closer examination it too reveals a Romantic perspective that matches Bodmer's brilliant brush.

Maximilian's family ruled a tiny Rhineland territory at the intersection of European political conflict and economic development. During the seventeenth and eighteenth centuries his ancestors invited Lutherans, Calvinists, Catholics, and Jews to settle Neuwied and turn it into a town of flourishing crafts and manufacturing. The French Revolution and its aftermath exposed the territory to the contradictory ideological forces of the age as émigrés, Jacobins, and Napoleonic armies marched through. At the Congress of Vienna Neuwied and the surrounding territories were handed over to Prussia, but the princely family retained its offices and privileges. Neuwied soon became one of the liveliest economic centers of the Rhineland again, humming with modern industry, agriculture, and commerce. Maximilian's many siblings – he was the eighth of ten children – cultivated good relations with Prussia, as well as with their Nassau neighbors.[11]

Maximilian was heir to both the military traditions and the cultivation of the arts and sciences that flourished in his parents' home. From childhood he was interested in the natural sciences, but in 1802 he entered Prussian military service, took part in the battle of Jena, and was imprisoned on October 28, 1806, near Prenzlau. Released from prison, he retired to Neuwied and dedicated himself to the study of geography, natural history, and ethnography. During the winter semester of 1811–1812 he studied with Blumenbach at the University of Göttingen.[12] In 1813 he returned to Prussian military service and entered Paris with the victorious monarchs.[13]

When peace finally made it possible for Maximilian to pursue his scientific

---

11. Philipp Wirtgen, *Neuwied und seine Umgebung,* rev. 2nd ed., ed. Rudolf Blenke (Neuwied, 1902). On Neuwied in the eighteenth century cf. Franz Petri, Georg Droege, et al., *Rheinische Geschichte,* vol. 2: *Neuzeit* (Düsseldorf, 1976), 300.
12. Bernhard Gondorf, "Die Expedition von Maximilian Prinz zu Wied und Karl Bodmer in das innere Nordamerika," in Ulrich Löber, ed., *Prärie- und Plainsindianer. Die Reise in das innere Nord-America von Maximilian Prinz zu Wied und Karl Bodmer* (Mainz, 1993), 40, 58.
13. The most important synthesis of Maximilian and Bodmer scholarship in English is the magnificently illustrated volume by David C. Hunt, Marsha V. Gallagher, William H. Goetzman, and William J. Orr, *Karl Bodmer's America* (Omaha, Neb., 1984). See especially William H.

ambitions without interruption, he spent two years, from 1815 to 1817, in Brazil. This was a voyage of apprenticeship; Maximilian himself wrote of the difficulty of succeeding Alexander von Humboldt.[14] He followed the lead of his predecessor in his low estimation of the indigenous peoples of tropical America. "Crude insensitivity," he noted, "is . . . a main feature of the savage's character."[15] The work also depended on Blumenbach, whose arguments for the existence of a distinctive North American race he tried to verify.[16] The intensity of his ethnographic observations, however, already set his work apart from the masters'. The second volume opens with a chapter on one people, the Botocudo, which interrupts the narrative flow of his voyage account.[17] He described the history of their conflicts with the Portuguese, their physical features, their unusual custom of distending their lips, their body paint and decorations, their moral character, method of making fire, weapons, swimming skill, hunting techniques, diet, health, migration habits, family life, singing, dancing, death rites, and religion. On the subject of cannibalism, he refuted the general European belief that they regularly consumed human flesh, noting how easy it was to mistake a monkey arm and limiting the instances of cannibalism to acts of revenge.[18] Although horrified by their vengefulness, he recognized that they were capable of more admirable behavior: "If you treat them openly and in good faith, then they often prove in return to be very warm, and even faithful and devoted."[19] The Brazil voyage demonstrated Maximilian's fascination with exotic peoples, ability to live closely with them under difficult conditions, and dedication to close observation.

When he undertook his journey to North America fifteen years later – as on the first voyage, with his private means – it was with a sure sense of his

Goetzman, "Introduction: The Man Who Stopped to Paint America," in ibid., 5ff., which I have relied on for the dates of the travelers' itinerary. For the orthography of Indian names, I have followed the usage in this volume. Löber, ed., *Prärie- und Plainsindianer,* is a valuable recent addition to German scholarship. See also the definitive biography of Bodmer by Hans Läng, *Indianer waren meine Freunde. Leben und Werk Karl Bodmers, 1809–1893* (Bern and Stuttgart, 1976). I have also drawn biographical details from Friedrich Ratzel, "Neuwied: Max Prinz von Wied-N.," in *Allgemeine Deutsche Biographie* (1886; Berlin, 1970), 23: 558–564.

14. Maximilian, Prince of Wied, *Reise nach Brasilien in den Jahren 1815 bis 1817,* 2 vols. and atlas (Frankfurt, 1820), 1: 6.
     For background on the Brazil voyage, see idem., *Unveröffentlichte Bilder und Handschriften zur Völkerkunde Brasiliens,* ed. Josef Röder and Hermann Trimborn with Josefine Huppertz, Udo Oberem, and Karl Viktor Prinz zu Wied (Bonn, 1954).
15. Maximilian, *Reise nach Brasilien,* 1: 146; cf. his remarks on 78.   16. Ibid., 2: 66, 68.
17. Ibid., 2: 1–69. Cf. Alfred Métraux, "The Botocudo," in Julian H. Steward, ed., *Handbook of South American Indians,* vol. 1: *The Marginal Tribes,* Smithsonian Institution, Bureau of American Ethnology, *Bulletin* 143 (New York, 1963), 531–540.
18. Maximilian, *Reise nach Brasilien,* 2: 50–51.   19. Ibid., 2: 16.

own judgment. Volney and others, he wrote, had already provided good physical descriptions of the North American continent. His task as a writer, he continued, was to bring this landscape to life. "Little," he wrote, "has been done in the way of a picturesque description (*der anschaulichen Beschreibung*) of North America's nature, and one can rightfully assert that very few travelers have sketched a clear and vivid image of the latter's natural perspective (*Anschauung*) and qualities."[20] His ambition of bringing a foreign place to life for the reader was Humboldtian. But flora and fauna no longer engulfed the traveler, as they did for Humboldt on his voyage and for Maximilian too in South America. Instead, on "those wide plains, those sad, dreary prairies," the human beings took on new prominence.[21] By focusing on them, Maximilian ended his apprenticeship and set the agenda for his masterpiece.

Arriving in Boston on July 4, 1832, Maximilian visited New York and Phildelphia, traveled through the mountains of Pennsylvania to Pittsburgh, and then headed southwest to New Harmony, Indiana. There he fell sick (from cholera, he suspected) and ended up staying from mid-October 1832 until mid-March 1833. New Harmony was a utopian community but also an outpost of scientific research in the American interior. "Good-hearted Thomas Say," he reported after his trip to the naturalist Charles Bonaparte, "gave us a friendly reception at New Harmony, and we spent four winter months in his warm and instructive vicinity."[22] Say, an entomologist and conchologist, came from a prominent Philadelphia family and was himself a leading member of the Philadelphia Academy of Natural Sciences from the time of its founding in 1812 and of the American Philosophical Society. Before settling in New Harmony in 1825, he served as zoologist on scientific expeditions to the Missouri and Mississippi rivers.[23] Maximilian also made thankful mention of a second naturalist at New Harmony, Charles Alexandre Lesueur, who, he reported to Bonaparte, showered him with care and friendship while he was sick.[24] Lesueur was a widely regarded naturalist in France and the United States. From 1800 to 1804 he served as naturalist on the Baudin expe-

20. Maximilian, Prince of Wied, *Reise in das innere Nord-America in den Jahren 1832 bis 1834* (Koblenz, 1839–1841), 1: viii (hereinafter cited as *Reise*). The double reference to "Anschauung" suggests a way of looking that captures the typical form of natural objects.
21. Ibid., 1: ix.
22. Maximilian to Charles Louis Bonaparte, Neuwied, February, 16, 1835, Muséum National d'Histoire Naturelle, Paris (microfilm, American Philosophical Society).
   Bonaparte, a famous naturalist, had already visited the United States and provided Maximilian with letters of introduction. See ibid. Cf. "Bonaparte, Lucien Jules Laurent," in *Dictionary of Scientific Biography*, ed. Charles C. Gillispie (New York, 1975), 2: 281–283.
23. See "Say, Thomas," in *Dictionary of American Biography* (New York, 1935), 26: 401–402; and "Say, Thomas," in *Dictionary of Scientific Biography*, 12: 132–134.
24. "... lequel m'a accablé de soins et d'amitié lorsque je me trouvais malade." Maximilian to Bonaparte, February 16, 1835.

dition of 1800–1804 to the South Pacific. He arrived in the United States in 1816 and over the succeeding ten years spent much of his time in and around Philadelphia, gathering specimens in the area and playing a leading role in the Academy of Natural Sciences.[25] Besides these guides, Maximilian found an excellent library at New Harmony – a rarity, he noted to Bonaparte, in America.[26] His unplanned stay – a postuniversity fellowship, as it were – permitted him to assimilate the most advanced American learning of his time before proceeding to the crucial part of his journey.

From New Harmony he traveled to St. Louis, arriving there on March 24, 1833. After outfitting himself for the voyage into the interior, he relied on the American Fur Company and the United States government for his passage up the Missouri, traveling on company boats and staying at government forts. He spent the winter of 1833–1834 at Fort Clark, in the immediate vicinity of the villages of the Mandan and Hidatsa Indians. Departing April 14, he steadily made his way back home, traveling along the Ohio Canal and Lake Erie and viewing Niagara Falls before embarking from New York for Europe.

Maximilian did not hesitate to admire, indeed almost to take vicarious pride in Anglo-American expansion. In the opening words of his travel account, the subduing of a continent fills the visitor with wonder:

What gigantic progress has been made in recent years in knowledge of the vast continent of North America! A large part of this land, which just a few years ago was covered with almost unbroken primeval forests and a weakly scattered population of wild savages, has been made over through a mass migration from the Old World into a rich, blossoming state of great significance, largely civilized, and as explored and developed as our old Europe. A most energetic commercial life and an unbound, unlimited industry have brought about these gigantic steps forward for civilization in the United States, a spectacle to leave the onlooker astonished! Extensive prospering cities, with every kind of wonderful and public institution, are quickly erected, and every year adds to the number of place names, so that maps are only useful for a short time. The immigrant population pushes forward in waves, and only the sterility of the Northwest can set a limit to the current that overflows everything in its way.[27]

Like Tocqueville and Paul Wilhelm, Maximilian was not a primitivist of the kind that fled Europe for exotic places later in the nineteenth century; he had

---

25. Maximilian, *Reise* 1: 165, 196–197.
    On Lesueur see R. W. G. Vail, *The American Sketchbooks of Charles Alexandre Lesueur 1816–1837* (Worcester, Mass., 1938); Adrien Loir, *Charles-Alexandre Lesueur, artiste et savant français en Amérique de 1816 à 1839* (Le Havre, 1920); and "Lesueur (Charles-Alexandre)," in *Biographie universelle, ancienne et moderne* (Michaud) nouvelle édition (Paris, 1843–1865), 24: 345–346.
26. Maximilian to Bonaparte, February 16, 1835.   27. Maximilian, *Reise* 1: vii.

no desire to go native. Whatever sympathy he felt for indigenous peoples, he did not hesitate to praise the forces that were overwhelming them.

A world of difference nonetheless sets the second voyage apart from its predecessor. In Brazil, fear and repugnance limited his understanding of the Bodocudos. In North America he searched the bookstores and engraving shops of the big cities for good illustrations of indigenous peoples, only to be frustrated by willful ignorance:

How astonished I was not to be able to get a single usable [i.e., typical] picture of them in any of the big cities of this country, apart from some poor or very mediocre engravings in travel accounts. It is unbelievable how the original American people is hated and neglected by the foreign usurpers.[28]

Before encountering them, he was haunted by their absence; crossing through the Delaware Gap into rural Pennsylvania, he noted that no attempt was made even to preserve the bones and arrowheads of the expelled natives. "It saddened me to the think that not a trace is left of the entire indigenous population in the vast state of Pennsylvania! O land of freedom! !"[29] In New Harmony, too, he was disgusted by the white settlers' destruction of the vestiges of the local indigenous culture. Nobody in New Harmony, he noted, could even tell him the name of the Indian tribe that had lived there just a few decades earlier.[30] Whereas Maximilian had welcomed the work of missionaries and the eradication of native cultures in Brazil, in North America he anticipated the modern anthropologist's melancholy over the destruction of native cultures and the determination to rescue whatever one could for historical memory.

Maximilian was aware that he was observing peoples caught in the grip of rapid, often devastating social and political change. On the Mississippi he witnessed one of the most dramatic episodes of the era, the expulsion of the Sauk and Fox tribes from their lands. Settlers coveted the rich soil of Illinois and had quarreled for decades with the indigenous peoples of the northwestern portion of the state. The long-standing hostility between Sauk and Fox natives and encroaching Anglo-Americans broke out for the last time in the Black Hawk War of 1832, a brief, futile act of indigenous resistance.

The Sauk and Fox were warrior peoples who to the end of the eighteenth century compelled tactful treatment from Europeans. Historically distinct, they had united in opposition to the French. The Sauks were the larger, more prestigious group, numbering about 4,800 in 1804, and were noted for their

28. Ibid., 42.   29. Ibid., 76–77.   30. Ibid., 185.

skill at political organization; the Fox numbered about 1,600.[31] They were peoples used to working closely with settlers; trappers of different nationalities often took wives from families of influential warriors.[32] In 1804 the Sauk and Fox made a peace treaty that the United States understood as ceding a large amount of land, a claim the Sauk and Fox did not recognize. More treaties followed in 1815 and 1816; again the Indians believed that they were making specific peace agreements, while the United States claimed that they were giving up property. One stretch of land in particular around Rock Island, Illinois, was especially coveted by both sides. Violent incidents mounted after 1800 between Sauk and Fox and pioneers. Cautious chiefs temporized; young warriors, eager for glory and social rank, chafed at restraint.[33] The government subagent for the Sauk and Fox wrote in 1826:

The Indians say, that the white peoples [sic] thirst after land is so great, that they are never contented until they have a belly full of it, they compare a white settlement in their neighborhood to a large drop of Raccoons grease falling on a new blanket, the drop at first is scarcely perceptible but in time covers almost the whole blanket.[34]

In the years leading up to the outbreak of war, William Clark treated the Sauk and Fox as especially proud, dangerous negotiating partners. After wrangling to get them to sit down with their Indian enemies, he reported: "Those Sacs and Foxes have more national character than any tribes we have within the Superintendency and a firm and decisive course is necessary to be pursued with them."[35] Clark was confident that the Sauk and Fox would ultimately recognize that they had no choice but to follow the dictates of the American government. The caution of the chiefs made this a reasonable guess, but he underestimated the desperation of peoples who knew that they were on the verge of being driven from their land.[36] In the spring of 1832 a band of about 1,000 Sauk, Fox, and Kickapoo Indians crossed the Mississippi to assert their

31. William T. Hagan, *The Sac and Fox Indians* (Norman, Okla., 1958), 5–8.
32. Ibid., 14–15.
33. See the excellent introduction by Anthony Wallace, "Prelude to Disaster: The course of Indian–White relations which led to the Black Hawk War of 1832," in Ellen M. Whitney, compiler and ed., *The Black Hawk War, 1831–1832,* vol. 1: *Illinois Volunteers* (Springfield, 1970), 16, 20–21, 23–24.
34. Thomas Forsyth to James Barbour, Rock Island [Illinois], June 15, 1826, in National Archives, Letters Received by the Office of Indian Affairs, 1824–1881, microfilm no. 234, Sac and Fox Agency 1824–1833, roll no. 728. This comment is part of a long ethnographic survey of the Sauk and Fox and appears in the third page of the section titled "Hunting" (262).
35. Clark to McKenney, St. Louis, June 19, 1830, in ibid.
36. See William Clark to E. Herring, St. Louis, April 8, 1832; and Clark to Secretary of War, St. Louis, May 1, 1832; in National Archives, Letters Received by the Office of Indian Affairs, 1824–1881, microfilm no. 234, St. Louis Superintendency (1832–1835), reel 750.

claim to Illinois land around the Rock River. Government-organized militias quickly hunted them down and broke their resistance.[37]

Black Hawk's recollections recalled his defeat in a language of freedom and honor:

[Black Hawk,] is now a prisoner to the white man, but he can stand the torture. He is not afraid of death. He is no coward – Black Hawk is an Indian. He has done nothing of which an Indian need be ashamed. He has fought the battles of his country against the white man, who came year after year to cheat his people and take away their lands.[38]

For his people, the war initiated a period of terrible hardship. After settling them in Iowa, the United States coveted their land and evicted them; they were then settled on poor land in Kansas on the Osage River, where they suffered from attacks from southern Plains tribes. The government again forced out most of the Sauk and Fox in 1863, and they ended up in Oklahoma. At the end of the nineteenth century, prowess in war remained the ideal of most young Indian men, who had little opportunity for formal education.[39]

Maximilian and Bodmer arrived in St. Louis just in time to witness Clark's meeting with Keokuk and a Sauk and Fox delegation pleading for the release of Black Hawk and the other prisoners. This was their first chance, he noted, to witness Indians "in their original state."[40] Maximilian did not hint at (and perhaps was not aware of) any wrongdoing in American government behavior toward the Indians.[41] He portrayed a paternalistic Clark listening patiently to Indian entreaties, encouraging peaceable behavior, and advising them to keep an eye on Black Hawk and his companions if they should be released.[42] Yet he was also sympathetic to the delegation. "They are strong, well-built men, many of taller than average height, broad, muscular, and corpulent" was his impression of these first Indians he met.[43] Able to observe Keokuk and his companions at leisure, Maximilian felt ever more drawn to them: "They were far from being solemn and still; on the contrary, one often observed lively and hearty laughter. If you approached them in good faith and spoke to them, then some had a really pleasant, friendly expression, while others were cold and appeared hostile."[44] Maximilian and Bodmer joined the

---

37. Wallace, introduction to *Black Hawk War*, 1–2.
38. Cited in ibid., 43.
39. Hagan, *Sac and Fox*, 215–218, 223, 225–226, 241, 243, 245, 250.
40. Maximilian, *Reise* 1: 232.
41. "Ihr Gebiet östlich des Mississippi verkauften sie 1805 an die Vereinten Staaten," he reported without comment. Ibid., 240.
42. Ibid., 242–243.   43. Ibid., 233.   44. Ibid., 241.

Sauk and Fox on their boat ride to Jefferson Barracks, where he could see them entertained by the steamship, making themselves up in small mirrors, quietly smoking their pipes, or singing in chorus.[45] At Jefferson Barracks he witnessed the painful reunion between the quiet, broken Black Hawk and his visitors. "It was touching to look on Black Hawk in his old age, as was the entire scene of reunion, and several observers shared in this mood."[46] Maximilian took the role of witness to a historical tragedy, divided between his admiration for Anglo-American civilization and the peoples resisting its inexorable advance.

Maximilian's central experience was his winter stay of 1833–1834 among the agricultural peoples of the Upper Missouri. He came as a late observer to the Mandans and their neighbors, the Arikaras and Hidatsas. They were at the center of a trade network that reached to the present-day Yellowstone Park area, the Great Lakes, and the Gulf of Mexico.[47] While often charming and hospitable, they were not easily taken in by the designs of European visitors and proved to be tough bargainers and cautious political negotiators. Lewis and Clark spent a difficult winter among them in 1804–1805 in which they inadvertently worsened the relations among the rival tribes of the area. Despite their diplomatic errors, they made a serious attempt during their five-month stay at systematic ethnography and came away with respect for the Mandans.[48] Other American and Canadian visitors, vying for their trade or traveling for pleasure, set down conflicting impressions of the Mandans and their neighbors. A Canadian trader who arrived at the same time as Lewis and Clark, Charles Mackenzie, took a liking to Indian life and had no hesitation about adopting Indian dress to advance his trade ambitions, much to the disgust of other white visitors.[49] The Anglo-Canadian surveyor and trader David Thompson, who visited from December 29, 1797, to January 10, 1798, admired their orderliness but also discovered a culture whose *joie de vivre* did not accord with his notions of propriety. They loved gambling, dancing, fine clothes, and amorous adventure. "The curse of the Mandanes [sic]," he wrote, "is an almost total want of chastity: this, the men with me knew, and I found

---

45. Ibid., 243.   46. Ibid., 245.
47. See Roy W. Meyer, *The Village Indians of the Upper Missouri: The Mandans, Hidatsas, and Arikaras* (Lincoln, Neb., 1977), 15–16.
48. See James P. Ronda, *Lewis and Clark among the Indians* (Lincoln, Neb., 1984), esp. 95–97, 105, 114–119. The Upper Missouri agriculturalists have been unusually well served by this book and by Meyer, *Village Indians,* two exemplary ethnohistories.
49. *Les Bourgeois de la Compagnie du Nord-Ouest: Récits de voyages, lettres et rapports inédits relatifs au nord-ouest canadien,* ed. and introd. L. R. Masson, vol. 1: Charles Mackenzie, *The Mississouri Indians: A Narrative of Four Trading Expeditions to the Mississouri* [sic], *1804–1805–1806, for the North-West Company* (Quebec, 1889), 318, 329ff., 383.

it was almost their sole motive for their journey hereto . . ."[50] A trader from a prominent New Jersey family involved in the fur trade, Alexander Henry the Younger, who set out for the Upper Missouri in July 1806, was equally disturbed by the immodesty of young Mandan women, who bathed without regard for the presence of men. Henry was also disgusted by the young women who "plagued" him with their advances and by the couples he heard dancing, singing, and making love at night.[51] A few years later an English naturalist, John Bradbury, gave a dismal picture of a victory procession in a village of the Arikaras. He wrote of returning warriors:

> They were painted in a manner that seemed as if they had studied to make themselves hideous. Many of them had the mark which indicates that they had drunk the blood of an enemy. This mark is made by rubbing the hand all over with vermillion, and by laying it on the mouth, it leaves a complete impression on the face, which is designed to resemble and indicate a bloody hand.[52]

He traveled in the company of a gentleman adventurer from Baltimore, H. M. Brackenridge, who blamed the local epidemics on the dirt and disorder of their villages. Even the disdainful Brackenridge had some good things to say about the Arikaras (he thought some of the women attractive and admired their artistic taste), but he commented that he and Bradbury, once inclined to sympathy with Indians, "now both agreed that the world would loose [sic] but little, if these people should disappear before civilized communities."[53] There was no consensus among white visitors about the Hidatsas, Arikaras, and Mandans. While some were charmed, others viewed them with civilized disdain or prudish condemnation.

The American government's Indian agents took an especially bleak view of their charges. "It is my opinion," reported Major John Dougherty in 1827,

> that much remains to be done among the red skins on the Missouri River. We have there many numerous tribes bordering on our frontier, who are constantly at war with each other, so much so, that no man is safe in passing to & from the villages of these roving bands – Starvation is at this time one of the leading causes of their disputes, the game has left them, they know not how to till the soil, and many of them starve half

50. David Thompson, *David Thompson's Narrative, 1784–1812*, ed. and introd. Richard Glover (Toronto, 1962), 177. On their orderliness, see 175. Thompson concluded that only Christianity "can give force to morality," and hoped that the United States would send missionaries soon (178).
51. Alexander Henry, *The Journals of Alexander Henry the Younger 1799–1814*, ed. and introd. Barry M. Gough (Toronto, 1988), 1: 218–219.
52. John Bradbury, *Travels in the Interior of America, in the Years 1809, 1810, and 1811 . . .*, 2nd ed. (London, 1819), 168.
53. H. M. Brackenridge, *Journal of a Voyage Up the River Missouri, Performed in Eighteen Hundred and Eleven*, 2nd. rev. ed. (Baltimore, 1816), 163.

their time, the natural consequence is the hungry worm is constantly gnawing on them and keeps them prowling over the country like so many hungry wolves out and devouring any thing notable that comes in their way.[54]

When another agent, John B. Sanford, actually went as far north as the agricultural villages, his impressions were equally depressing. The Arikaras, he wrote in July 1833, had abandoned their villages, and where they were, neither friends nor enemies could say; during the previous winter, one of their war parties had ambushed and killed three men from the American Fur Company. As for the Mandans and Hidatsas, their conduct merited grudging approval: "deportment tolerably good – not as good as heretofore." In general, he noted:

As it regards the relation of the Indian Tribes or Nations towards each other – I will only say that they are (as usual) at war with each other – & will always continue so. They are hereditary foes and the facility with which they procure food, gives them ample leisure to indulge in their hate & propensity for war.[55]

To Sanford the Upper Missouri was anything but romantic; all he saw was a border country whose uneasy peace was threatened by hunger, greed, and vendetta.

How different was the spectacle that greeted Maximilian when he reached the region! From Fort Clarke his party took a steamboat a few miles past the Mandan and Hidatsa villages. Along the way, Indians teemed by the river to watch the novelty; handsome male warriors gathered on shore, while their Indian companions on board the boat were relaxed, removing insects from their hair and biting them between their teeth. At midday Hidatsas rode out of their villages to admire the steamboat, the boat stopped in meadow bushes, and Maximilian admired his admirers:

The most beautiful, powerfully built people of all ages and sexes, in highly distinctive, finely worked and stylized costumes, were clustered before the astonished viewer, and suddenly there was so much to see and to observe here that one anxiously used every instant just to take in the main features of the panorama. The Hidatsas really are the largest and best formed Indians of the entire course of the Missouri; in this respect as in the elegance of their dress only the Crows can compare, though they perhaps exceed even them in the latter regard. Their faces were for the most part painted vermilion, a practice the North Americans share with the Brazilians and many other South Americans; their long hair hung in broad or narrow braids down their back; to

---

54. Dougherty to McKenney, St. Louis, September 14, 1827, in National Archives, Letters Received by the Office of Indian Affairs, 1824–1881, microfilm no. 234, Upper Missouri Agency (1824–1835), reel 883.

55. John B. Sanford to William Clark, St. Louis, July 26, 1833, in ibid., St. Louis Superintendency (1832–1835), roll 750.

the side of each eye and from the forehead down they wore a long string of white and azure coral beads alternating with shells, and their head was adorned with feathers in their hair. One saw oneself viewed with awe by these curious faces with their different expressions! Here a cold wild look, there an unlimited frozen curiosity, there a simple goodwill came to expression. Their torsos were generally naked, the beautiful brown skin on the arms sometimes decorated with brilliant broad arm bands of white metal, in their hand they carried their weapon, the bow and the axe, on the back a mantle sometimes of otter fur and very finely decorated; their leather leggings were covered with braids of their defeated enemies' hair or colorfully dyed horse scraps as well as many leather fringes and finely embroidered with strips of dyed porcupine needle or glass beads in the liveliest colors. Laughing and showing their ivory teeth, these beautiful strong people gave free rein to their feelings, and the unnatural and ugly fashions and the various dress items of white people must often serve as the material for telling remarks, which these children of nature know very well how to make. All of these Indians had dressed themselves in their most magnificent fashion, and they did not fail to achieve their end; for they made, at least on us foreigners, a vivid impression![56]

It is a moment of approximate equality: the whites may astonish them with their new invention, but the Hidatsas have not lost their strength and confidence. The fragility of the equal standing between the two sides – soon, we know, the steamboat will overwhelm the bareback riders – heightens the significance of the moment, turning it into a poignant late manifestation of a form of beauty about to disappear.

Maximilian had neither political ambitions nor commercial interests nor Anglo-American puritanism to keep him from confronting a culture with mores different from his own. His descriptions of Mandan women's sexual freedom was frank and matter-of-fact. While noting their pride and dislike of systematic work – qualities he had condemned in Brazilian Indians – he emphasized the Mandans' quickness and understanding. Some had a decided talent for drawing and music, and others argued with him about philosophical questions.[57] Against Volney and other critics of American Indians he wrote:

Even if man in all his varieties does not receive the same abilities from his Maker, I at least am convinced that the Americans in this respect do not lag behind the whites. Some of the Mandans had a great deal of hunger for knowledge and a strong impulse to learn something new about higher matters. If they were not so dependent on the prejudices inherited from their ancestors, many of them would be easy to teach.[58]

One can see here how ambivalence pervades Maximilian's relationship to American Indians: within a racialist paradigm he brings us close to a people

56. Maximilian, *Reise*, 1: 411–412.   57. Ibid., 2: 135.   58. Ibid., 2: 134–135.

for whom he has developed a genuine affection. At times Maximilian fixes their features with the impersonal precision of a naturalist, but he also shares his enthusiasm for these vain, quick, vivacious fellow human beings.

The Mandans' mythology, social organization, ceremonial organization, kinship system, economic practices, and crafts were complex and interrelated, too much so for Maximilian to explore them adequately. Sometimes his own limitations closed him off; even though he recorded some of their myths at some length, he was too dismissive of them as superstition to make much use of them. In other ways the Mandans probably closed themselves off from him, for they were guarded about areas that they considered sacred knowledge. Kinship patterns did not take up much of his attention at a time when no theory of kinship had yet been developed, and he could hardly have imagined its significance for later generations of ethnologists. Nonetheless Maximilian was able to grasp the Mandans *as* a society with its own forms of social organization. He was especially successful in outlining Mandan age societies. These were age-ranked groups (with separate series for men and women) that only selectively admitted members, growing more stringent at each ascending level. On the Indian side, these societies were not considered sacred, and members did not have to hesitate to share information about them with an outsider. Maximilian, for his part, could readily grasp the significance of male social bodies that were warrior clubs, honoring and preparing their members for the rigors of battle. A trader or priest might have regarded such organizations with indifference or contempt; Maximilian singled them out for attention.[59] German university training, Humboldtian insistence on exact observation, and Maximilian's talent for focused observation resulted in a new kind of portrayal of the Mandans.

Maximilian's description of the social lives of the Mandans and other Native peoples reached its greatest degree of insight in conjunction with Karl Bodmer's art. Their joint production, in turn, cannot be understood in isolation but must be viewed as a product designed for an age of Restoration.

Maximilian's travel account was a work for the libraries of aristocrats. Out of 277 subscribers (who pledged in advance to purchase the work), 103 were titled individuals or aristocratic institutions such as royal libraries.

---

59. See, for example, Maximilian's description of the ceremony and dance of the Dog society and the Bull society in ibid., 142–143 and 309–310.

Alfred W. Bowers captures the richness of the Mandan and Hidatsa worlds in *Hidatsa Social and Ceremonial Organization* (1963; Lincoln, Neb., and London, 1992) and *Mandan Social and Ceremonial Organization* (Chicago, 1950). See especially the description of the Dog societies and the Bull society in *Hidatsa*, 194–199. Cf. Virginia Bergman Peters, *Women of the Earth Lodges: Tribal Life on the Plains* (North Haven, Conn., 1995), 49–64.

Kings, princes, dukes, and counts – that is, the aristocratic upper end of the nobility – figured prominently among the names. The Prussian royal family, the queen of Hanover, the duke of Nassau, several Russian princes, the Danish royal family, Crown Prince Maximilian of Bavaria, Archduke Joseph of Hungary, and the Austrian Alexander zu Sayn-Wittgenstein-Hohenstein were among the buyers. Maximilian wrote and controlled the production of the illustrations as a high-ranking noble addressing his social peers.[60]

The man assigned to amuse and instruct the princes of Europe with his pictures came from a modest family of craftsmen and artists. Born in Zurich, Karl Bodmer was thirteen when his mother's brother, Johann Jakob Meier, a well-known landscape painter, took him into his atelier in 1822. The next year, Bodmer improved his craft on a walking tour of Lake Como (one of the earliest tourist areas in Europe and a favorite of the Romantics, with its ancient villages, palaces, craggy heights, and placid lake). In 1828 he moved to Esslingen (near Stuttgart) and in the same year to Koblenz. There he worked for Jakob Hölscher, a prominent publisher, who had high regard for his work. It may have been Hölscher who brought the gifted young artist to the attention of Maximilian.[61] Bodmer was not educated in the high academic tradition; rather, he came from the world of draftsmen. This artisan background was, in its own right, an important part of the story of travel illustration. As Bernard Smith has noted with regard to art of the Pacific, draftsmanship was more effective than academic art in representing non-European peoples.[62] Maximilian, like the scientists on the Cook expedition and other expeditions of the late eighteenth and early nineteenth centuries, furthered the naturalist tendency of a draftsman education by expecting his artist to produce an empirically accurate representation of what he saw. Yet to describe Bodmer's paintings simply as a triumph of scientific accuracy would be to miss a large part of their significance. They are works of Romantic imagination, distinguished by their attempt to give psychological depth to their subjects, to represent their disconcerting strangeness for the European visitor, and to provide lasting images of a disappearing Native aristocracy.

The picture atlas accompanying Maximilian's text is a large, lavish work. It includes two parts: thirty-three vignettes and forty-eight plates. The vignettes

---

60. The subscription list is published in Maximilian, *Reise,* 2: v–xvi. Many of the aristocrats subscribed indirectly through book dealers, whose names are listed before theirs in the list.
61. Läng, *Indianer waren meine Freunde,* 117–122. See also the valuable recent summary and overview of the scholarly literature by H. W. von Kittlitz, "Bodmer, Karl," in *Allgemeines Künstlerlexikon. Die Bildenden Künstler aller Zeiten und Völker* (Munich and Leipzig, 1996), 12: 88–90.
62. Bernard Smith, *Imagining the Pacific: In the Wake of the Cook Voyages* (New Haven, 1992), chap. 1, esp. 28.

are smaller pictures, of a kind suitable for framing and wall mounting if the owner chose; the plates are full-sized illustrations. About half of the vignettes are scenes of places that follow the itinerary of the voyage, starting with the Boston lighthouse, taking the reader through such places as Bethlehem (Pennsylvania), Pittsburgh, the Ohio and Wabash rivers, St. Louis, and the Missouri River, and returning via Lake Erie and New York harbor. The vignettes illustrate people and nature and landscapes – Crow Indians at Fort Clark, beaver dams, Blackfeet on horseback, the Mandan Mandeh-Pahchu and Hidatsa Indians. The plates also include some scenes of places and a large number of scenes of Indian life, including portraits, ceremonies, rituals, and Indian art and artifacts. The illustrations concentrate on ethnography at the expense of natural history. Even though Maxmimilian was a trained natural-ist and was strongly interested in the flora and fauna he observed on the voy-age, he largely excluded it from the atlas, instead creating a volume in which the Indians are clearly the center of attention, with just enough nature and civilization to serve as background.

The ethnographic character of Bodmer's art emerges clearly in his selec-tion of Sauk and Fox illustrations for the atlas. His choice was a striking one: not the famous actors in the story but two young warriors, a Fox named Wakusásse and a Sauk named Massika (Fig. 9). They were both "hand-some," and Massika had "a bold, savage face" (*ein kühnes, wildes Gesicht*) and an aquiline nose. His friendliness was especially expressive: his dark eyes sparkled, and his snow white teeth shone in his dark brown, usually vermilion-dabbed face."[63] The young men's beauty was attractive in its own right. But artist and painter simultaneously used the portraits as scientific sam-ples: Maximilian described the appearance of the Sauk and Fox in great detail, and he carefully commented on a detail like Wakusásse's feather, his decora-tion for having stolen a horse, "in his eyes a great act of heroism."[64] The illus-trations and text monumentalize free men. Qualities like "bold" and "savage" are here admired as the manifestations of their fearlessness. Massika's smile, like the jocular behavior of the warriors on the way to Jefferson Barracks, is the expression of a man not yet overwhelmed by the white invasion. Together the illustration and description are supposed to record a social and ethnic *type*, precisely what Maximilian sought in vain when he scoured the book and engraving stores of the East Coast. The ambition is still traceable to Hum-boldt's interest in typologies, but Maximilian extends it to human subjects.

The Romanticism of Bodmer's style emerges clearly from the comparison with a contemporaneous Neoclassical sculptor and artist, Ferdinand Pettrich.

63. Maximilian, *Reise*, 1: 237–238.   64. Ibid., 236.

9. *Massika – Wakusásse.* From Maximilian, Prince of Wied, *Reise in das innere Nord-America in den Jahren 1832 bis 1834,* 2 vols. and atlas (Koblenz, 1839–1841), illustrations by Karl Bodmer, atlas plate 3. Courtesy of the Edward E. Ayer Collection, The Newberry Library, Chicago.

After training first in his father's atelier and then under the tutelage of the famous Danish sculptor Bertel Thorvaldsen in Rome, Pettrich arrived in the United States at age thirty-seven in 1835 as an accomplished and successful artist. He, too, seems to have been genuinely fascinated by Indian subjects and attempted to convey them with specificity and dignity. Sketches of Sauk and Fox warriors from 1842 permit comparison with Bodmer's representations of Massika and Wakusásse. One shows a delegation of native warriors negotiating with American government officials in Washington, D.C. The entire sketch has a frozen, formal symmetry, with the seated figure at the center flanked by the two extremes of the couple lying to the left and the couple standing to the right; the two dark couples to the left and right give balanced depth to the background, and the extra figure on the left adds variety without disturbing the rigorous design of the whole. Individual sitters strike a variety of handsome poses; the most important is the penultimate right-hand figure, who is delivering a speech; his costume has been virtually transformed into a toga, and as he towers over his translator, he is a figure of Greek grace. The dramatic rhythm of the picture sweeps from the lying to the seated to the

10. *Council of the Sacs and Foxes at Washington City.* Sketch by Ferdinand Pettrich, 1842. From Newberry Library, Ayer Collection, Pettrich Sketch Book, Folder 1, 35a. Courtesy of the Edward E. Ayer Collection, The Newberry Library, Chicago.

standing Indian, their attention fixed on his words and his raised arm. They are Indians – the feathers and breechskins signal that much – but the composition and costumes make a pointed comparison with classical predecessors and almost completely overwhelm the ethnographic subject (Fig. 10). The same is true of Pettrich's magnificent sculpture *The Dying Tecumseh.* It shows the famous leader of a failed Indian confederation in a pose modeled on the ancient sculpture of *The Dying Gaul.*[65] (Fig. 11) Once again, ethnographic touches like the tomahawk only accentuate the power of the classical form, which can encase contemporary events in ancient precedents. As in the Hellenistic model, the representation is ambiguous. Its subject is beautified and dignified, but in the manner of a worthy enemy who in turn reflects glory back on the victors strong enough to conquer him; the sculpture is civilization's trophy.[66]

65. In the years leading up to his death in 1813, Tecumseh, a Shawnee warrior, attempted to unify Indian peoples in a political confederation that would transcend tribal interests. For a short biographical survey see R. David Edmunds, "Tecumseh," in *Encyclopedia of North American Indians,* ed. Frederick E. Hoxie (New York and Boston, 1996), 620–621. Cf. the analysis in Richard White, *The Middle Ground: Indians, Empires, and Republics in the Great Lakes Region, 1650–1815* (Cambridge and New York, 1991), 514–517.
66. For another interpretation of the sculpture see Julie Schimmel, "Inventing 'the Indian'," in *The West as America: Reinterpreting Images of the Frontier,* ed. William H. Truettner (Washington, D.C., 1991), 169–170. For a discussion and picture of *The Dying Gaul* see *The Dictionary of Art* (London, 1996), 13: 463.
   On Pettrich see Hans Geller, *Franz und Ferdinand Pettrich. Zwei sächsische Bildhauer aus der Zeit des Klassizismus* (Dresden, 1955), especially the friezes reproduced on 155,

11. *The Dying Tecumseh.* Ferdinand Pettrich, 1856. Courtesy of National Museum of American Art, Smithsonian Institution, Transfer from the U.S. Capitol.

Bodmer's art is not lacking in its own European allusions. Its effectiveness is sometimes heightened by its synthesis of ethnographic details entirely "other" with recognizable signs of majesty. For example the Hidatsa leader Péhriska-Rúhpa surveys the surrounding plain. We view him from below, and he does not acknowledge us but looks out toward a distant object. The slight turn of the head also has the effect of turning the picture from a static portrait into a more dynamic study, his attention concentrated on some distant object of interest, perhaps game, perhaps friend or foe. His leather robes and leggings make his form as solid as a statue, with wide shoulders and broad creases hanging almost to the ground. The long pipe suggests a scepter or spear; it is a recognizable sign of his mastery of the surrounding land (Fig. 12).

Bodmer constructs many other images of political and military leadership. The Mandan warrior Mató-tópe is honored with two images of his leadership status. One, comparable to the picture of Péhriska-Rúhpa, shows him in full dress, his spear hovering over the land in an ostentatious gesture of domination (Fig. 13). The second picture presents Mató-tópe's body as the precise record of a military career:

which illustrate the theme of progress from savagery to civilization. There is also valuable background information on the Roman milieu and a discussion of Pettrich in Friedrich Noack, *Deutsches Leben in Rom 1700 bis 1900* (Stuttgart and Berlin, 1907), esp. 210, 228, 311.

12. *Péhriska-Rúhpa.* From Maximilian, *Reise in das innere Nord-America,* atlas plate 17. Courtesy of the Edward E. Ayer Collection, The Newberry Library, Chicago.

13. *Mató-Tópe.* From Maximilian, *Reise in das innere Nord-America,* atlas plate 13. Courtesy of the Edward E. Ayer Collection, The Newberry Library, Chicago.

Famous distinguished warriors wear all sorts of highly ostentatious wood signs in their hair indicating their wounds and heroic actions; thus for example Mató-tópe had fastened through his hair a carved wood knife, painted red and about the length of a hand, because he had stabbed a Cheyenne chief with the knife, as well as six miniature wood sticks, painted red, blue, or yellow, with a yellow nail driven in at the upper end, which signified as many bullet wounds as he had received. He attached the split feather of a wild turkey to the fine arrow in his hair, and on the back of his head he wore a large bundle of yellow owl feathers tipped in red dye as a sign of the Meniss-Ochatä (Dog Society). His face was painted half red and half yellow, his body daubed reddish brown, with small stripes on top that were formed by running fingers through the paint. On his arm from the shoulder down he had seventeen yellow stripes which indicated his deeds, and on his breast the figure of a hand in yellow paint as sign that he had taken a prisoner. A warrior decorated in this way needs more time for his toilette than the most elegant Parisian lady.[67]

The picture is empirical documentation. Maximilian pores over the body in order to make it an intelligible document. At the same time, it has direct appeal to aristocratic viewers: they could admire this written and visual description of Mató-tópe's body as a counterpart to their own ideal of heroism in battle. The Mandan warrior is at once an exotic primitive and an accomplished member of the original noble calling. Here as in the landscape portraits, Bodmer's art is well calculated to interest his audience (Fig. 14).

The same tension between nearness to and distance from European models characterizes Bodmer's illustrations of Mandan ceremonies. The men of Mandan society underwent a lifetime of training and selection for a warrior elite. From boyhood on, males who felt qualified could apply for admission to a succession of societies, for which they had to demonstrate their courage, probity, and skill. As they ascended, they also had to pass through painful rituals that Europeans viewed as forms of torture but that the Mandans considered to be forms of exchange with the gods in return for power.[68]

One of the ceremonies Bodmer was able to view on March 7, 1834 (Maximilian was sick at the time), was the spring dance of the Dog society, which gathered many of the Mandan leaders. The applicants had already proven their courage in battle and their good judgment in keeping domestic order.[69] In the medicine lodge where the Dogs first gathered, Bodmer saw Mató-tópe, "who, however, very exalted as a result of his high value as Dog, did not want

---

67. Maximilian, *Reise*, 2: 111.
68. See Peters, *Women of the Earth Lodges*, chaps. 3–6, on how the Mandans developed ceremonies that were nodal points for different aspects of their communal life.
69. Bowers, *Hidatsa Social and Ceremonial Organization*, 194–198. This society was also sometimes called the "Real Dogs" to distinguish it from several other Dog societies.

14. *Mató-Tópe, geschmückt mit den Zeichen seiner Kriegsthaten.* From Maximilian, *Reise in das innere Nord-America,* atlas plate 14. Courtesy of the Edward E. Ayer Collection, The Newberry Library, Chicago.

to recognize him."[70] In the afternoon the Dogs moved to the vicinity of the fort, and a group of onlookers watched the twenty-seven or twenty-eight society members, all clothed in their full splendor. An astonishing costume set apart the society's four highest members:

Four of them – the Real Dogs – wear a colossal hat or gear on their head whose raven or magpie feathers, with little down feathers fastened to the tips, reach far over their shoulders. The extended, upright tail of a wild turkey or an eagle is fastened to the middle of this unformed mass of feathers. These four main Dogs wear a long strip of red cloth around their throat which hangs down their back to their calves and in the middle of the back is tied in a bow.[71]

Among the Hidatsas, one of the Dog society members was Péhriska-Rúhpa. Bodmer captured his likeness in full ceremonial costume, transformed from the dignity and isolation of field duty to the *mania* of the dance, his head dehumanized, his jaw jutting and teeth projecting forward, his back bent, shoulder contorted and arm muscles tensed. Maximilian describes him soberly and precisely, with pride in the accuracy of Bodmer's representation and only a hint of irony marking distance from this bizarre figure (Fig. 15). Bodmer also depicted another male club, the Bull society. Widespread among Plains peoples, the dances they held four times a year among the Mandans and Hidatsas acted out different moments in the life of the animal.[72] Maximilian relates that the two bravest members, who were never supposed to flee from an enemy, wore a full-sized artificial bull's head over their own heads; these two men danced on the outside of the ring and imitated all the movements and moods of the animal[73] (Fig. 16).

Bodmer portrayed ecstatic dances unlike anything that his audience would run into at a European ball. And yet the content of the ceremonies would not be without meaning for fellow warriors across the ocean. In the pictures of the Real Dog and of the Bull Dance he captures moments of charismatic leadership in the making, when the participants enhance the strength and courage that would make them victors on the battlefield.

Maximilian's and Bodmer's aristocratic vision converged with the work of other travelers. The American artist and travel writer George Catlin preceded by one year their journey to the Upper Missouri. From an old Connecticut family with gentlemanly ambitions, and politically allied to Andrew Jackson's opponents in Washington, he wrote about and painted Indians in a spirit of sympathy with the moral and aesthetic qualities of these "lords of the for-

70. Maximilian, *Reise*, 2: 109.   71. Ibid., 2: 310.
72. Bowers, *Hidatsa Social and Ceremonial Organization*, 198–199.
73. Maximilian, *Reise*, 2: 142–143.

15. *Péhriska-Rúhpa, Mönnitarri Krieger im Anzuge des Hundetanzes.* From Maximilian, *Reise in das innere Nord-America,* atlas plate 23. Courtesy of the Edward E. Ayer Collection, The Newberry Library, Chicago.

16. *Bisontanz der Mandan Indianer.* From Maximilian, *Reise in das innere Nord-America,* atlas plate 18. Courtesy of the Edward E. Ayer Collection, The Newberry Library, Chicago.

est." He too was captivated by Mató-tópe, whom he called "a high-minded and gallant warrior, as well as a polite and polished gentleman," painting him in a classical pose and making use of the spear to suggest domination of the land.[74] In 1837 a third ethnographic adventure began when the Scottish baronet William Drummond Stewart took the Baltimore artist Alfred Jacob Miller along with him for a tour of the American Rockies. Stewart's two nov-

74. See George Catlin, *Illustrations of the Manners, Customs and Condition of the North American Indians with Letters and Notes Written during 8 Years of Travel and Adventure Among the Wildest and Most Remarkable Tribes Now Existing* (London, 1866), 1: 2, 114.

    The founding work of recent Catlin scholarship, with a systematic inventory and analysis of his pictures, is William H. Truettner, *The Natural Man Observed: A Study of Catlin's Indian Gallery* (Washington, D.C., 1979). On Catlin's portrait of Mató-tópe, see ibid., 178–179. For another fine analysis of Catlin's use of classical allusion, see Truettner's comments on Catlin's portrait of Keokuk, 142–143.

    On Catlin's political affiliations, see Brian W. Dippie, *Catlin and His Contemporaries: The Politics of Patronage* (Lincoln, Neb., and London, 1990).

    The ties between Catlin's art and the racialist science of his time – which are far closer than has hitherto been appreciated – are discussed in the imaginative dissertation of Bridget L. Goodbody, "George Catlin's Indian Gallery: Art, Science, and Power in the Nineteenth Century" (Ph.D. diss., Columbia University, 1996).

    Catlin's personal and family papers provide occasional glimpses into the family's mentality. See, for example, the description of George's father, Putnam Catlin, by George's nephew, Horace Putnam Hartshorn, in Catlin Family Papers, Archives of American Art, Roll 3023, 1387; and Putnam's letter to his son praising his artistic endeavors and providing

els about his adventures and Miller's paintings and sketches sought to establish the relationship between the Indian and Scottish aristocracies, comparable in their primitive, manly vigor.[75] All three of the major Romantic artists of the American West (and the patrons of Bodmer and Miller as well) praised the primitive vigor and dignity that characterized the peoples of the Plains. To be sure, there were significant differences among their admirers: Catlin was more comprehensive in the breadth of his Indian "Gallery"; Bodmer was more precise and benefited from Maximilian's scientific training; Miller was superior to the others in psychological insight. Yet they shared a vision of European and native elites as allied in their "pure" form by an aristocratic ideal.

Maximilian's ethnography is well known to historians of the American West but has been virtually forgotten by students of European intellectual and cultural history. Yet here, too, there are important contemporary parallels. His travel account belongs to an emerging appreciation for the anthropological foundations of politics and society. There was a widespread awareness in the early nineteenth century that theirs was an age of revolution, in which the French Revolution was only the beginning of an ongoing transformation. Many thinkers experienced this as a chronic condition of instability. The great tradition of sociological and anthropological thinking culminating in Nietzsche's publication in 1872 of *The Birth of Tragedy* (with its discovery of a community of ecstatic experience underlying the rational forms of organization in ancient Greek and modern European society) was a search for the underlying principles that could invigorate modern society. Again and again, from the beginning to the end of the century, social thinkers returned to categories of the sacred as the force that welded anarchic human beings into communities. Maximilian was not a theorist, but his work laid bare the kinds of rituals that gave indigenous societies their powerful unity.

Maximilian wrote about these things with considerable discretion. It was remarkable, however, for a member of the social and cultural elite to write about them at all. By the 1830s, the great efflorescence of Romantic scholarship was coming to an end, and a more positivist spirit had invaded the German universities. The paradigmatic area of learning for this transformation was the study of ancient Greece. In the late eighteenth and early nineteenth centuries, thinkers and poets alike turned to the ancient Greeks for sublime

a long list of European artists, March 26, 1821, Archives of American Art, Roll 2136, 532–536, National Museum of American Art.

75. I am indebted here to the remarkable work of Lisa M. Strong, "Image of Indian–White Contact in the Watercolors of Alfred Jacob Miller, 1837–60" (Ph.D. diss., Columbia University, 1997).

ideals; decades later, a deadening dedication to producing correct texts and a focus on the classical period to the exclusion of everything earlier or later dominated the universities. In a secondary school system and a university system in which classics were the dominant discipline of the human sciences, and even archaic and Hellenistic studies were devalued, the study of "savages" was a wild choice.[76] Scholars like Johann Jacob Bachofen and Jacob Burckhardt, Maximilian's contemporaries in nearby Basel, shared his preoccupation with ritual, ceremony, and the establishment of authority in archaic societies. They rebelled against the authority of the positivists in Berlin and turned to preclassical periods of Greek history for an understanding of the prerational foundations of Greek culture.[77] This alone was enough to put them on the margins of the scholarly world of their time. Maximilian was far stranger when he traveled from his Rheinland home to the Upper Missouri and experienced what more bookish contemporaries could only read about in their classical texts: the rites that formed a unity between man, nature, and the gods.

76. On classical studies in nineteenth-century Germany see Suzanne Marchand, *Down from Olympus: Archaeology and Philhellenism in Germany, 1750–1970* (Princeton, N.J., 1996).
77. See Lionel Gossman, *Orpheus Philologus: Bachofen versus Mommsen on the Study of Antiquity, Transactions of the American Philosophical Society,* 73/5 (1983); idem., "Basle, Bachofen and the Critique of Modernity in the Second Half of the Nineteenth Century," *Journal of the Warburg and Courtauld Institutes* 47 (1984), 136–185; idem., "Jacob Burckhardt as Art Historian," *Oxford Art Journal* 11/1 (1988), 25–32. Particularly notable in Burckhardt is the emphasis on religion as the historical force that can form a unified people. See Jacob Burckhardt, *Gesamtausgabe* (Berlin and Leipzig, 1929–1934), 8–9: *Griechische Kulturgeschichte,* ed. Felix Stähelin, esp. 9: 55–56. The Renaissance, by contrast, demarcated for Burckhardt the beginning of the modern process of fragmentation. See Burckhardt, *Gesamtausgabe,* vol. 5: *Die Kultur der Renaissance in Italian. Ein Versuch,* 1–2.

Epilogue: A World of New Aristocrats

The social theorists of the nineteenth and early twentieth centuries predicted the collapse of hierarchy. Tocqueville announced it in the first volume of *Democracy in America:* the withering away of aristocracy and the advance of democracy as providential events that political action could channel but not halt. A comparable sense of irresistable movement underlies Marx's anticipation of revolution from *The Communist Manifesto* to *Capital,* Mill's anxieties about the fate of freedom of expression in *On Liberty,* and Weber's account of the erosion of privilege in "Politics as a Vocation." Their starting point was the same as this book's: the democratic revolutions of the late eighteenth century and the collapse of legal hierarchy in France. The starts and stops of the following years, the alternation of revolutions and restorations, seemed to confirm that princes and generals could only postpone the formation of an egalitarian society, whether viewed with Marx as a triumph of justice over age-old exploitation or with the others we have named as an invitation to tyranny.

At the end of the twentieth century, we can recognize that contemporaries were overly impressed by the French Revolution and underestimated the inventiveness of European elites. Political events defied the logic of social theory. If European aristocracies lost their legal ground, they regrouped around a shared way of life. Education, dress, occupation, residence, leisure, friendship, marriage, and taste could give expression to a set of values that defined a socially superior coterie and marked it off from the rest of society.[1] Hierar-

---

1. Two books have pursued this line of thought with brilliant insight for contemporary France: Pierre Bourdieu, *Distinction: A Social Critique of the Judgment of Taste,* trans. Richard Nice (Cambridge, Mass., 1984); and Jean-Philippe Mathy, *Extrême-Occident: French Intellectuals and America* (Chicago, 1993). For a longer historical perspective on the concept of status, see *Economy and Society: An Outline of Interpretive Sociology,* ed. Guenther Roth and Claus Wittich (New York, 1968), 1: 305–307.

chical social orders did not simply dissolve and give way to a civil society of equals; rather, alongside the elimination of legal differences, culture (propped up, of course, by power and wealth) became a new marker of social gradations. The English country house and the Paris salon served as centers for these reinvented aristocratic cultures. Germany lacked a comparable institution for mediating an exalted world of deportment and thought, but the dynamism of the great Prussian landholders and favorable legal and social conditions made the German Empire a place of unusually strong aristocratic influence.[2] Aristocratic refashionings may have struck contemporaries as anachronisms, but in retrospect we may view them as important and original nineteenth-century creations.

Travel was one of the activities that furthered this transformed aristocratic culture. In the decades after 1815 the distinction emerged between travel and tourism as aristocratic and middle-class modes of going abroad. The tourist could sign up with Thomas Cook or rely on his Baedeker for a safe and reliable trip.[3] Men like Maximilian and Tocqueville, by contrast, made journeys that called for resources of money, education, and social connection available only to the aristocratic few. Their travel writings memorialized their achievements for their contemporaries, teaching them how a man of high social rank was supposed to comport himself in and interpret the larger world. Successors could follow their routes, use their example as inspiration for travels to other parts of the world, or imaginatively relive their experiences.

Through their travel writings we can measure how the aristocratic culture of the nineteenth century differed from its old regime predecessor. It contained a new savage accent: the nineteenth-century aristocrat recoiled from the preceding century's hint of rococo decadence and went abroad to recover the rough virtues of his primitive cousins. The aristocratic travelers to North America turned their journeys into symbolic quests for contact with a primitive aristocracy that put them in touch with their own inmost selves. Through these meetings European travelers asserted their savage nobility – their ability to socialize with native leaders, win their respect, and receive acknowledgment

---

2. For European-wide comparisons, see especially the rich collection of essays in *Les noblesses européenes au 19. siècle,* Actes du colloque de Rome, 21–23. novembre 1985 (Paris and Padua, 1988). On the unusual strength of the German aristocracy see ibid., esp. Gérard Delille, "Introduction," 10–11, and Christof Dipper, "La noblesse allemande à l'époque de la bourgeoisie. Adaption et continuité," 165–197.

  Two other recent collections with references to further literature are Hans-Ulrich Wehler, ed., *Europäischer Adel 1750–1950 (Geschichte und Gesellschaft* Sonderheft 13, Göttingen, 1990); and Armgard von Reden-Dohna and Ralph Melville, *Der Adel an der Schwelle des bürgerlichen Zeitalters 1780–1860* (Wiesbaden and Stuttgart, 1988).

3. On the emergence of the distinction between the tourist and the traveler in this period see James Buzard, *The Beaten Track: European Tourism, Literature, and the Ways to Culture, 1800–1918* (Oxford, 1993).

of comparable social standing. These were not tourist experiences, for they had to undergo all the trials of the wilderness in order to befriend a Plains warrior. Although they might seem like parodies of the meetings that took place between Indians and Europeans as military allies in earlier times, their encounters also showed off aristocratic military qualities in an age when class tensions simmered beneath the orderly surface of European society.

Did travelers gaze down on non-European "others" from a consistent stance of superiority? Some did; others, however, reworked their aristocratic culture through encounters with non-European elites. The aristocratic brotherhood was not limited to North America. Oceania provides striking parallels: the obsession with genealogies, haughtiness, love of combat, and will to power of native elites in places like Hawaii and New Zealand impressed travelers as rivals to the most baroque excesses of European lords and ladies. This kind of admiration could turn into an asset of colonial administration. In India, British administrators invented a quasi-feudal hierarchy of native aristocrats culminating in the monarchy of Queen Victoria. And in late-nineteenth-century Africa, British and German administrators experimented with different recipes for collaboration, invoking loyalty to monarchy and gentlemanly lifestyles in order to link settlers and native elites to the metropolis. Culture could serve not just as a means of asserting difference, but also to turn native and European elites into political collaborators.[4]

Cultural as well as political appropriations followed the Romantic travel tradition. By the time George Catlin arrived in Paris with a troupe of Indians and his collection of paintings in 1845, the cultural elite of the capital, including George Sand and Eugène Delacroix, knew the cultural code for responding to the sight of Indians; they were to be honored as fellow aristocrats. Charles Baudelaire initiated the transition to primitivism in modernist art when he commented on Catlin's painting in his essay on the Salon of 1846 (which included two of the artist's entries). Catlin, he wrote, "has captured the proud, free character and the noble expression of these splendid fellows in a masterly way. . . . With their fine attitudes and their ease of movement, these savages

---

4. See Adelbert von Chamisso, *A Voyage Around the World with the Romanzov Exploring Expedition in the Years 1815–1818 in the Brig* Rurik, *Captain Otto von Kotzebue,* trans. and ed. Henry Kratz (Honolulu, 1986); and Jules Dumont D'Urville, *Voyage de La Corvette L'Astrolabe Exécuté par Ordre du Roi, pendant les années 1826–1827–1828–1829 . . .: Histoire du Voyage,* div. 1, vol. 2, part 2 (Paris, 1830); Bernard Cohn, "Representing Authority in Victorian India," *The Invention of Tradition,* ed. Eric Hobsbawm and Terence Ranger (Cambridge, 1984), 165–209; and Terence Ranger, "The Invention of Tradition in Colonial Africa," ibid., 211–262. In the late nineteenth century and the first half of the twentieth century, British officers developed a comradely admiration for the gentlemanly and martial qualities of the Gurkhas of Nepal who served under them; see Lionel Caplan, *Warrior Gentlemen: "Gurkhas" in the Western Imagination* (Providence, R.I., and Oxford, 1995).

make antique sculpture comprehensible."[5] The remarks belonged to Baudelaire's larger preoccupation, inspired partly by Chateaubriand, with the "savage" as an alternative to bourgeois Europe and an ally of the aristocrat in a democratic age.[6] He was the first of a succession of artists who turned to native peoples for a heroism, vitality, and expressiveness that were being eradicated from the modern world. An especially haunting memory of the French identification with Indians was a pen-and-ink drawing by the Symbolist artist Rodolphe Bresdin. A bohemian artist whose eccentric life was celebrated by his contemporaries, Bresdin identified to the point of madness with Chingachgook, the Indian hero of *The Last of the Mohicans* (Fig. 17). The picture shows Bresdin himself dressed up as an Indian, contemplating a strange assortment of objects: a sun reminiscent of earlier sun symbolism going back to Natchez legends, manufactured goods, and a simian bust atop a ladder vaguely suggesting an evolutionary hierarchy. What a contrast there was between Bossu's frontispiece and Bresdin's self-portrait! In a little over a century, the clarity of Enlightenment verities about *l'homme sauvage* and *l'homme policé* had given way to a modernist dream of merging with the primitive.[7]

The legacy of Romantic travel did not just rest with cultural elites, however. American Indians became the aristocratic heroes of widely read Westerns. Gustave Aimard predicted to his French audience that the Indians of the Southwest and Mexico would one day rise up and conquer their Spanish and Anglo oppressors: "and that will be just, for they are heroic natures, richly endowed, and capable, under good direction, of undertaking or carrying out great things."[8] A mass readership of Germans, too, identified with Indians.

5. Charles Baudelaire, "The Salon of 1846," in *Art in Paris, 1845–1862: Salons and Other Exhibitions Reviewed by Charles Baudelaire*, trans. and ed. Jonathan Mayne (London, 1965), 71. Cf. the discussion of the visit in Hugo Honour, *The New Golden Land: European Images of America from the Discoveries to the Present Time* (New York, 1975), 238.
6. See Baudelaire's pairing of the dandy, an aristocratic figure, and the savage in his famous essay "Le Peintre de la Vie Moderne" (1863), *L'Art Romantique*, ed. Jacques Crépet (Paris, 1925), 88–91.
7. On Bresdin see *Prints by Rodolphe Bresdin/Gravures de Rodolphe Bresdin*, An Exhibition Organized by the Norman Mackenzie Art Gallery, University of Regina (Regina/ Saskatchewan, Canada, 1981), which reproduces three different versions of this picture. For biographical background see E. Benezit, ed., *Dictionnaire critique et documentaire des peintres, sculpteurs, dessinateurs et graveurs de tous les temps et de tous les pays . . .*, 10 vols. (Paris, 1974), 2: 299–300. A fascinating exhibition first drew my attention to Bresdin's self-portrait: "Graphic Tours: Travel and Nineteenth-Century French Works on Paper," the Art Institute of Chicago, Department of Prints and Drawings (January 14–April 17, 1994), organized by Margo Thompson et al.
8. Gustave Aimard, *The Indian Scout: A Story of the Aztec City* [*L'Éclaireur*] (1859; London and New York, 1910), 214. The National Union Catalogue of Pre-1957 Imprints lists five French and fifteen English editions.
   On French admiration for Indians in the second half of the nineteenth century see Honour, *The Golden Land*, 238–240; and Christian F. Feest, "The Indian in Non-English Literature," *Handbook of North American Indians* (Washington, D.C., 1988), 4: 582–583.

17. Rodolphe Bresdin, French, 1825–1885. *A North American Indian,* pen and ink (1878), 16.8 × 13.6 cm, Gift of Walter S. Brewster, 1923.348 Photograph © 1998, The Art Institute of Chicago. All Rights Reserved.

The fantastically successful Karl May – sometimes called the best-selling German writer of all time – fashioned a nationalist myth with his masterpiece, *Winnetou* (1892). Yankees, learns the German hero of the book, are opportunists who stand for nothing more than brute force, while the real Indians, like his friend Winnetou – the ones not yet corrupted by Anglo-American civilization – are born noblemen. Germans play a special role as mediators, for they combine European knowledge with Indian honor.[9] Through Karl May, the self-promotion of a handful of elite travelers became the fictional fare of hundreds of thousands of Germans. In the age of high imperial competition with the United States, they eagerly received his images of noble Germans befriending aristocratic Indians, both of them misused by scurrilous Yankees.[10] May conforms to the later nineteenth-century tendency to adopt hierarchical habits of thinking – but to transfer them from strata within a society to the relationship between nations. These nations, in turn, had the status of natural species or races, each stamped with a timeless character. This popularization of Europe's romance with Indians brings our story to an ironic conclusion: the comparison that had once set transatlantic peers apart from the rest of their societies now defined entire peoples of Europe, despite all the democratic politics of the modern era, as aristocrats.

9. Karl May, *Winnetou*, trans. Michael Shaw (New York, 1977).
10. See especially the insightful interpretation by Peter Uwe Hohendahl, "Von der Rothaut zum Edelmenschen. Karl Mays Amerikaromane," in *Karl Mays "Winnetou". Studien zu einem Mythos*, ed. Dieter Sudhoff and Hartmut Vollmer (Frankfurt, 1989), 214–238, which points to the French Wild West writer Gabriel Ferry, as well as Heckewelder and Catlin, as important sources. See also Helmut Schmiedt, *Karl May* (Frankfurt, 1983), which emphasizes Catlin but also points out that May's personal library contained all sorts of things, including geographical, ethnological, and religious works, and a great deal of Nietzsche (52–53); and Gert Ueding, ed., in Zusammenarbeit mit Reinhard Tschapke, *Karl-May-Handbuch* (Stuttgart, 1987), which offers an overview of May scholarship. There is a witty discussion of Karl May, with reproductions of covers of *Winnetou*, in Honour, *The Golden Land*, 242–244.

Feest, "The Indian in Non-English Literature," offers a general overview of the German reception of Indians, 583–586.

A Note on Guides to Research

The footnotes to the text provide detailed references for readers who seek documentation or detailed reading on specialized topics. A separate listing of a few of the guides to printed works and primary source materials relating to late-eighteenth- and early-nineteenth-century European travelers to North America, however, may be of use to readers interested in further research.

The basic body of sources for the history of travel is the printed travel accounts, and the researcher who wishes to work in this area should consult the available guides to travel literature. For French travel to North America, scholars are now well served by Durand Echeverria and Everett C. Wilkie, Jr., *The French Image of America: A Chronological and Subject Bibliography of French Books Printed Before 1816 Relating to the British North American Colonies and the United States,* 2 vols. (Metuchen, N.J., and London, 1994). Still valuable for the older as well as the later period, with brief sketches that bring some of the more important travelers to life, is Frank Monaghan, *French Travellers in the United States, 1765–1932* (New York, 1933). For German travelers see Peter J. Brenner, *Der Reisebericht in der deutschen Literatur. Ein Forschungsüberblick als Vorstudie zu einer Gattungsgeschichte (Internationales Archiv für Sozialgeschichte der Literatur,* Sonderheft 2, Tübingen, 1990); and idem., ed., *Der Reisebericht: Die Entwicklung einer Gattung in der deutschen Literatur* (Frankfurt am Main, 1989). For pre-nineteenth-century German travelers see Paul B. Baginsky, *German Works Relating To America, 1493–1800: A List Compiled From the Collections of The New York Public Library* (New York, 1942). For the early nineteenth century see Wilhelm Engelmann, ed., *Bibliotheca Geographica. Verzeichniss der seit der Mitte des 18. Jahrhunderts bis zu Ende des Jahres 1856 in Deutschland erschienenen Werke über Geographie und Reisen, mit Einschluss der Landkarten, Pläne und Ansichten,* 2 vols. (1857; Amsterdam, 1965).

Since the early twentieth century, American scholars have transcribed and made reproductions of archival materials relating to the history of New France; see Henry Putney Beers, *The French in North America: A Bibliographical Guide to French Archives, Reproductions, and Research Missions* (Baton Rouge, 1957). The most important sources for the history of colonial Louisiana are described in Archives Nationales, *Inventaire des Archives Coloniales. Correspondance à l'arrivée en provenance de la Louisiane. Tome I (articles C¹³ᵃ 1 à 37)*, ed. Marie-Antoinette Menier, Etienne Taillemite, and Gilberte de Forges, introd. Jean Favier (Paris, 1976). There is a large collection of transcribed (and, in a few cases, photographically reproduced) French sources in the Illinois Historical Survey of the University of Illinois, Urbana-Champaign, which is described in Maynard J. Brichford, Robert M. Sutton, and Dennis F. Walle, *Manuscripts Guide to Collections at the University of Illinois at Urbana-Champaign* (Urbana, Chicago, and London, 1976).

The reports and correspondence of U.S. government officials complement the writings of travelers on Indians: see Edward E. Hill, *The Office of Indian Affairs, 1824–1880: Historical Sketches* (New York, 1974); and *American Indians: A Select Catalog of National Archives Microfilm Publications* (Washington, D.C., 1995). The American Philosophical Society has served for over two centuries as a repository of materials relating to exploration and the history and anthropology of American Indians. Its holdings are listed in John F. Freeman, ed., with Murphy D. Smith, *A Guide to Manuscripts Relating to the American Indian in the Library of the American Philosophical Society* (Philadelphia, 1966); and Stephen J. Catlett, ed., *A New Guide to the Collections in the Library of the American Philosophical Society* (Philadelphia, 1987).

Index

Aimard, Gustave, 168
American Indians, *see* North American
    Indians
American Philosophical Society, 28–30,
    140
Anglo-American character, 4, 36, 37, 40,
    68–74, 103, 117, 121–122, 130,
    142, 170
anthropology, 7n, 47, 135, 139
Arikaras, 145, 146
aristocracy
    Anglo-American elites and, 6, 112
    compared to Indians, 1, 2, 20, 23, 38,
        58, 119, 167, 168
    decadence in old regime, 43, 59, 166
    defined, 2n
    incest and, 45
    reinvention after 1789, 1–2, 32–33,
        37–38, 39, 63–64, 112, 166
    Scottish, compared to Indians, 76, 162
    see also nobility
Atala (Chateaubriand), 3, 39, 41, 42–43,
    76, 94
    heroism in, 53–54
Atwater, Caleb, 111, 112

Bachofen, Johann Jacob, 163
Balzac, Honoré de, 75
Baudelaire, Charles, 167–168
Baudry des Lozières, Louis-Narcisse,
    33–34

Beaumont de la Bonnière, Gustave de,
    96, 99
Benjamin, Walter, 8
Bernardin de Saint-Pierre, Jacques
    Henri, 45–46, 137
Birth of Tragedy, The (Nietzsche), 162
Bismarck, Otto von, 123, 129
Black Hawk, 144, 145
Black Hawk War, 118, 142–145
Blackfeet, 2, 81, 151
Blosseville, Ernst de, 100–101
Blumenbach, Johann Friedrich, 135–136
    influence of, 138, 139
Bodmer, Karl, 4, 138, 149–151, 154–161,
    162
    Romanticism of, 150, 151
    training, 150
Bonaparte, Charles Louis, 140
Boon, James, 10
Bossu, Jean-Bernard, 27–28, 168
Bülow, Dietrich von, 115n
Brackenridge, H. M., 146
Bradbury, John, 146
Bresdin, Rodolphe, 168
Buffon, Georges-Louis Leclerc de, 31,
    137
Burckhardt, Jacob, 163

Calhoun, John, 107
Canada, 48, 51, 96
    Indians of, 3, 13–14, 26

Canada (*cont.*)
  missionaries in, 20–22
  social system in, 18–19
  soldiers in, 22–23
  travelers in, 84, 87, 96
Capital (Marx), 165
Carheil, Étienne de, 20
Castelnau, Francis de La Porte,
  86–90
Catlin, George, 6, 138, 159, 160–161,
  167
Cavelier de La Salle, Réné-Robert, 48
Cercle des Philadelphes, 33
Chamisso, Adelbert von, 5
Champlain, Samuel de, 22
Charlevoix, Pierre François Xavier de,
  53n
Chateaubriand, François-René de, 92,
  93, 94, 100, 137, 168
  critique of the Enlightenment in, 40,
    47, 59
  early life, 39–41
  identification with Indians, 3, 45, 47,
    59, 133
  itinerary in America, 40
  political evaluation of America, 51–52,
    59–60
  Romantic departure from eighteenth-
    century models, 41, 42, 45–47
  Romantic religiosity of, 42, 43, 45,
    53–54
Chateaubriand, Jean-Baptiste Auguste
  de, 40, 93
Cherokees, 78, 128
Chevalier, Michel, 73–74, 98
Chickasaws, 50, 78
Choctaws, 50, 106
Clark, William, 132, 143, 144
Colton, Calvin, 110–111
Communist Manifesto, The (Marx), 165
Constant, Benjamin, 41
Cooper, James Fenimore, 75, 84, 92
Courrier des États-Unis, Le, 78, 90
Crepieul, François de, 20

Crèvecoeur, Michel Guillaume St. Jean
  de, 36–38, 39
Crows, 2, 133, 147, 151

De L'Allemagne (Staël), 5
De Pauw, Cornelius, 31–32, 122
De Smet, Jean-Pierre, 79–82
degenerationism, 31–32, 122
Delacroix, Eugène, 76–77, 167
democracy
  as challenge to elites, 3–4, 66–68
  sociology of, 60, 68, 69, 70
  see also hierarchy, Tocqueville, Anglo-
    American character
Democracy in America (Tocqueville),
  87, 96–98, 104–107, 110, 119
"Des États-Unis et de leurs habitants"
  (Castelnau), 86–87
Detchéparré, 50, 58
Detroit, 101, 108, 109, 110
Discourse on Inequality (Rousseau),
  24–25
Dougherty, John, 146–147
Dronôt de Valdeterre, 49
"Drunken Boat, The" (Rimbaud), 87–89
Duden, Gottfried, 118–120, 122
Dumas, Alexandre, 75
Dumont dit [de] Montigny, Jean Ben-
  jamin François, 55n
Duponceau, Peter, 28
Dying Gaul, The, 153
Dying Tecumseh, The (Pettrich), 153

Ellsworth, Henry Leavitt, 124, 126–127,
  128–129
Émile (Rousseau), 46
Enlightenment
  crisis of its interpretation of Indians,
    32–33, 34, 35, 37
  criticism of Indians, 30–35
  idealization of Indians, 1–2, 13–14,
    26–28
  secularization of missionary reports
    in, 22

see also Neoclassicism, "noble savage," republicanism
equality
  liberal ideal of, 14–17
  see also Anglo-American character, democracy, hierarchy
exile, 2, 6, 39, 40, 41, 42, 43, 72, 89–90, 104, 106–107, 121

forests
  as Romantic setting, 45, 60, 66, 83, 86, 87, 92, 102
Forster, Georg, 135
Fort Rosalie, 49, 52–53
Fourier de Bacourt, Adolphe, 70n
"Fourteen Days in the Wilderness" (Tocqueville), 101–104
freedom
  aristocracy and, 98, 104–105
  Indians and, 23, 99, 104, 109
  nobility and, 17
French Revolution
  influence on travel writing, 32–38, 78–79, 138
Fürstenwärther, Moritz von, 117

Gall, Ludwig, 117n
Genius of Christianity, The (Chateaubriand), 41
Germania (Tacitus), 101
Gerstner, Clara von, 121
Granier de Cassagnac, Bernard-Adolphe, 71
Grasset de Saint-Sauveur, Jacques, 13–14
Gravier, Jacques, 52
Great Sun, the (Natchez ruler), 57
Guizot, François, 94–95

Heckewelder, John, 30n
Henry, Alexander (the Younger), 146
Hidatsas, 141, 145–148, 151, 154
  social and ritual life, 157–159
hierarchy

defenses of, 57, 68
Enlightenment critique of, 24
in the old regime, 17
in New France, 18–19
social theory and, 165–166
History and Class Consciousness (Lukács), 9
History of Louisiana (Le Page du Pratz), 54–59
Hubert, 49
Hudson (valley), 83–84
Hugo, Victor, 71
Humboldt, Alexander von, 5, 83, 136–137, 139, 140, 149
  Romantic theory of travel, 137
Hurons, 30, 59, 87
Hyde de Neuville, Jean-Guillaume, 72, 74, 83

Iroquois, 13–14, 19–20, 21–22, 87, 99
Irving, Washington, 122, 124, 127–128

Jackson, Andrew, 159
  Indian policies of, 6, 77–78, 106–107
  populist politics of, 3
Jacobins
  impact on travel writing, 34–35
Jefferson, Thomas, 28
Jesuits (Society of Jesus), 20–22, 64, 71, 79–82, 95
Journey into Northern Pennsylvania and the State of New York (Crèvecoeur), 37
Julius, Nicholas Heinrich, 120
July Revolution
  influence on travel writing, 3
  Tocqueville and, 95–96
Junaw-sche Wome, 131

Keating, William K., 107, 108

La Rochefoucault-Liancourt, François de, 35–36, 37–38, 39

Le Moyne de Bienville, Jean-Baptiste, 48–49
Le Page du Pratz, Antoine Simon, 54–59
  admiration for Natchez, 56–57
  Chitimacha woman and, 55–56
Le Peletier de Rosanbo, Aline-Thérèse, 40, 93
Le Peletier de Rosanbo, Louis, 40
Le Peletier de Rosanbo, Louise-Madeleine, 93
Le Petit, Mathurin, 53
Lafitau, Jean-François, 21–22, 28
Lahontan, Louis-Armand de, 22–23
Lamoignon de Malesherbes, Chrétien-Guillaume, 40, 93
landscape
  influence on human society, 102, 137
  see also degenerationism
Last of the Mohicans, The (Cooper), 75–76, 168
Latrobe, Charles Joseph, 124, 128–129
Leatherstocking Tales (Cooper), 75
Lenau, Nicholas (Nikolaus Franz Niembsch Edler von Strehlenau), 121–122
Lesueur, Charles, 140–141
Letters from an American Farmer (Crèvecoeur), 37
Lettres sur L'Amérique du Nord (Chevalier), 74
Lewis and Clark Expedition, 107, 145
Ingénu, L' (Voltaire), 30–31
Long, Stephen H., 107
Louisiana, French, 28
  as inferno, 48–49, 52
  misrule of, 48–49, 50–51
  propaganda on behalf of, 48, 51, 52, 58
  settlement of, 47–49
  see also Mississippi (valley), New France
Luckner, Felix von, 133–134
Lukács, Georg, 9

Mackinac Island, 86, 110
Mackenzie, Charles, 145–146
Mandans, 2, 141, 145–149
  social and ritual life, 149, 157, 159
Mandeh-Pahchu, 151
Marx, Karl, 97, 165
Marxism
  interpretation of old regime, 17
Mató-tópé, 154, 157, 161
Maximilian, Prince of Wied, 4, 134, 166
  biography, 138
  itinerary in America, 137–138, 139–141
  journey to Brazil, 138–139, 142
  modern social thought and, 162–163
  travel account, 149–151
May, Karl, 170
Mengarini, Gregory, 82
Menominees, 89
Merlin, Maria de Las Mercedes, 70–71, 74
métis, 19, 104
Michaux, André, 28
Milbert, Jacques-Gérard, 83–86
Mill, John Stuart, 97, 165
Miller, Alfred Jacob, 138, 161–162
Mississippi (river), 106–107, 130, 131, 143
Mississippi (valley), 41, 45
  as paradise, 42, 48, 52
  French settlement of, 19
  see also Natchez (region)
Missouri (valley), *see* Upper Missouri
Mohicans, 84–86
Montaigne, Michel de, 13n, 100
Montesquieu, Charles-Louis de, 92, 93, 100
Montlezun, 68–69, 72, 74
Montulé, Édouard de, 72–73, 74, 98

Narrative of the Captivity and Adventures of John Tanner, A (Tanner), 100
Natchez (Indians), 47–48

aristocratic character of, 59
missionaries and, 52–53
political history of, 48–51
social hierarchy, 56–57
war with French, 47, 50–51, 58
Natchez (region), 49–50, 55, 131
Natchez, Les (Chateaubriand), 41–42, 76
Native Americans, *see* North American Indians
nature
state of, 25, 28, 46, 101
see also degenerationism, North American Indians, Rousseau
Neoclassicism, 5, 21
in literary treatment of Indians, 42, 89, 125, 127
in visual art, 13–14, 28
see also Pettrich
New France, 19, 24
nostalgia for, 4, 51, 65, 75, 76, 79, 84, 87, 92, 168
see also Canada, Louisiana, Mississippi Valley
New Harmony (Indiana), 140–141
New York (state), 40, 83–84, 101, 108
Niagara Falls, 43, 66, 122, 141
Nietzsche, Friedrich, 162
nobility
after 1789, 123
crisis of, 2–3, 43
in the old regime, 17–18
see also aristocracy
"noble savage," 23–24, 28, 30
critiques of, 34–35, 100–101
North American Indians
alcoholism among, 36, 90, 100, 108
as anarchists, 25, 105
as aristocrats, 1–3, 5, 37–38, 54, 58, 59, 92, 117–118, 159–162, 166–167, 170
authentic versus inauthentic, 36, 76, 102, 128, 131
as democrats, 3, 5, 13–14, 34

extermination of, 89, 90–91, 106, 112, 120
as hunters, 26, 30, 37, 60, 99, 100, 110, 112, 119, 124–125
love of freedom, 26, 27, 59–60, 99, 104, 109–110
physical beauty, 102, 110, 147–148
religion of, 26, 28, 42, 43, 52, 54
as Teutons, 101, 119

Odérahi (Palisot de Beauvois?), 30n, 46–47
Ojibwas (Chippewas), 4, 107, 109, 111
social system, 105
Oklahoma Territory, 122, 124–129, 144
On Liberty (Mill), 165
Orientalism (Said), 8
Osages, 2
history, 125, 126
travelers' impressions of, 125–128, 132–133
Ottawas, 100, 109, 111

Pagès, Pierre-Marie-François de, 27
Palisot de Beauvois, Ambroise-Marie-François-Joseph de, 30n, 46n
Paul et Virginie (Bernardin de Saint-Pierre), 45–46
Paul Wilhelm, Duke of Württemberg
itinerary in America, 129–130
views of Indians, 131–133
Pavie, Theodore, 90
Péhriska-Rúpa, 154, 159
Peale, Charles Willson, 30
Périer, Étienne de, 49
Pettrich, Ferdinand, 151–153
Philadelphia, 28, 68, 73, 96, 140
Philosophical and Political History of the Establishments and Commerce of Europeans in the Two Indies (Raynal), 26
Philosophical Research on the Americas (De Pauw), 31–32, 122

Plenty Coups, 133
Potawatomis, 111, 131–132
Pourtalès, Albert de, 122–129
    admiration for Indians, 124–126
    biography, 123
    itinerary in America, 124
*Protestant Ethic and the Spirit of Capi-
    talism, The* (Weber), 69

race
    American Indians as a, 86–87, 120,
        128, 148–149
    theories of, 102, 106, 136, 148
Raumer, Friedrich von, 120
Raynal, Guillaume-Thomas, 26–27, 30,
    100
René (Chateaubriand), 3, 41, 42, 76
    crisis of nobility in, 43–45
    heroism in, 45
republicanism, 32n
    criticisms of, 42, 127
    in the Enlightenment, 24
    and interpretation of Indians, 5,
        13–14, 26, 40
Restoration, 94
    influence on travel writing, 63,
        149–150
Riedesel, Frederike Charlotte Luise von,
    115n
Rimbaud, Arthur, 87–89
Romanticism, 5, 150, 162
    cultural comparison and, 6–8, 9–10
    in literary treatment of Indians, 90,
        110–111
Rousseau, Jean-Jacques, 5, 24–26, 34, 40,
    46, 100
    "savages" and, 25–26

Saginaw (Michigan), 102, 103–104, 109
Said, Edward, 8
Saint-Victor, Jacques de, 98n
St. Louis, 79, 80, 118, 132, 144, 51
Salish ("Flatheads"), 80–83
Salzbacher, Joseph, 121

Sand, George (Amandine Aurore Lucie
    Dupin), 75, 167
Sanford, John B., 147
Sauk and Fox, 2
    artistic representation of, 151–153
    history of, 142–143, 144–145
    see also Black Hawk, Black Hawk
        War
"savage," 30
    Europeans as, 37, 45, 47, 124, 125,
        127, 133–134, 141–142
    homme policé and, 23n, 27, 36, 47,
        168
    nature as, 101, 102
Say, Thomas, 140
Schlegel, August von, 5
Schlegel, Friedrich, 135
Schwartz, Stewart, 9
Schoolcraft, Henry, 108–110
slavery, 58, 59, 71, 73, 109
Staël, Germaine de, 5, 41
Stewart, William Drummond, 161–162
Stung Serpent, 57

Tacitus, 101
Tanner, John, 100
Thiers, Adolphe, 73–74
Tocqueville, Alexis de, 35–36, 69, 70, 87,
    91, 119, 133, 165, 166
    on Algeria, 99
    ambivalence toward American
        democracy, 96–98
    and American Indians
        as aristocrats, 1, 4, 92, 99, 104, 112
        as extreme of freedom, 104, 112
        as impure "savages," 102
        as objects of comparative analysis,
            105
        as objects of curiosity, 92, 99, 101
        as pure "savages," 102–103
        as victims of Anglo-Americans,
            103, 104, 106–107
    aristocratic liberalism, 92, 93–94
    Chateaubriand and, 94

critique of Anglo-Americans, 103,
106–107
fear of revolution, 93
family background, 93, 94
French politics and, 94–96
itinerary in America, 96
on slavery, 104
racial analysis rejected by, 86–87, 102,
104, 106
sociological method, 92, 104–105,
106
Tocqueville, Hervé de, 94
travel
aristocratic culture and, 64–65
as *Bildungsreise*, 130, 135
grand tour, 64–65, 72–73, 129
revitalization of aristocratic identity
through, 59, 129, 133–134,
166–167
scientific, 28–30, 129, 135–138
travel writing, 6–10
French and German compared, 133
travelers, Anglo-American
views of American Indians, 6,
107–112, 145–147
see also United States
travelers, British, 146
compared to Continental travelers,
5–6
see also Latrobe, Stewart
travelers, French
admiration for American democracy,
72–74
disillusionment with American
democracy, 37, 40, 65–66, 68–
71
military accounts by, 22–23
missionary accounts by, 20–22, 52–54,
78–83
post-1815 attitudes toward North
America, 65–66

Romantic view of Indians, 4
scientific accounts by, 28, 32n, 83–
86
social composition, 63–64, 66
travelers, German
class divisions among, 4, 116–118
critics of democracy, 117, 121–122,
125–126, 142
impact of economic change on, 4,
116
lack of imperial background, 115
populist writers, 118–120
pre-Revolutionary, 115

United States
treatment of Indians, 36, 77, 82, 89,
91, 107, 109, 111, 112, 119, 121,
124, 127, 128–129, 131–132,
143–144, 146–147
westward expansion of, 4, 74, 78, 119,
120, 130, 141,
Upper Missouri, 80
Anglo-American travelers in, 145–147
Catlin in, 138, 159–161
Maximilian and Bodmer in, 138, 145,
147–151, 154–159, 163

Verein zum Schutz deutscher Einwan-
derer in Texas (society for the
Protection of German Immi-
grants in Texas), 116
Views of Nature (Humboldt), 137
Volney, Constantin-François Chasse-
beuf de, 34–35, 37, 148
Voltaire, 30–31

Weber, Max, 69
Wette, Ludwig de, 120–121
White, Richard, 9
Winnabagos, 111
Winnetou (May), 170